The Power of Attorney Book

BY ATTORNEY DENIS CLIFFORD

EDITED BY LISA GOLDOFTAS

ILLUSTRATIONS BY MARI STEIN

PLEASE READ THIS

NOLO PRESS 950 PARKER STREET
BERKELEY CA 94710 415 549-1976

PRINTING HISTORY

Nolo Press is committed to keeping its books up-to-date. Each new printing, whether or not it is called a new edition, has been revised to reflect the latest law changes. This book was printed and updated on the last date indicated below. You might wish to call Nolo Press (415) 549-1976 to check whether there has been a more recent printing or edition.

New **PRINTING** means there have been some minor changes, but usually not enough so that people will need to trade in or discard an earlier printing of the same edition. Obviously, this is a judgment call and any change, no matter how minor, might affect you.

New **EDITION** means one or more major, or a number of minor, law changes since the previous edition.

FIRST EDITION	July 1985
Second Printing	February 1986
Third Printing	January 1987
SECOND EDITION	April 1988
Second Printing	September 1988
THIRD EDITION	March 1990
Second Printing	June 1990
EDITOR	Lisa Goldoftas
ILLUSTRATIONS	Mari Stein
BOOK DESIGN	Jackie Clark
COVER	Toni Ihara
INDEX	Sayre Van Young
PRINTING	Delta Lithograph

Nolo books are available at special discounts for bulk purchases for sales promotions, premiums, and fund-raising. For details contact: Special Sales Director, Nolo Press, 950 Parker Street, Berkeley, CA 94710.

Clifford, Denis.
    The power of attorney book / by Denis Clifford : illustrations by
Mari Stein.
        p.   cm.
    ISBN 0-87337-123-2 : $19.95
    1. Power of attorney--United States--Popular works.   2. Power of
attorney--United States--Forms.   I. Title
KF1347.Z9C56   1990
346.73'029--dc20
[347.30629]   90-32736
                                                                  CIP

Printed on recycled paper

ACKNOWLEDGEMENTS

My thanks and appreciation to all the people who helped me create, update and revise this book—Jackson Chin, for his excellent research; Mary Willis of The Berkeley Coop Consumer Group Legal Services, pioneers in the durable powers of attorney for health care; Linda Moody, and the Trauma Foundation of San Francisco; Marian Gray, who provided so much useful information about durable powers of attorney for health care in California; Edie Rogers, of Alta Bates Hospital; Dave Steinberg of the *San Francisco Examiner*; John McCabe, National Conference of Commissioners of Uniform State Laws; Naomi Puro, for all her assistance; and those at Nolo Press whose hard work and expertise contributed to this book—Lisa Goldoftas, for her fine editing; Stephanie Harolde, for preparing so many drafts of the manuscript so well; Jackie Clark, for her excellent design and production; David Freund, for his fine proofreading and eye to detail; Mari Stein, artist and illustrator; and to all my friends and colleagues at Nolo Press.

CONTENTS

CHAPTER 4
SAMPLE FORMS AND CLAUSES FOR
FINANCIAL DURABLE POWERS OF ATTORNEY

CHAPTER 5
STATUTORY FINANCIAL DURABLE POWERS OF ATTORNEY

CHAPTER 6
DURABLE POWERS OF ATTORNEY FOR HEALTH CARE

CHAPTER 7
SAMPLE DURABLE POWERS OF ATTORNEY
FOR HEALTH CARE FORMS AND CLAUSES

This book provides you with the information, forms and instructions necessary to create your own conventional or durable power of attorney. It enables you to design documents to meet your specific needs and covers common situations for which powers of attorney are used.

Before going further, let's start with some basics. A power of attorney is, physically, a document in which one person (the "principal") gives another person (the "attorney in fact") legal authority to act on her behalf. Depending on how the document is drafted, it may be effective for a designated period of time or it may be open-ended and remain effective even if the principal becomes incapacitated. A power of attorney does not remain valid when the person creating it dies.

A conventional power of attorney, which has been available for hundreds of years, basically gives someone authority to handle your financial affairs for a defined reason or time. By law, it becomes ineffective if you become incapacitated. A conventional power of attorney might be used to carry out business decisions if you can't be reached while on an extended vacation.

This book focuses on durable powers of attorney, which are designed to give someone authority to make necessary financial and medical decisions on your behalf or to implement decisions you've already made in case you're incapacitated. A durable power of attorney can be drafted so that it does not go into effect unless you become incapacitated—which allows you to retain all control over your affairs unless and until incapacity occurs. If it does, you've determined what restrictions and directions are imposed on the person you've named to act for you.

A durable power of attorney can provide you with the security and peace of mind of knowing you've arranged to have your affairs handled in the manner you desire, by the person you've chosen, if you become incapacitated.

If you don't establish a durable power of attorney, the problem of who will make important financial and medical decisions for you if you become incapacitated won't go away. Normally a family member or friend will be put to the trouble and expense—your expense, incidentally—of petitioning a court to appoint someone to make decisions for you. In short, should you become incapacitated, the existence of a durable power of attorney will likely appear as a minor miracle to those close to you.

Example

Fred developed the first symptoms of Alzheimer's disease several years ago. Recently his mental acuity deteriorated to the point where he is unable to handle his financial affairs or make medical decisions for himself. However, while still competent, Fred executed durable powers of attorney, placing authority over both his finances and health care decisions in his brother Benjamin's hands. This means no court proceedings are necessary. Benjamin can sign checks, make bank deposits, sell securities, make vital health care decisions—including methods of treatment for Fred—and do whatever else is necessary to manage Fred's affairs sensibly.

Drafting a durable power of attorney is generally not a complicated matter from a legal point of view. This book covers the basic practical decisions you must make to establish durable powers of attorney and provides step-by-step instructions on how to draft them to suit your needs. It also includes sample forms for both basic types of durable powers of attorney: financial/asset management and health care.

How to Use This Book

The Power of Attorney Book allows residents of all 50 states and the District of Columbia to prepare:

- Conventional powers of attorney;

- Durable powers of attorney for finances; and

- Durable powers of attorney for health care.

The Power of Attorney Book provides you with guidelines to help you decide whether you can prepare your own durable powers of attorney or if you'll need to see a lawyer. In some states, I believe you must have your completed work reviewed by an attorney, as explained in detail in subsequent chapters.

You don't need to read this entire book. In general, you must read and understand the information necessary to prepare the forms for the state where you live and to reflect your individual desires. Be sure you read all chapters applicable to your situation before you start making decisions and actually drafting documents. To make informed decisions, you'll need to understand how durable powers of attorney work, both for finances and for health care, and what your basic options are. Here's a basic outline of how to proceed:

- Read Chapter 1, "Understanding Powers of Attorney," and Chapter 2, "Information for Attorneys in Fact." You're then ready to turn to the chapters that help you prepare the types of powers of attorney you want.

- *Conventional powers of attorney* for use in all states are covered in Chapter 9.

- *Durable powers of attorney for finances* are discussed generally in Chapter 3. Forms are presented in Chapter 4—except certain specific statutory forms for residents of California and New York, which are discussed in Chapter 5. Residents of Alaska, Connecticut, Illinois, Minnesota and North Carolina should also review Chapter 5, since those states also have special statutory forms.

- *Durable powers of attorney for health care* are discussed generally in Chapter 6. Specific forms for residents of all states except California, Idaho, Nevada, Rhode Island and Vermont are presented in Chapter 7. Forms for Californians are discussed in Chapter 8 and are presented as Forms 13, 14 and 15 of the Appendix. Special statutory forms are contained in the Appendix for: Idaho (Form 7), Nevada (Form 8), Rhode Island (Form 9) and Vermont (Form 10). The Appendix also includes non-mandatory statutory forms for the District of Columbia (Form 11) and Illinois (Form 12).

Living Will Note: This book explains what a living will is and how it relates to a durable power of attorney for health care (see Chapter 6, Section G). A tear-out California living will form is contained in the Appendix as Form 16.

The *Power of Attorney Book* enables you prepare two separate durable powers of attorney—one for finances and one for health care. I strongly believe these documents should be separate, even if you want one person to represent you (i.e. be your attorney in fact). Some states legally require that a durable power of attorney for health care be separate from a financial durable power of attorney, and more states are likely to require this separation soon. Because issues in health care and finances differ widely, preparing two durable powers of attorney helps you focus on the specifics of each concern when you prepare the documents. For all these reasons, information and the forms for the two types of durable powers of attorney are presented in separate chapters.

CHAPTER 1

UNDERSTANDING POWERS OF ATTORNEY

A. Legal Terms

This chapter provides an overview of different types of powers of attorney. A "power of attorney" is a written document signed by one person authorizing another person to act for her. There's not much technical legal language connected with powers of attorney, but to make sense of what follows, you need to understand several essential legal terms.

1. Principal

The person who creates the power of attorney document is called the "principal." If you draft and sign a power of attorney, you're the principal. Anyone can create a valid power of attorney—that is, be a principal—except:

- Minors (people under age 18 in most states, but perhaps another age, depending on state law);

- Persons who aren't legally competent; and

- Those deprived of their civil rights (certain felons).

2. Attorney in Fact

The person who is authorized to act for the principal is called an "attorney in fact." (In some states, this person is also referred to as an "agent.") Any competent adult can serve as an attorney in fact and most definitely doesn't have to be a lawyer. In other words, you may designate whomever you choose—your spouse, best friend, or Aunt Faye—as your attorney in fact.

3. Incapacity

There are various words used to describe the condition of being unable to handle one's own financial matters and/or health care decisions. The terms include "incompetent," "disabled" and "incapacitated." This book generally uses the term "incapaci-

tated," as it seems to be the least pejorative and most clinically accurate description of that condition. It's important to realize that "incapacity" generally isn't precisely defined by state law and is basically a medical—not legal—decision. The term basically refers to the loss of those physical or mental abilities necessary to minimally function in life.

A determination of whether a person is incapacitated is usually made by one or more doctors. The most common causes of incapacity are problems associated with advancing age, such as heart attacks, strokes, and Alzheimer's disease. Incapacity can also be caused by serious accidents, drug or alcohol addiction, degenerative diseases and mental illness.

The term "incapacity" is applied to many different physical realities. Sometimes an incapacitated person is permanently unable to manage any of his own affairs, while other times there may be a reasonable chance of recovery. A person might be unable to handle financial matters, but still be able to make personal medical decisions. In some situations, a person can handle his own personal day-to-day finances, but cannot manage investments. A person could move in and out of periods of incapacity caused by physical or mental illness.

4. Conventional Power of Attorney

The conventional power of attorney is designed primarily to give another person the temporary right to completely or partially manage one's financial affairs. Often the attorney in fact is restricted by the principal to one transaction (e.g., "to sell my 1986 Buick"). The conventional power of attorney usually terminates at a time specified in the document, or when the principal becomes incapacitated or dies. It's a useful legal method to authorize the handling of many short-term financial and business matters when the principal won't be available.

Example

Mary is purchasing a house. The closing becomes delayed to the point when it will occur during her long-planned vacation to Paris. Not wanting to postpone either her vacation or the closing, Mary designates her friend, Phil, as her attorney in fact. She gives Phil the power to handle all aspects of the closing, including document signings, while she's away.

Numerous financial situations can be conveniently handled by using a conventional power of attorney—from banking transactions, to IRS hearings, to paying bills, to handling expenses of a friend's minor children on a temporary basis. Practical uses of a conventional power of attorney and sample forms are presented in Chapter 9.

5. Durable Power of Attorney

A durable power of attorney gives someone authority to make necessary financial or medical decisions if the principal becomes incapacitated. It is valid from the date signed and remains valid regardless of the principal's subsequent disability or incapacity. A durable power of attorney normally terminates only if the principal dies or revokes it. A durable power of attorney is reasonably short and generally not difficult to prepare. It allows the principal to privately select the person she wants to manage her affairs without the necessity of court review or notification to any governmental or public agency.

Unlike some legal documents which by their very nature narrowly restrict your choices, durable powers of attorney are flexible legal tools adaptable to your needs. With very few limits, you can put in whatever specifications, qualifications and limitations you wish on the person you choose to manage your financial affairs or make medical decisions. This book discusses major problems you might face regarding limits and qualifications, and presents choices for solving those problems.

A durable power of attorney can be drafted so the principal maintains all power over her affairs until and unless she becomes incapacitated. It can delegate only the authority the principal chooses, under whatever restrictions and limits she provides. No formal transfer of title of assets is required, and the principal can always revoke it unless she becomes incapacitated.

In sum, a durable power of attorney can provide you with the security and peace of mind of knowing you've arranged to have your affairs handled in the manner you desire, by the person you've chosen, if you become incapacitated.

6. 'Springing' Durable Power of Attorney

This important type of durable power of attorney becomes effective only if the principal becomes incapacitated at some future time. If the principal never becomes incapacitated, a springing durable power of attorney never goes into effect, and the principal retains all control over her assets and medical care. But if the principal does become incapacitated, the durable power of attorney "springs" into use. In other words, the principal creates a legally valid method for handling her affairs during any future period of incapacity. Any durable power of attorney can be drafted as a "springing" one. (Specific uses of different types of springing durable powers of attorney are covered in detail in Chapters 3 and 6.)

Example

Martha, an elderly widow, wants to insure that her closest friend, Patricia, will make decisions for her should she become incapacitated. Martha presently feels fine and has no intention of relinquishing power over her own affairs. So Martha prepares a springing durable power of attorney, naming Patricia as attorney in fact. If Martha never becomes incapacitated, Patricia will never have authority over her or her finances. However, should Martha's doctors conclude that she's no longer fit to manage her own affairs, Patricia can step in without the necessity of any court action.

7. Financial Durable Power of Attorney

A financial durable power of attorney is created to allow management of one's finances without court proceedings. It allows an attorney in fact to handle the money and property affairs for an incapacitated principal. A durable power of attorney for finances can go into effect immediately upon signing or it can be "springing," if that's what you want.

Example

Celina, who is ill, lives with her daughter, Nancy. Celina's primary source of income is Social Security payments. Celina prepares a springing durable power of attorney for financial management so that if she becomes incapacitated, Nancy has authority to cash or deposit her checks and pay her bills.

Of course, the principal's financial situation can be far more complicated than Celina's. If the principal has an active, complex investment portfolio or owns a substantial business, deciding who should serve as attorney in fact may require careful thought. How the attorney in fact's powers should be structured may raise a number of difficult questions and call for the creation of a fairly involved, custom-designed durable power of attorney, which may require an attorney's help.

Financial durable powers of attorney can be useful if an incapacitated principal must move into a nursing home or a long-term hospital care facility. Within the terms permitted by law, the attorney in fact can take action to prevent all of the principal's money from being used up for medical or housing costs, and try to preserve assets for the principal's family.[1]

Under a durable power of attorney for finances, the attorney in fact can handle all basic financial matters. This includes paying bills, managing bank accounts, depositing checks, handling taxes, and taking charge of house repairs and maintenance. As stated, a durable power of attorney can be specially drafted to handle far more involved and sophisticated financial needs. In sum, the financial durable power of attorney is a flexible tool which can be geared to any level of financial complexity.

8. Durable Power of Attorney for Health Care

A durable power of attorney for health care authorizes the attorney in fact to make medical and health care decisions for an incapacitated principal. It can also be used to express desires the principal wishes to make legally binding and wants her attorney in fact to carry out. It may be designed either to take effect immediately or "spring" into effect in the future upon the incapacity of the principal. One major use of a durable power of attorney for health care is to create binding instructions regarding the use, or non-use, of life-sustaining procedures if the principal is incapacitated

---

[1]Planning to avoid consuming all one's assets in these situations is discussed in *Eldercare: A Consumer's Guide to Choosing and Financing Long-Term Care*, by Joseph Matthews (Nolo Press), *Social Security, Medicare and Pensions: A Sourcebook for Older Americans*, by Joseph Matthews and Dorothy Matthews (Nolo Press), and *Avoiding the Medicaid Trap*, by Armond Budish (Henry Holt).

and suffering from a terminal illness. (See Chapter 6, Section F.)

California law authorizes a specific form of durable power of attorney for health care (covered in Chapter 8). Idaho, Nevada, Rhode Island and Vermont also now require that a specific form of durable power of attorney for health care be used. As of the date of the printing of this edition, no other state requires a particular form for a durable power of attorney for health care. However, the District of Columbia and Illinois have adopted statutory forms, which are suggested but not mandatory.

As is discussed in Chapter 6, it's generally accepted that any state which has authorized durable powers of attorney permits health care decisions to be delegated to the attorney in fact, although in some states (identified in the chart in Section B of Chapter 6), you need to check with an attorney to see what's legally permitted.

9. Living Will

A "living will" is a document you can use in most states to express your desires regarding use of life-sustaining procedures.[2] A living will should always be used in conjunction with a durable power of attorney for health care. Information about specific state laws, living wills and how you can prepare and use one with a durable power of attorney is covered in Chapter 6, Section G. For residents of California, a tear-out California living will form is provided in the Appendix as Form 16.

---

[2]Despite the similar name, a "living will" is not a conventional "will" used for designating how property should be distributed after a person's death. Nor is a "living will" the same as a "living trust," which is an estate planning device used to transfer your property, outside of probate after your death.

B. The Need for Two Separate Durable Powers of Attorney

This book enables you to prepare two types of durable powers of attorney—one for health care and one for finances. If you want both types, you should prepare two separate documents, even if you appoint the same person as your attorney in fact in both. The reasons for this are:

- There may be different laws in your state governing each type of durable power of attorney. Charts showing each state's laws for durable powers of attorney for finances are in Chapter 3, Section B. Those for health care are in Chapter 6, Section B.

- Each durable power of attorney will be used for a very different purpose and presented to vastly different people and organizations.

- People active in preparing durable powers of attorney generally agree that it's wiser to prepare two separate documents.

For all these reasons, the information on and the form of the two types of durable powers of attorney are presented in separate chapters.

C. The Human Element

Most of this book is devoted to practical and legal aspects regarding drafting powers of attorney. But here in the beginning, it's important to note that deep feelings and concerns often underlie these practical legal documents. Accordingly, it's appropriate to say a few words before proceeding to the logistics of creating your documents.

Any power of attorney—especially a durable power of attorney—is a document which transfers tremendous power either in the present or, in the case of a springing durable power of attorney, possibly sometime in the future. Even though a power of attorney can be revoked at any time (as long as the principal remains competent), you should never create a durable power of attorney unless you're confident you have a thorough understanding of the authority you plan to transfer.

1. Selecting an Attorney in Fact

Once you decide to establish a power of attorney, you'll need to make one big decision, followed by a number of smaller ones. Your most important decision will be the selection of your attorney in fact (discussed in more detail in Chapter 3, Section G and Chapter 6, Section D(3)). Common sense dictates that the attorney in fact be someone whom you, the principal, completely trust. Fortunately, most of us know at least one such person—usually a family member or close friend. However, if there's no such trustworthy person in your life, then a power of attorney is a bad idea.

Legally, your attorney in fact is a "fiduciary," which means she owes a duty of complete good faith and trust to you. But in the real world, if the attorney in fact breaches her duty and manages your affairs in a careless or dishonest way, the existence of this legal duty will probably do little good. Why? Because your recourse, or that of your family or friends, would be to sue the attorney in fact for breach of duty. Lawsuits are burdensome and expensive, and even a

successful one is notoriously difficult to collect. If you wind up having to sue an attorney in fact, you ironically become deeply entwined with the very legal system a power of attorney was designed to avoid.

2. Special Considerations Regarding Durable Powers of Attorney

It's important to acknowledge that anyone who considers adopting a durable power of attorney is by definition dealing with the possibility of being incapable of handling her own affairs. Obviously, no one likes to consider her own frailties, let alone the fact she might become so incompetent she can't manage her finances or make personal medical decisions. Facing the truth that you or someone you care about may become incapacitated is a powerful and often courageous act.

In this context, it's easy to understand why one might procrastinate preparing a durable power of attorney. A healthy person may simply want to avoid thinking that he could someday become incapacitated. A person who is ill, and may soon become so incapacitated that he can't manage his affairs, may attempt to deny that reality. There's no magic formula that can eliminate or diminish the feelings and fears which may cause people to postpone preparing a durable power of attorney. What can be offered are a few common sense suggestions.

- Despite superstitions, thinking about one's potential incapacity doesn't increase the possibility it will occur.

- A springing durable power of attorney, which goes into effect only in the event one becomes incapacitated, means there's absolutely no loss of control if incapacity doesn't occur.

- If incapacity does occur, someone who hasn't established a durable power of attorney setting out her wishes will likely have less control over what happens to her. Almost inevitably lawyers and courts will become involved in decision-making.

Aside from problems of trust and feelings of mortality, other important issues can arise with a durable power of attorney. An attorney in fact, acting under a durable power of attorney for health care, may likely become involved in emotional and moral dilemmas. For example, should an incompetent principal continue to receive artificial feeding when there's no hope for recovery? This can be a disturbingly real issue, not an academic question. An attorney in fact may be wrenched by powerful emotions if he needs to make a life-or-death decision for a loved one. (These matters are discussed further in Chapter 6.)

Another common and worrisome situation can develop if an ill person resists the honest efforts of loved ones trying to help her recognize she may soon be unable to handle her own affairs and should now prepare a durable power of attorney. This can cause very touchy problems. While you should never coerce a person to give up the right to handle her own affairs, you also don't want to wait too long—especially if you'll be left to deal with a legal mess if no durable power of attorney is prepared.

Problems can sometimes develop if the person urging an ill person to sign a durable power of attorney is the same one who will serve as attorney in fact. If the ill person's family or close friends are opposed to the durable power of attorney, they could file a court challenge claiming "undue influence" in establishing the durable power of attorney, and there could be a nasty legal battle.

Personal conflicts between family members or close friends may cause disagreement with the principal's selection of attorney in fact, or about the nature and extent of the authority delegated. This sometimes occurs when there are long-standing feuds among family members. If you foresee personal conflicts like these, it's wise to consider ways to defuse them in advance. Perhaps a discussion with people who are a little leery of your choice of attorney in fact might help.

As a general rule, if there's a significant chance that someone will challenge the legitimacy of the durable power of attorney or contend that the principal was coerced into it, it's wise to see an attorney. Discuss what specific steps can be taken to minimize the chances that the durable power of attorney could be ruled invalid in a lawsuit.

D. Revoking a Power of Attorney

As long as the principal is mentally competent, she can always revoke (invalidate) any power of attorney, durable or not. It's important to remember this as you proceed through the book. Also keep in mind that a springing durable power of attorney doesn't bind you from the date you sign it, but only if you become incapacitated in the future. In other words, it's a voluntarily adopted form of protection which you can revoke before it goes into effect. (Information and forms covering revocation of powers of attorney are provided in Chapter 10.)

Example

Susan prepares a springing durable power of attorney naming her closest friend, Tina, as her attorney in fact. Three years later, they have a bitter fight. Susan simply prepares a one-page document which revokes the durable power of attorney. Susan then prepares a new document, naming her sister Joan as her (new) attorney in fact.

E. Court Proceedings for an Incapacitated Person

Court proceedings to give someone legal authority to handle the financial affairs and/or personal and health care of an incapacitated person usually can be avoided if a durable power of attorney has been prepared in advance. Doing this is desirable where one's personal situation is relatively harmonious—after all, why needlessly involve a court in your affairs? Let's pause and explore this legal area, and see when court proceedings are advisable and when a durable power of attorney may be used instead. While the law of each state varies in detail, the following discussion is based on general legal principles, and should give you a good overview of what's involved.

Court proceedings to handle an incapacitated person's affairs go by several names in different states. They may be called custodianships, guardianships, conservatorships or curatorships. For simplicity, this book refers to this sort of court proceeding as a "conservatorship" with the incapacitated person known as the "conservatee" and the person appointed by the court to handle the conservatee's affairs as the "conservator."

Regardless of what they're called, these court proceedings are basically the same. They all involve a court determination of whether a conservator should be appointed to have legal authority to manage the financial and/or personal affairs—including medical decisions—of the conservatee.

The appointment of a conservator is a serious act. It means the conservatee will lose a number of the most basic aspects of life, such as the right to control her own money, make medical decisions for herself or choose where she will live. The conservatee may lose the right to manage even a small allowance, vote, travel or drive a car. And while a conservatorship isn't necessarily permanent, it may only be ended by a subsequent court action, something that often isn't easy. In addition, court proceedings are public and there's an inherent stigma attached to people who have been publicly determined to be unable to feed, clothe or take care of themselves or their finances. To top things off, conservatorships are time-consuming and relatively costly.

A conservatorship proceeding begins when a petition is filed with a court, usually in the county where the proposed conservatee lives. It is typically filed by the proposed conservatee's spouse, relatives or close friends, and could even be filed by the proposed conservatee. The petition alleges that the proposed conservatee is incapacitated and cannot manage his own affairs. Filing this petition normally requires a lawyer who is familiar with conservatorship law and local court rules of procedure.[3]

The matter is set for a court hearing, and certain people—including the proposed conservatee, spouse and close relatives—are formally notified. At the hearing, the proposed conservatee and others may testify about the need for a conservatorship. The proposed conservatee has a right to his own lawyer, and he has the right to contest the proceeding.

A judge determines from the evidence whether the proposed conservatee is incapacitated and if so, selects the conservator. If there's no opposition to the petition, the hearing can be routine—albeit often upsetting and embarrassing. If there's opposi-

---

[3] In California, conservatorship proceedings may be handled without an attorney by using *The Conservatorship Book*, by Lisa Goldoftas and Carolyn Farren (Nolo Press).

tion, the hearing can become very nasty, with one side trying to prove the incapacity of the proposed conservatee, and the other side strenuously arguing the opposite. The potential conservatee may have to to testify unless a doctor states that he or she is unable. The conservatorship petition can even evolve into a full scale trial, along with inevitably complicated and expensive proceedings.

The conservator is usually selected by the conservatee, if he is competent enough to make that decision. If the conservatee does not express his preference, or if the court decides the conservatee's choice wasn't in his own "best interests," state law generally provides a priority list for who shall serve.[4] The court also has a big loophole allowing it to appoint whomever it determines best. In other words, it's even possible the conservatee will wind up with some crony of the judge managing his finances. If so, there's a distinct possibility that the conservator will pay himself handsomely for his services.

Once appointed by a court, the conservator may handle the conservatee's property and finances or have authority over his personal, medical and health care. One person may be assigned to manage both personal and property matters.

The appointment of a conservator is usually just the beginning of court proceedings, even if no one objects. Often the conservator must post a bond, pay premiums from the conservatee's money, and return to court if the required amount of bond changes. It handling finances, the conservator must have the property appraised at the conservatee's expense and prepare and file a full inventory with the court.

The conservator may opt to go back to court to obtain guidance or permission from a judge, or legal proceedings may be required by law for certain financial transactions. Detailed reports must be prepared

and periodically filed with the court by the conservator. Even matters that are entirely routine can potentially be contested or appealed, so someone who is disgruntled can fight every major action the conservator takes and have a field day in court. The conservator is entitled to receive compensation for his work. And of course, the attorney handling the case may also receive "reasonable" fees for services.

1. When is a Court Proceeding Needed?

You may wonder if all this court involvement and expense would ever be desirable. Usually it isn't—after all, a durable power of attorney can accomplish the same thing with no need to set foot in court. But here are several situations where a conservatorship may be necessary.

- *No Advance Preparation.* A court proceeding is generally inescapable once a person becomes incapacitated if there was no advance planning. While this situation is avoidable by simply preparing durable powers of attorney, this is sometimes easier said than done. As I suggested, some people just aren't willing to face up to the possibility of their own incapacity. If they don't, a conservatorship is a better alternative than forgery. (A court proceeding may not be required for some married couples, as discussed in Chapter 3, Section C(3).)

- *Need for Personal Supervision.* In rare instances, a person's situation may require detailed court supervision. Thus, if a person feels there's no one she trusts sufficiently to handle her financial affairs as an attorney in fact, a conservatorship can be desirable.

- *Likelihood of a Family Fight.* In situations where there are strong disagreements about how to handle a family member's finances or medical care, it may make sense to initiate conservatorship proceedings from the start, rather than rely on a durable power of attorney. In bitterly

---

[4]For example, the laws of a number of states, including California, provide that the conservator shall be the spouse, then an adult child, then a parent, and then a brother or sister of the conservatee.

contested situations, the court's controls, reviews and scrutiny can be helpful. Needless to say, this sort of contested situation is most likely to develop if a person has considerable assets. No one ever gets very worried about who will manage the financial affairs of people who own nothing but a 1970 Volkswagon and an elderly cat.

- *Reluctance to Serve as Attorney in Fact.* If no one is willing to serve as an attorney in fact, there may have to be a conservatorship proceeding. This situation can arise for various reasons. The would-be principal may have very tangled, murky finances, and no one willing to take on the job and risk of handling them. Or those close to an extremely ill person may decide that a conservatorship is preferable to a power of attorney. If someone is seriously abusing himself, suffering from insanity or some other gravely destructive emotional state, there might be a need to severely restrict his or her liberty. This type of restriction cannot be imposed through a durable power of attorney, but requires the direct sanction of the state through a court proceeding.

F. Using a Durable Power of Attorney to Avoid Court Proceedings

As you know, if a person becomes incapacitated and unable to handle his financial affairs or health care decisions, someone must have legal authority to take over. The issue is, what is the most convenient, least burdensome method to authorize this? In most instances, a durable power of attorney has many advantages over a conservatorship proceeding.

In a durable power of attorney for finances, you normally provide the attorney in fact with the exact same powers to manage your finances that a court grants a conservator—but you completely avoid the need for legal proceedings. An attorney in fact for finances normally has the right to:

- Handle the principal's bank account and pay the principal's bills;

- Collect all money owed the principal, including wages, government benefits or other income and negotiate with people or institutions who have claims against the principal;

- Maintain the home and any other real estate belonging to the principal; and

- Handle the principal's assets ranging from stock accounts to automobiles.

If the principal wants, he can use his durable power of attorney to impose limitations on the attorney in fact's authority.

Example

Steve creates a springing durable power of attorney, naming Ed as his attorney in fact. Steve doesn't want to risk the loss of his beloved auto, a 1970 yellow Jaguar XKE. So he simply states in the durable power of attorney document, "My attorney in fact shall have no authority to sell, encumber or transfer my automobile, a 1970 Jaguar XKE, license plate: LEMON."

Similarly, under a durable power of attorney for health care, an attorney in fact has authority to make medical decisions for an incapacitated principal, and to carry out the principal's written instructions. This includes such vital matters as:

- Enforcing the principal's written directions stating her desires regarding use of life-sustaining procedures;

- Deciding an appropriate medical treatment if the principal hasn't left binding instructions; and

- Having authority to visit the principal in a hospital.

Use of a durable power of attorney is usually the wisest method for handling the possibility of incapacity, but you shouldn't draft anything until you understand both the details of how they will work (i.e., read this book) and consider the other available options. Basically, there are two other legal options:

- A conservatorship (see Section E of this chapter); or

- Some other out-of-court method for handling your affairs if you become incapacitated. (These methods, including use of an "inter vivos," or "living," trust, are discussed further in Chapter 3, Section C(4) and Chapter 6, Section C.)

There is, of course, always another possibility—faking it. Should you become incapacitated, this involves someone in your family acting without legal authority on your behalf by forging your signature on checks, bills of sale, tax returns, etc., and asserting the right to make medical decisions on your behalf. This may work for a while, but it's risky, as well as illegal. Forging a name to a check, even with the best of intentions, is just plain dumb, especially when the fully legal alternative of use of a durable power of attorney is so convenient.

G. Legal Requirements to Establish Durable Powers of Attorney

One of the major benefits of a durable power of attorney is how few formal legal requirements are involved. Generally, those legal requirements are:

- *Words Stating the Principal's Intention*. The document must use words clearly demonstrating that the principal intended to create a durable power of attorney. This isn't hard to accomplish. For example, the durable power of attorney forms in this book have standard phrasing stating that the principal "willfully and voluntarily intends to create by this document a durable power of attorney" (or similar wording).

- *Appoint an Attorney in Fact*. The durable power of attorney must appoint at least one attorney in fact (there can be more), and contain some descrip-

tion of his or her powers (this can be very general);

- *Sign and Date the Document*. The document must be signed by the principal, and should be dated.

- *Review the Document Periodically*. Although very few states impose a time limit on the interval between the creation of a springing durable power of attorney document and a decision that incapacity exists, it's wise to review and renew the document every five to seven years to make sure it will be accepted.

In some states, the conditions listed above are the only legal requirements to establish a durable power of attorney. However, there are other actions which should be undertaken even if they're not formally required. The actions are essential to ensure your durable power of attorney will be accepted by people or institutions in the real world and include:

- *Type the Document*. A durable power of attorney should be double-space typed or word-processed on good white bond paper. Our society expects legal documents to be typed, and is suspicious of handwritten ones, even though they may meet all technical legal requirements.

- *Notarize the Document*. In my opinion, any durable power of attorney should be notarized. Financial durable powers of attorney authorizing the attorney in fact to handle real estate are generally required by law to be notarized. And some state laws require all durable power of attorneys for finances to be notarized whether or not you own real estate. As a practical matter, any durable power of attorney—whether for finances or health care—should be notarized, or there's a serious risk it won't be accepted.

- *Filing or Recording the Document*. "Recording" means that the power of attorney document is photocopied (often on microfilm) and maintained by an official state record keeper, usually going by a name like "county recorder of deeds." In most states, there's a separate county recorder of deeds office for each county. If the attorney in fact may buy or sell real estate, the durable power of attorney should be recorded. It normally isn't required that the document be filed or recorded with any state or judicial agency, although Arkansas, Missouri, North Carolina and South Carolina do have special filing/recording requirements for durable powers of attorney for finances. In any other state, though, recording can be one additional way to promote acceptability. Recorded documents may be more acceptable to bank officials or other financial personnel.

- *Keep the Document in a Safe Place.* The notarized, signed original durable power of attorney must be kept in a safe, convenient place. If the durable power of attorney becomes effective upon signing by the principal, the attorney in fact should keep the original. In the more typical case where a springing durable power of attorney is created, the original should be retained by the principal and kept in some place where it's also accessible to the attorney in fact. A safety deposit box isn't the best place to store a springing durable power of attorney, unless the attorney in fact is a co-tenant with access to the box. Bear in mind that if—or when—the attorney in fact begins to serve, he must quickly be able to obtain the original document. Without being able to show the original, the attorney in fact may not be able to exercise his authority.

- *Witnessing.* Having a document witnessed means that competent adults see the principal sign that document, and then those adults also sign as witnesses to the authenticity and competence of the principal. Generally, a power of attorney, whether durable or conventional, does not legally require witnessing (the few exceptions, such as the California durable power of attorney for health care, are noted in subsequent chapters). However, witnessing can be a good idea. It's often not hard to do, and the fact that a power of attorney has been witnessed can make it look more official, and therefore more acceptable in the real world.

Finally, to clear up any misconceptions you may have picked up talking to Uncle Albert, whose second wife was a legal secretary, here's what isn't required to create a valid durable power of attorney. The attorney in fact legally doesn't have to sign the durable power of attorney document. No formal transfer of title of the principal's assets to the attorney in fact is required. There are no legal administrative requirements imposed on the attorney in fact—i.e., no required reports to courts or administrative agencies.

H. How to Use this Book to Prepare Durable Powers of Attorney

Here are the steps you'll need to take to prepare your durable powers of attorney.

Step 1: Read the Overview Chapters

Read the overview chapters which explain each type of durable power of attorney in detail and provide guidelines on their preparation:

- Chapter 3 for Financial Durable Powers of Attorney; and

- Chapter 6 for Durable Powers of Attorney for Health Care.

Step 2: Decide on the Type(s) of Powers of Attorney You Want

Before you decide to create a durable power of attorney, make sure you understand:

- The different types of powers of attorney, and which best suits your needs (for example, both financial and health care powers of attorney may either be springing or standard);

- Alternatives to durable powers of attorney (see Chapter 3, Section C(4) and Chapter 6, Section C);

- The important role of your attorney in fact (See Chapter 3, Section G and Chapter 6, Section D(3); information for attorneys in fact is contained in Chapter 2); and

- Ways of enhancing acceptability of your durable power of attorney (see Chapter 3, Section E and Chapter 6, Section A(1).

Step 3: Prepare Your Draft Documents

Each overview chapter directs you to appropriate chapters which contain sample forms, optional clauses and detailed instructions on how to prepare your documents. Forms for financial durable powers of attorney are presented in Chapters 4 and 5. Forms for durable powers of attorney for health care are presented in Chapters 7 and 8. There are tear-out forms in the Appendix.

Step 4: Prepare Your Final Documents

Regardless of whether you re-type a durable power of attorney or fill in the blanks of a form contained in the Appendix, carefully follow the preparation guide-lines in the appropriate chapters.

Step 5: Have the Documents Signed, Dated and Notarized

It is crucial that each durable power of attorney be signed, dated, and notarized. (As mentioned, it can't hurt to have the document witnessed, although it's rarely required). Instructions on how to do this are contained in the appropriate chapters.

Step 6: Record and Distribute the Documents as Needed

Depending on the requirements of your state, and whether you own any real estate, you may need to record a copy of your financial durable power of attorney with the county recorder of deeds. The attorney in fact should be given a copy—and perhaps the original—durable power of attorney. You should also consider giving copies to any institutions or agencies with which the attorney in fact is likely to deal.

Step 7: Keep Your Original Power of Attorney in a Safe, Convenient Place

The original, signed durable power of attorney, should always be kept in a safe place to which the attorney in fact has easy, convenient access.

CHAPTER 2

INFORMATION FOR ATTORNEYS IN FACT

A. Introduction

Many readers of this book will be friends or family members of someone who might need a durable power of attorney. In some instances, the person you care about may face the prospect of incapacity in the near future because of illness or age-related problems. Or, perhaps the person is simply prudent and wants to prepare for the possibility of becoming incapacitated, however remote that now seems. Regardless of the reason, you'll naturally want to help someone you care about make provisions for future decision-making.

Anyone considering serving as an attorney in fact should be aware that the position commits one to serious responsibilities. Bear in mind that no one can be forced to serve in that capacity—it's a voluntary job from which the attorney in fact can legally resign at any time. However, practically speaking, once a person begins to serve and function as an attorney in fact, it isn't easy to quit—either morally or legally. Additionally, the resignation of an attorney in fact may result in the need for a court proceeding unless the durable power of attorney document provides for a successor.

If you have been or might be asked to serve as attorney in fact, you may have a number of questions you want answered before you agree to serve. What exactly are you committing yourself to? What legal and ethical duties are involved in serving in this position? What practical problems will arise if the principal becomes incapacitated and you start handling her business affairs or health care?

Particularly with a durable power of attorney for health care, an attorney in fact may have to make serious, weighty decisions. For example, difficult questions concerning use of life sustaining equipment may arise. How unlikely do a patient's chances of recovery have to be before his condition is "hopeless?" What action should an attorney in fact take if hospital personnel are reluctant to follow medical instructions in a durable power of attorney? It's appropriate to pause and consider what someone who serves as attorney in fact is actually getting into both from practical and legal viewpoints.

B. Practical Concerns

The most important concern for the attorney in fact, as with the principal, is trust. The attorney in fact must trust the principal and feel confident that the principal is being open and honest. If you've been asked to serve as an attorney in fact but have doubts about your ability to trust the principal, decline the job. No underlying motivation, such as obligation or guilt, is a sound basis for accepting these important responsibilities.

An essential step you must take before accepting the position is to assess the principal's personal and family situation. Will others close to the principal support you? Are you walking into a nest of jealousy and suspicion? Are you willing to spend the energy to deal with whatever conflicts and tensions may be involved? This is an area where it's important to be realistic. Once you take on the role, it won't be easy to change your mind.

Assuming the presence of trust and relative family peace, the attorney in fact must next evaluate the overall situation. How much time might be involved in serving as attorney in fact? What types of decisions might you be called on to make? Do you know what the principal's assets are, and do you have the expertise to manage them? What health care decisions might be required? How do you feel about dealing with hospitals and doctors? Do you have the time, energy and willingness to do whatever the job requires? All these practical concerns, and any others you deem significant, should be considered, discussed and resolved with the would-be principal before you agree to serve as attorney in fact.

1. Special Considerations for Durable Powers of Attorney

If you begin to serve as attorney in fact upon signing of a durable power of attorney by the principal, it doesn't matter whether the principal now is, or later becomes, incapacitated. However, if you are to serve only if and when the principal becomes incapacitated (i.e., the principal uses a "springing" durable power of attorney), it's obviously vital that you know exactly how this determination will be made and that you feel comfortable with the process.

The method adopted by the forms in this book is certification of incapacity by a doctor—or by two doctors if the principal chooses. This can seem so reasonable that some people may overlook considering which doctor will make the determination. As prospective attorney in fact, carefully discuss the issue of incapacity with the would-be principal. Does he have a personal doctor he trusts to make this important decision? If so, has that doctor been asked if she'll be willing to make a determination of incapacity? If there's no personal doctor, what hospitals or other medical resources are available to make the determination of incapacity?

Finally, if you plan to take on the responsibility of being an attorney in fact under a durable power of attorney for health care, talk with the would-be principal about his wishes for health care. Also ask yourself these questions:

- Is the principal likely to cooperate with my best efforts and honest judgment when it comes to health care decisions or the finding of incapacity by a physician?

- Do I know and feel comfortable with the principal's general approach to health care?

- If the principal states in his power of attorney that he wants to be disconnected from life-support equipment if he is diagnosed with a terminal condition, do I feel comfortable with implementing this decision?

If the answer to any of these questions is "No," red flags are flying and you may want to seriously reconsider taking on the responsibility of serving as attorney in fact.

2. Legal Technicalities Required of an Attorney in Fact

If you actually need to serve as an attorney in fact, you need to know whether your state's laws impose any technical requirements for paperwork you handle, especially for financial matters. For example, in California, when an attorney in fact signs a document for a principal which must be notarized, a specific form of notary acknowledgement must be used. Candidly, it's my impression that many people, including many lawyers, aren't aware of this obscure California requirement, and in most cases it would be ignored. Still, this is obviously not the safest course of action. If you are actually called upon to serve as an attorney in fact for an incapacitated principal, it's sensible to check with a knowledgeable expert—a lawyer or a reliable financial adviser—to learn the rules for properly executing documents, and any other technical requirements.

C. Legal Concerns for Durable Powers of Attorney

This section covers the legal concerns of those serving as attorneys in fact under a durable power of attorney. Because durable powers of attorney are relatively new, there's no developed body of law specifically concerned with the duties and powers of attorneys in fact. However, there are ample laws and cases concerning "agents" and "fiduciaries," who are essentially the legal equivalents of attorneys in fact. There is also much legal precedent relating to attorneys in fact under conventional powers of attorney.

These laws and cases indicate that attorneys in fact will be held strictly accountable for acting in the principal's best interests—that is, doing what's best for her (in legalese, this is called a "fiduciary duty"). This strict legal standard will not arise in most simple situations. For example, if the attorney in fact's basic function will be to sign for the principal's retirement check, deposit it in a bank and pay for the principal's basic needs, there will probably be little possibility of uncertainty or dispute. However, if the principal has more complicated finances or needs, events may not flow so smoothly.

Under traditional legal principles, an attorney in fact is legally required to:

- Act in good faith and be able to demonstrate that she has done so (i.e., keep adequate records; faithfully follow the principal's expressed medical wishes, even if her own desires conflict);

- Never allow any conflict of interest between the principal and herself, such as being personally involved with, or stand to profit by, any transaction where she represents the principal; and

- Never commingle (mix) the principal's funds with her own.

These legal standards may impose rather demanding duties on an attorney in fact beyond the obvious requirement of acting honestly. For example, if the principal has complicated finances, the attorney in fact may have to keep detailed financial records distinctly separate from any other records she maintains. Fortunately, the principal can insert clauses in his durable power of attorney allowing the attorney in fact to act sensibly without being artificially restricted by fiduciary duties.

Assuming you feel comfortable knowing that you'll be held to a high standard of trust and care should your management of the principal's affairs ever be questioned, you should next consider the following practical legal concerns before agreeing to serve.

1. Will You Be Compensated as Attorney in Fact?

In family situations, an attorney in fact is normally not paid if her duties won't be complicated or burdensome. However, there are plenty of situations when compensation makes sense, and some where it's virtually essential, given the amount of time and effort the attorney in fact will devote to the job.

If you, as attorney in fact, are likely to devote significant time managing the principal's property and finances, or attending to an ill principal's medical care, compensation seems fair. Certainly, this issue should be discussed and resolved by the proposed attorney in fact and would-be principal. If you are to be compensated as attorney in fact, this should be stated in writing in the durable power of attorney document. (See sample clauses in Chapter 4, Section E(2)(e).) The rate of compensation should also be set out. This can run from "reasonable compensation, as determined by the attorney in fact," to a set hourly rate, to any other method agreed upon.

(FIDUCIARY - A VERY SPECIAL KIND OF RELATIONSHIP)

2. What "Standard of Duty" Will Be Required of the Attorney in Fact?

As previously noted, the attorney in fact is always a "fiduciary," and must act in good faith to and for the principal. The same standards apply whether or not the attorney in fact is paid. But suppose you, as attorney in fact, in good faith make an error of judgment or a careless mistake? Are you willing to accept potential liability to the principal or his heirs for your mistakes? If you want to be protected from liability for your possible negligence or bad decisions, you can have the principal specify that the attorney in fact can only be liable for willful misconduct, which means intentionally doing something wrong (see Chapter 4, Section E(2)(f)).

Example

Jim and Edward have been living together for 25 years. They have a joint checking account and share all basic living expenses. Each names the other as his attorney in fact in springing durable power of attorney documents. If one actually serves as the other's attorney in fact, technically, he isn't allowed to "commingle" (i.e., share or pool) the principal's funds with his own. But this is exactly what they have been doing all along. What can Jim and Edward do to deal with this problem? Fortunately, the law allows them to make specific provisions to allow commingling of funds, and excusing any liability for innocent mistakes made when handling the other's money as his attorney in fact.

3. May the Attorney in Fact Engage in "Self-dealing?"

"Self-dealing" means taking part in activities where the attorney in fact personally stands to benefit—for example, if an attorney in fact borrows some of the principal's money for her own use. As noted above, an attorney in fact normally has no right to commingle the principal's money with her own or otherwise engage in self-interested business dealings. Permission for self-dealing given in the power of attorney document means that the attorney in fact has the authority to engage in transactions which would otherwise be a conflict of interest, including purchasing the principal's property for herself. Authorizing the attorney in fact to self-deal can be unwise from the principal's point of view—why open up a potential can of worms? But there are many situations where permitting self-dealing by the

attorney in fact is desirable, especially if the principal is appointing a person such as a spouse, family member, business partner or other person whose affairs are already intertwined with his (see Chapter 4, Section E(2)(g)).

Example 1

Jack and Alice are best friends. Both are involved in real estate. Jack wants Alice to serve as his attorney in fact. They have been involved in many real estate transactions together: shared ownerships, shared sales, sales to one another, purchases from one another. Currently Jack and Alice are involved in several shared projects, including some involving other people. Jack doesn't want to risk disrupting these projects, or curtailing Alice's ability to do business, so Jack specifically states in his durable power of attorney that Alice may, in her capacity as attorney in fact, buy or sell Jack's property to herself, as long as the transaction reflects fair market prices.

Example 2

Art appoints his son, Michael, as his attorney in fact. Art knows his summer home may have to be sold to raise cash, and he wants Michael to have the first chance to buy it. So he specifically provides in his financial durable power of attorney that his attorney in fact has first choice to buy Art's summer home at the fair market price if the attorney in fact determines the home should be sold.

4. What Records Must be Maintained by the Attorney in Fact?

If nothing in the durable power of attorney document provides otherwise, the attorney in fact is legally required to keep accurate and separate records for all transactions he engages in for the principal. This is true whether or not the attorney in fact is compensated for her time. The attorney in fact must be able to demonstrate where and how all the principal's money has been spent. This is particularly important if an attorney in fact wishes to resign and turn her responsibility over to a successor.

Keeping detailed records may be fine in legal theory, but sometimes it may be burdensome and unnecessary in reality. If you feel that this is the case, talk with the principal about adding language to the durable power of attorney to relax the normal record keeping duties. A common way to do this is to state that the attorney in fact only need to keep those records she deems necessary.

Example

Sarah appoints Kathryn, her daughter (a poet with three children), to serve as her uncompensated attorney in fact. Sarah receives income from her savings, two IRAs, Social Security, and stock dividends. She doesn't want Kathryn to have to bother with keeping records of income and expenses, aside from what's required for bank and tax purposes. So she states in her durable power of attorney document that no distinct record keeping is required.

It's clearly important for a prospective attorney in fact to consider what record keeping is appropriate. Once the attorney in fact and the principal reach agreement, then the principal should write up a clause setting forth what has been agreed on and insert it into the durable power of attorney document. Especially if the attorney in fact is likely to be too busy to keep detailed records, she'll want to be sure the principal has adopted a record keeping standard that will work. If the principal has complicated finances, you as prospective attorney in fact may want an express provision that you can hire an accountant, or other financial adviser, as you deem appropriate.

Important: If you're the attorney in fact, it's wise to start with thorough, complete records of the principal and review them to make sure they're in order before incapacity occurs.[1] If you can't cooperate satisfactorily with the principal on getting clear records, this is a good tip-off you may face serious trouble if you agree to be attorney in fact.

5. Can the Attorney in Fact Legally Resign?

Generally, there's no legal prohibition which prevents an attorney in fact from resigning, for any reason. However, leaving a disabled principal on the lurch could be considered a breach of duty, or just plain wrong. Also, there's the possibility that the attorney in fact herself could become disabled, or be otherwise unable to continue serving. The best way to handle these concerns is for the principal to name at least one successor attorney in fact in the durable power of attorney document should the original attorney in fact stop serving for any reason.

D. Common Sense Conclusion

After raising all these concerns and issues, let's recall that in most situations, the person the principal wants to serve as attorney in fact will readily agree to do so, and no serious problems will be raised. A prospective attorney in fact should be careful when deciding if it's wise to serve, but there's no need to ignore common sense, good feelings, and most likely, years of intimate connection out of a fear that serving as attorney in fact will result in a horrible legal morass. In most situations, serving as attorney in fact involves little legal risk and is a loving and generous thing to do for a close family member or friend.

---

[1] One good way to organize and maintain records is by using *For the Record*, by Carol Pladsen & Ralph Warner (Nolo Press), a computer program where you can keep and update all important records.

CHAPTER 3

FINANCIAL DURABLE POWERS OF ATTORNEY

A. Introduction

This chapter focuses on durable powers of attorney used for handling a person's financial affairs and assets. They are referred to in this book as "durable powers of attorney for finances" or simply as "financial durable powers of attorney."

Before you plunge into drafting any documents, it's important that you gain a more thorough understanding of how financial durable powers of attorney work. As you read this chapter, you may want to make notes of ideas, problems, thoughts and decisions that occur to you. Carefully consider what major choices you'll make when you prepare your own durable power of attorney.

After you finish this chapter, proceed to Chapter 4, which provides you with specific sample forms and clauses you can use, adapt, or modify to design your own financial durable power of attorney.

If you live in California or New York, also read Chapter 5, which discusses statutory "short form" financial durable powers of attorney available in those states. Statutory short forms can be used as a substitute for the general forms discussed in the bulk of this book to create a specifically authorized durable power of attorney. Readers who live in Alaska, Connecticut, Illinois, Minnesota and North Carolina—which also have statutory short forms—may benefit from reading Chapter 5, because although the statutory "short forms" aren't required, they may offer advantages to non-statutory forms.

Once you've learned what you can do in a financial durable power of attorney, you can use one of the tear-out, fill-in-the-blanks forms in the Appendix to prepare your draft.

Note on Health Care: "Incapacity" obviously raises problems concerning health care matters. Financial durable powers of attorney are generally "springing"—i.e., they become operational only if the principal becomes incapacitated. Unless yours are unusual circumstances, you'll also want to authorize someone to make health care decisions for you as well, in the event you become incapacitated. Often the simplest and wisest choice is for you to authorize the same person to handle decision-making in both areas, even though you create two separate documents. Read Chapter 6 for an overview of durable powers of attorney for health care, and then either Chapter 7 or 8 (depending on your state) for instructions on drafting one.

B. State Laws Affecting Financial Durable Powers of Attorney

All 50 states and the District of Columbia (Washington, D.C.) permit some form of durable power of attorney for finances. The legal right to establish a financial durable power of attorney is drawn from one of three distinct sources, depending on your state's laws.

What difference does the legal basis authorizing a financial durable power of attorney make? For the purpose of this book, it can make an important difference. Depending on the legal basis your state uses, the forms contained in this book will either work for you without modification, or should be reviewed by an attorney. The forms in this book are modeled on the Uniform Durable Power of Attorney Act,[1] which has been adopted by some, but not all, states.

The charts in Section B(1) below provide you with a detailed breakdown regarding each state's legal basis for financial durable powers of attorney:

- *Chart 1:* Lists those states which have adopted a form of the Uniform Durable Power of Attorney Act without substantial changes. If your state has adopted a version of that Act, you can be confident that the general information and forms presented in this book are valid in your state.

---

[1] "Uniform" Acts are drafted by a centralized commission of lawyers and legal scholars.

- *Chart 2*: States listed in this chart have adopted a part of the Uniform Probate Code that authorizes durable powers of attorney. The Uniform Probate uses almost identical language in authorizing durable powers of attorney as the Uniform Durable Power of Attorney Act. If your state is listed in Chart 2, and authorizes durable powers of attorney on the basis of provisions of the Uniform Probate Code, the information and forms presented here are also substantially accurate. However, as some states changed certain minor details when adopting the Uniform Probate Code, the possibility exists that in your state there's a minor variation in legal requirements from those set out here. In other words, if your state is listed in Chart 2, it may be a good idea to check your final draft with a lawyer.[2]

- *Chart 3*: States which impose limits or special conditions on durable powers of attorney for finances are listed in Chart 3. These states authorize durable powers of attorney on a basis other than those described above, or have imposed serious restrictions on the Uniform Durable Power of Attorney Act or Uniform Probate Code. For example, Arkansas, Missouri, North Carolina and South Carolina each impose distinct filing or recording requirements (e.g., filing with a county recorder, or registering with the probate court clerk). In states like these, you need to know actual local practice, as well as the specifics of the law, to be sure your durable power of attorney will prove viable. If your state is listed in Chart 3, I must advise you to check your work with an attorney. However, despite the necessity

for this warning, in many cases you'll discover that the basic substance of the forms provided in this book complies with your state's law. (How to find an attorney, and what you should expect to pay, is covered in Chapter 11.)

1. Charts Summarizing State Laws

Set out below are Charts 1-3. When you've found your state, make sure you understand the consequences of its categorization as explained above.

CHART 1: STATES WHICH HAVE ADOPTED THE UNIFORM DURABLE POWER OF ATTORNEY ACT

Alabama	Montana
California	Nebraska
District of Columbia	North Dakota
Delaware	Pennsylvania
Idaho	Tennessee
Indiana	Vermont
Kansas	West Virginia
Massachusetts	Wisconsin

CHART 2: STATES WHICH HAVE ADOPTED SOME FORM OF THE UNIFORM PROBATE CODE PROVISIONS FOR DURABLE POWERS OF ATTORNEY

Alaska	Maryland	Oregon
Arizona	Michigan	Rhode Island
Colorado	Minnesota	South Dakota
Connecticut	Nevada	Utah
Hawaii	New Jersey	Washington
Iowa	New Mexico	Wyoming
Kentucky	New York	
Maine	Ohio	

---

[2]To emphasize this point, here is an excerpt from the Official Report of the Uniform Probate Code Commission regarding the durable power of attorney provisions adopted by the states listed in Chart 2: "Because of the numerous variations resulting from the manner of adoption of the Probate Code by various jurisdictions, it is not feasible to note the difference in the individual sections of the Code between the Official text and the counterpart text in adopting jurisdictions."

CHART 3: STATES THAT RECOGNIZE SOME FORM OF A DURABLE POWER OF ATTORNEY

Arkansas	Mississippi	South Carolina
Florida	Missouri	Texas
Georgia	New Hampshire	Virginia
Illinois	North Carolina	
Louisiana	Oklahoma	

Repeat Warning: In these states, it's essential that you check out the law before relying on the information and forms presented in this book to prepare a financial durable power of attorney.

C. Assessing Your Need for a Financial Durable Power of Attorney

To determine whether to prepare a financial durable power of attorney, you'll need to figure out whether you need one—and if so, what kind.

1. Do You Need a Financial Durable Power of Attorney?

Practically everyone with assets or income could benefit from a financial durable power of attorney. Prime candidates are older people and those with serious health conditions such as upcoming operations or life-threatening illnesses. If a person becomes incapacitated and unable to handle his financial affairs, inevitably there will be practical matters to be handled. Bills must be paid, bank deposits made, insurance and benefits paperwork dealt with. Many other matters may have to be handled, from purchasing Christmas presents to administering complex business interests. In most cases, a durable power of attorney is the wisest method of handling all these financial affairs.

2. What Type of Financial Durable Power of Attorney Do You Need?

As explained in Chapter 1, Section A, you have two choices for your durable power of attorney when it comes to managing your finances:

- A *standard financial durable power of attorney,* effective upon your signing (or on some other specific date you specify); or

- A *"springing" financial durable power of attorney,* effective only if you become incapacitated and are unable to handle your financial affairs.

Some people worry that a springing financial durable power of attorney relinquishes authority over their property upon signing. It doesn't. By the very terms of the document, it doesn't "spring" into effectiveness unless and until incapacity occurs.

Others worry about how incapacity is determined. Obviously, no one wants to wake up one morning to find that several family members or friends had a midnight meeting and decided she was incompetent. There's no precise functional state law definition of "incapacity." It's a factual matter determined by medical custom and practice. Normally, a durable power of attorney document specifies that the determination of incapacity must be made in writing, by a doctor (you can provide the name of the doctor empowered to make the determination). It's wise to discuss this matter with your doctor, and have an agreement that he'll be willing to make a determination regarding your capacity or incapacity. If this isn't safeguard enough for you, you can prepare a durable power of attorney which requires a second medical opinion before incapacity can be found (see Chapter 4, Section E(2)(a)).

Which type of financial durable power of attorney is best for you depends, of course, on your circumstances. If a person knows, or reasonably believes, that she's likely to become incapacitated soon, a standard durable power of attorney, effective upon signing, probably makes the most sense. For example, a person facing major surgery may authorize a durable power of attorney effective the day of the surgery. A person with a serious degenerative disease who knows he's rapidly losing the ability to manage business affairs probably would authorize a durable power of attorney effective upon signing.

However, most people don't need a durable power of attorney effective immediately or in the imminent future, because they're not in immediate danger of incapacity. Instead, they want to act now, to be prepared for the possibility that they might become incapacitated someday. These people need a springing durable power of attorney, effective only if they become incapacitated. A springing durable power of attorney is a kind of risk-free legal insurance, protecting you only if you need it.

3. Spouses and Financial Durable Powers of Attorney

What about spouses? If one spouse becomes incompetent, does the other need a durable power of attorney to handle both their finances? The answer here is that a durable power of attorney certainly can't hurt, and in some instances may be essential.

In community property states—Arizona, California, Idaho, Nevada, New Mexico, Texas, Washington and Wisconsin—either spouse has some legal rights to manage the community property.[3] In community property states, the additional authority provided by a durable power of attorney isn't needed as long as each spouse wants the other to manage the community property. However, if an incapacitated spouse owns valuable separate property, a durable power of attorney is wise, as the other spouse has no inherent legal authority to manage that property. Separate property includes property owned prior to marriage and property received by one spouse after marriage as a result of a gift or inheritance.

In non-community property states (all other states and the District of Columbia), there's more reason for spouses to create durable powers of attorney for asset management. In non-community property states, legal authority to manage property exists only for the person whose name is on the title to that property. If property is held in one spouse's name, as is often the case, the other spouse has no legal right to manage that property without either a durable power of attorney or a court order.

Example

New York residents, Michael and Ellen have been married for 47 years. Their major assets are a home and stock. The home is owned in both their names as joint tenants. The stock was purchased only in Michael's name, and the couple has never transferred it into shared ownership. Michael becomes incapacitated and requires expensive medical treatment. Legally, Ellen cannot sell the stock to pay for medical costs. (She could sell her interest, not Michael's, in the house, or take a loan against it, but that isn't what she wants to do.) Practically, stockbrokers may allow a spouse to sell stock owned in another spouse's name—but then again, they may not. It's surely unwise to take that risk when it can so easily be eliminated with a durable power of attorney.

---

[3]For a thorough discussion of California community property law and separate property, see *California Marriage and Divorce Law*, by Ralph Warner, Toni Ihara and Stephen Elias (Nolo Press).

4. Alternatives to a Financial Durable Power of Attorney

There are alternative methods to durable powers of attorney for handling financial problems arising from incapacity. Two have been mentioned previously: conservatorships (court proceedings) and ignoring the problem (faking it). As explained in Chapter 1, Sections E and F, neither of these methods is usually desirable. Two other methods for handling financial problems of possible incapacity are living trusts and joint tenancy, particularly for bank accounts. Let's explore both.

a. Living Trusts

A "living trust"—often called an "inter vivos trust"—is an arrangement where title to property is transferred by its living owner (called a "settlor") to a trust, managed by a "trustee." In a living trust, the settlor and the trustee are the same person. The trust property is controlled by the settlor while she is alive. After the settlor dies, a successor trustee transfers the trust property to the beneficiaries chosen by the settlor. The primary purpose of a living trust is to avoid probate, the costly court process required for property left by a will.[4] For this reason, it's common to transfer into a living trust those assets that are most expensive to probate, such as real estate and valuable securities.

What does all this have to do with incapacity? The answer is that, in a living trust, the settlor may also provide for what shall be done with the trust property if she becomes incapacitated. A standard provision states that, if incapacity occurs, the successor trustee shall manage the trust property for the benefit of the settlor.

Although a living trust can provide extensive authority for another person to handle your financial affairs upon incapacity, it's generally advisable to create a durable power of attorney even if you create a living trust. There may be assets or financial matters which you never transfer to the trust, so the successor trustee has no authority over these. Normally, you would appoint the same person to be the successor trustee and the attorney in fact.[5]

Example

Mary, a widow, owns a prosperous clothing manufacturing company. To avoid probate, she transfers the company stock into a living trust, naming her brother, Herb, as successor trustee. If Mary becomes incapacitated, Herb will become acting trustee, and manage the trust (i.e., the manufacturing company) for Mary's benefit. Mary also prepares a durable power of attorney to cover whatever assets are not transferred to the trust (e.g., her personal bank accounts) and names Herb as her attorney in fact.

b. Joint Tenancy

Joint tenancy is a form of equally shared property ownership. The key to joint tenancy is that when one owner dies, the other owner(s) automatically own that deceased person's share of the property.

Except for bank accounts, joint or shared ownership of property isn't a sensible method for handling one owner's incapacity. For example, problems can arise if real estate is owned in joint tenancy. If one owner becomes incapacitated, the other would have no legal authority to sell or refinance the incapacitated owner's share.

In a joint tenancy bank account, either (or any) of the joint owners can make deposits or withdrawals. This right can enable a healthy joint tenant to take care of the financial needs of the incapacitated

---

[4] For information about use of living trusts, see *Plan Your Estate: Wills, Probate Avoidance, Trusts and Taxes*, by Denis Clifford (Nolo Press).

[5] A successor trustee of a living trust cannot be given authority to make medical decisions for you, unlike an attorney in fact, so a health care durable power of attorney is also recommended if you establish a living trust. (See Chapter 6.)

person simply by paying bills from the joint account. However, if the incapacitated person receives income (other than cash), the other joint bank account owner has no legal right to sign or endorse checks made out to the incapacitated person. In practice, checks are often deposited to a joint account by stamping them with "For Deposit Only," so it might be possible—if not technically legal—to get an incapacitated person's checks into a joint account. But if the incapacitated person has other financial interests, from home ownership to stocks to a business, joint tenancy bank accounts can't help. It's unwise to rely on a joint bank account to handle financial problems arising from incapacity.

D. Scope of Financial Durable Powers of Attorney

Durable powers of attorney are very flexible legal tools, capable of being tailored to your precise needs and circumstances. With a few limits, discussed in this section, you can make your durable power of attorney as broad and general or as narrow and specific as you desire.

1. Deciding on the Scope

Unless restricted by you (the principal) in the durable power of attorney document itself, your attorney in fact normally has very broad power over your assets. Thus, your attorney in fact can sell, transfer or encumber your property as she thinks best. The attorney in fact can use your assets to pay for any of your obligations, including all debts, home maintenance costs, taxes, insurance premiums, wage claims, medical care costs, child support, alimony and your personal allowance. The attorney in fact can execute deeds, make gifts, pay school expenses, endorse and deposit checks.

In short, because of the broad flexibility of a durable power of attorney, the attorney in fact can be granted almost all the powers that you enjoy yourself or which could be granted to a conservator through a court proceeding. However, unlike a conservatorship, you can limit the power you grant, or place conditions upon the attorney in fact. You can accomplish this by including restrictions in the durable power of attorney document.

Example 1

Ilana, who's elderly and frail, prepares a springing durable power of attorney authorizing her niece, Patricia, to be her attorney in fact in the event Ilana becomes incapacitated. Ilana trusts Patricia. However, Ilana is nevertheless fearful that her home might somehow be sold, even though Patricia has promised she would never do that. So Ilana writes into her durable power of attorney a provision stating, "In no event shall my attorney in fact have authority or power to sell, transfer or otherwise encumber my home at 222 Fern Street, Greendale, Alabama."

Example 2

Theodore Post, who is ill, decides to appoint his son, Jason, as his attorney in fact to handle his financial affairs. Theodore has two other children, Nancy and Ed, who don't live in Theodore's state. Nancy and Ed aren't on the best of terms with Jason. To try to prevent suspicion or conflict between his children over Jason's handling of Theodore's finances, Theodore decides to require Jason to prepare quarterly reports of all financial transactions he engages in as attorney in fact and deliver them to Nancy and Ed. To accomplish this, Theodore inserts the following clause in his durable power of attorney: "The attorney in fact shall prepare quarterly reports of all financial transactions he engages in for or with any asset of the principal. A copy of each such report shall be mailed to Nancy Byrne and Edward Post within 14 days of preparation."

The possibilities of what can be specified in a financial durable power of attorney and what can be excluded or limited are nearly endless. What's important is for you to carefully think about your own situation. Do you simply want to turn all your property over to the management of your attorney in fact if you become incapacitated? If so, fine. Preparing the paperwork will consist of little more than filling in the blanks on a prepared form. But if you intend to impose specific restrictions and limitations, you'll need to pin down exactly what controls you want. There's no one approach to accomplish this that's right for everyone. It's important that you take time to focus on your needs. Make some notes and start thinking of your desires, fears, hopes and circumstances. Talk over your concerns with a trusted friend or family member. That way, as you get deeper into financial durable powers of attorney, you'll be working up the answers to your own problems as you go along. (Clauses for customizing your financial durable power of attorney are included in Chapter 4, Section E.)

CUSTOMIZING YOUR FINANCIAL DURABLE POWERS OF ATTORNEY

To give you an idea of the range and flexibility of durable powers of attorney, here are a few options you may consider adopting:

- You can use two or more attorneys in fact, and you can prescribe that they must act unanimously or that a majority prevails.

- You can determine what happens in the event of conflict between attorneys in fact. You can compel binding arbitration, give one attorney in fact final authority, or specify other ways of dealing with disagreements.

- You can require that your attorney in fact keep certain records and make them available to specific people.

- You can impose any control over your property you want and describe how certain property should be managed.

- You can prohibit your attorney in fact from doing whatever has not been delegated in the durable power of attorney document.

- You can authorize your attorney in fact to make gifts—or you can eliminate that authority.

- You can define what you mean by incapacity (as long as your definition isn't unreasonable), including requiring a second medical opinion before you're found to be incapacitated.

---

2. Costs of a Durable Power of Attorney

In most instances, the only cost you pay to create a durable power of attorney is the price of this book. However, in some situations there may be some additional costs, such as:

- *Attorney's Fees.* If you have your durable power of attorney reviewed by a lawyer, you'll have to pay her fee. This fee shouldn't be large, at least by lawyers' standards (see Chapter 11 for details on how to hire and pay a lawyer to review your document).

- *Attorney in Fact's Compensation.* If you decide your attorney in fact is to be compensated for her services, those fees will be paid from your property.

- *Fees for Accountants and Experts.* If your finances require use of professionals, such as accountants or financial advisers, the attorney in fact will pay these fees from your assets.

- *Recording Fees.* If your attorney in fact will be buying or selling real estate, or state law requires it, you'll need to record the durable power of attorney. This cost is nominal (usually $5.00 to $15.00).

3. Arrangements for Minor Children

A durable power of attorney has limited use in arranging for the care of one's minor children (people under age 18 in most states) if one becomes incapacitated. Several problems can arise if a person with minor children becomes incapacitated, such as:

- Who will have custody and care of the children (serve as the children's personal legal guardian)?

- Who will manage the children's property, if they legally own or inherit any?

- How will the children's financial needs be met?

If there's another person who also has legal custody of the children, such as a spouse or ex-spouse, that person will be responsible for the children and their property. But if there's no other person who already has legal custody, then a court will have to determine who will become the children's guardian. The guardian may be responsible for caring for the children, their property, or both.

A durable power of attorney cannot be used to give anyone authority to care for your children. Your children are not property, and you cannot delegate guardianship of them in any durable power of attorney. The best you can do is set forth in writing your nomination for a personal guardian of your children, should that need arise, along with an explanation of the reasons for your choice. This type of nomination can be quite persuasive to a court. Although a will is the best place for this nomination, it can't hurt to repeat it in your durable power of attorney. (See Chapter 4, Section E(2)(r).)

A durable power of attorney also can't be used to delegate responsibility for managing property legally owned by your children. Again, a property guardian must be appointed by court proceeding. However, a durable power of attorney can be used to have some or all of a parent's property managed for the benefit of her children. The attorney in fact can be directed to use the principal's assets to pay for the children's needs. The clauses creating this direction can be as detailed and specific as you want them to be. (See Chapter 4, Section E(2)(j) for specific clauses.)

4. Durable Powers of Attorney and Wills

As you know, a durable power of attorney legally terminates upon death of the principal. An attorney in fact cannot be given authority to handle the principal's post-death affairs, such as payment of debts, burial arrangements or transfer of assets to inheritors. Moreover, an attorney in fact cannot make a will (a document used for designating how property should be distributed after a person's death) for the principal. However, an attorney in fact can be given authority to make gifts while the principal remains alive, including gifts designed to save on estate taxes.

A principal can create other legal documents, such as a will or living trust, to give the same person who serves as attorney in fact authority to handle the principal's affairs after death. Don't rely on a durable power of attorney for estate planning purposes. Be sure you've also made effective arrangements for the handling of your affairs after your death. (See Section H(1) of this chapter.)

5. Combining Use of Conventional and Durable Powers of Attorney

If desired, you can use a durable power of attorney in conjunction with a conventional power of attorney. In Chapter 1, Section A(4), there's an example of use of a conventional power of attorney by Mary, who authorizes her attorney in fact to handle the closing of her home purchase while she's in Paris. Because a conventional power of attorney no longer works if the principal becomes incapacitated, Mary could also prepare a separate springing durable power of attorney so she's protected if she becomes disabled or incapacitated (including while on her trip).

6. Considerations of Small Business Owners

If you're a sole proprietor of a business, a durable power of attorney can be a very useful method of allowing someone else to run that business if you become incapacitated. The document lets you designate who should take over and allows you to delegate precisely the authority you determine is needed. In addition, you can incorporate whatever safeguards or limits you want in the durable power of attorney document. Because no court proceedings are required, if you become incapacitated, there should be no disruption of your business—your attorney in fact steps in right away and continuity is preserved. Obviously, this sort of power of attorney should be worked out in close consultation with the person you plan to appoint as your attorney in fact.

If you're an owner of a shared business, provisions for handling incapacity should be included in the governing partnership agreement, or corporate bylaws. Those rules can't be overridden by a durable power of attorney (e.g., the CEO of IBM can't simply appoint his successor as his attorney in fact.) Owners of a shared small business can appoint each other as attorneys in fact if that's consistent with their basic agreement.

7. Reviewing, Revoking and Ending Durable Powers of Attorney

As of the latest printing of this book, no state has imposed a statutory time limit on the validity of financial durable powers of attorney. However, state laws in this area are subject to change or revision. Because of problems with acceptability which can arise over a document signed many years ago (see Section E of this chapter), this book urges you to redo and re-sign any springing durable powers of attorney you prepare every five to seven years, whether or not that is legally required in your state. People and institutions your attorney in fact will have to deal with are more likely to accept your document if the interval between its creation and your incapacity is relatively short.

Review and revision of your durable power of attorney are especially necessary if important facts change. For example, if the person you appointed as your attorney in fact in a springing durable power of attorney moves out of state, becomes ill, or is no longer personally close to you, a change should be made immediately and the appropriate parties or institutions notified.

In most circumstances, a durable power of attorney can be revoked by the principal at any time,

as long as he is legally competent. (The rare exceptions to this rule are covered in Chapter 10.) If the attorney in fact disputes the competence of the principal to revoke the durable power of attorney, there's an obvious problem. The attorney in fact may deeply believe that the principal doesn't know what he is doing, is deluded, etc. If so, there will probably have to be court proceedings to resolve the conflict.

Aside from revocation by the principal, or automatically by law, a durable power of attorney is terminated by death of the principal, or upon any earlier date specified in the document itself. However, it's normally not wise to specify a set termination date in advance. If you become incapacitated, there's no sure way to predict when you will recover, and you certainly don't want a durable power of attorney to end while you're still incapacitated.[6]

There's no generally accepted method for amending a durable power of attorney for finances. Rather than trying to invent an amendment form, and hope it will be accepted, I feel it's prudent to offer this conservative advice: If you want to revise or amend your document, revoke it completely and prepare a new one.

---

[6] In a conventional power of attorney, a set termination date is often sensible. This is discussed in more detail in Chapter 9.

E. Acceptability of Your Financial Durable Power of Attorney

"Acceptability" is the term used in this book to define the concept of "working in the real world." Obviously there's little point in establishing a financial durable power of attorney unless the people and institutions who will deal with your attorney in fact will accept her authority to act for you. If a person or institution, such as a bank, title company, insurance company, or government agency, absolutely refuses to accept the attorney in fact's authority, and the principal is incapacitated, there's little that can be done.[7] All of this means that it's wise to take the time to be sure any durable power of attorney you prepare will work. This shouldn't be difficult if you take the following steps.

1. Prepare Your Document Correctly

Make sure you've properly carried out all the necessary technical steps to prepare your form (I

---

[7] In theory, a rejected attorney in fact could file a lawsuit to compel an institution or person to accept his authority. Aside from the waste of time and money and uncertainty this would involve, durable powers of attorney are supposed to avoid lawsuits, not create them.

show you how to do this in Chapters 4 and 5). Include as part of your durable power of attorney specific clauses which expressly exonerate from any liability people or institutions who rely on the attorney in fact's authority. (The forms in Chapters 4 and 5 and the Appendix contain standard exoneration clauses.) Obviously, banks, brokers and others with whom your attorney in fact may have to deal are primarily concerned with their own self-interest and this sort of clause can work wonders when it comes to getting them to relax.

Check with an attorney if you live in a state which hasn't adopted a standard law governing durable powers of attorney for finances. (Review the charts in Section B(1) of this chapter, particularly Chart 3.) For example, in Florida, only "family members" can legally serve as your attorney in fact.

2. Contacting Financial Institutions

Give thought to your specific circumstances and see if there are any actions you can take prior to your incapacity to encourage acceptability. Usually there are. For example, since it's likely that your attorney in fact will be dealing with a particular bank, broker, insurer or other financial institutions, discuss your plans with institution officials, and place a copy of the durable power of attorney with their records.

If bank or other financial institution officials aren't familiar with durable power of attorney laws, they may be reluctant to accept the legal authority of your attorney in fact. Some education now can eliminate serious hassles for your attorney later. If the bank or other institution suggests that you use their form instead of the ones in this book, you'll probably want to do so. If you live in a state which has a statutory financial durable power of attorney form (Alaska, California, Connecticut, Illinois, Minnesota, New York and North Carolina), give serious consideration to using one of those forms to insure that no one can object to the legality of your form. (See Chapter 5 for more information on statutory financial durable powers of attorney.)

But what about a springing durable power of attorney? Isn't it premature to contact people and institutions about a document which may never go into effect? To some extent, the answer is "Yes," although it usually makes sense to place a copy of a springing durable power of attorney in your major financial institutions' records. Be sure to keep a list of everyone you've given copies. If you later revoke your financial durable power of attorney, contact each institution and give them your new document.

There's another act you can take with a springing durable power of attorney which should increase acceptability. This involves a question which may well arise concerning how outside people can confirm that the principal has become disabled. Do they simply have to take the attorney in fact's word for it? Obviously, people who handle money and are paid to be cautious may be reluctant to do so. To help solve this problem, you can provide, as part of your springing durable power of attorney, a form which can be signed by a physician stating that you've become incapacitated. (See the form in Chapter 4, Section 2E(a)(ii).) Should you ever become incapacitated, this form is signed by the doctor and attached to the original durable power of attorney document.

3. Record Your Document

If your attorney in fact will buy or sell real estate, recording is required. And in a few states (mentioned in Section B(1) of this chapter), recording is required. Otherwise, recording isn't essential. But some financial institution officials may be reassured by seeing that the principal took that step.

4. Periodically Review Your Documents

Review and prepare your durable springing power of attorney for finances at regular intervals. I recommend doing this every five to seven years. If the interval between signing a durable springing power of attorney and incapacity is very long, the power of attorney may be harder to get accepted.

F. Legal Limits of Financial Durable Powers of Attorney

Under the Uniform Durable Power of Attorney Act there are some limits on what the principal can delegate in a financial durable power of attorney. The laws of many states prohibit you from granting authority for a few specific acts. Fortunately, for the most part, these prohibitions are in areas that you wouldn't want to delegate anyway, so you really don't need to worry about them. Here's a brief summary:

1. Marriage, Adoption, Wills

An attorney in fact cannot be authorized to marry, adopt, or make a will on behalf of the principal. Why not? Because these acts are considered "too personal" for delegation.

2. Minor Variations in State Laws

There may be other minor restrictions in your state's laws on powers which can be granted to an attorney in fact. For example, in Tennessee, state law provides that the next of kin can petition a court to require an attorney in fact to post a bond. A bond is basically an insurance policy, generally issued by a surety company. If the variations in state law can have significant impact on your attorney in fact's authority, that state is listed on Chart 3 in Section B(1).

3. Community Property States

In community property states, such as Texas or Washington, a married principal cannot delegate to a non-spouse attorney in fact the authority to manage the other spouse's one-half share of the community property. Legally, a non-spouse attorney in fact can be appointed by a spouse to manage his or her own one-half share of community property, and all of his or her separate property. However, this could result in serious conflict between a spouse and the other spouse's attorney in fact. If you want to do this, see a lawyer. (For more information about financial durable powers of attorney, spouses, and community property, see Section C(3) above.)

4. Prior Legal Arrangements

Finally, there may be prior legal arrangements which prevent the principal from delegating authority over certain of his property, such as a contractual or partnership agreement.

Example
Mike wants his wife, Nancy, to be his attorney in fact to manage his finances if he becomes incapacitated. Mike is a house painter and partner in the M-J Painting Co. with his equal partner, Jack. Mike and Jack's partnership agreement provides that the other partner shall have exclusive authority to operate the partnership business if one partner becomes incapacitated. To prevent misunderstanding and conflict, Mike puts a clause in his durable power of attorney expressly excluding Nancy from having any authority over Mike's interest in the M-J Painting Co.

This example sounds tidy, doesn't it? In the real world, however, money matters often overlap and are intertwined with personal concerns, particularly when it comes to small businesses. If Mike and Nancy don't get along, or are likely to have conflict over money, there could be serious problems, and Mike should prepare very carefully, perhaps spelling out in great detail the scope of the arrangement in both his partnership agreement and durable power of attorney.

G. Some Advice on Choosing Your Attorney in Fact

In Chapter 1, it was emphasized that the most important decision regarding a durable power of attorney is selection of the attorney in fact. Chapter 2 discussed the concerns a person should address when deciding whether to serve as attorney in fact. Here it's appropriate to look deeper into what's involved in a principal's choice of an attorney in fact.

To remind you once more, the attorney in fact of a financial durable power of attorney has tremendous power over the principal's (your) property. If there's no person you trust sufficiently to give this great awesome power to, a durable power of attorney isn't for you. Don't try to make up for this lack of trust by restrictive provisions or controls over the attorney in fact in the document itself. Such restrictive controls can serve as a supplemental check to try to insure your wishes are carried out, but they're never an adequate substitute for trust.

Obviously, you should never name someone to serve as your attorney in fact without prior discussion and agreement. Common sense indicates this is unlikely to be a problem. What principal would be so foolish as to try to turn over management of her affairs to someone who might well decline the job?

In many situations, it's obvious who the attorney in fact should be. Often a spouse or loved one is the person you most trust to manage your finances. Or perhaps one member of your family is particularly good at managing business affairs, and you and other family members routinely ask her to help in these areas.

For some people, the choice may not be so clear. For example, you might decide that your attorney in fact needs business skills, knowledge or management abilities which the people closest to you don't have. Perhaps you're not sure who you want to be your attorney in fact, or there's no one person in your life who is the obvious choice. Perhaps your mate is old, or ill, and wouldn't be a good choice for attorney in fact. Or you may have no mate, but a number of friends and relatives. In this situation, there can be a potential for conflict from disgruntled family members or friends if someone they dislike is chosen the attorney in fact.

The only useful advise I can give you if you have doubts about who to choose as your attorney in fact is to ponder this issue carefully and discuss it with those closest to you. If you see the possibility of future conflict, try to defuse it in advance. While this book can't tell you who to choose as your attorney in fact, it can provide you suggestions on who to avoid:

- Don't choose someone who resides out of state to be your attorney in fact (or even your successor attorney in fact). This isn't legally permitted in many states, and is a bad idea in any case. The attorney in fact must reside nearby to carry out his duties and responsibilities properly and promptly.

- Don't name an institution (such as a bank) as attorney in fact. Again, this isn't legal in many states, and is definitely not desirable. Serving as attorney in fact is a personal responsibility, and there should be personal connection and trust between the principal and attorney in fact. If the person you trust the most happens to be your banker, name that person as attorney in fact, not the abstract entity of the bank.

- In general (but not always), it's not desirable to have co-attorneys in fact in a durable power of attorney for finances. This shared responsibility may make it cumbersome for the attorneys in fact to act effectively if one is out of town or they disagree. Also, some banks and other financial institutions prefer to deal with a single attorney in fact rather than joint ones.

1. Should You Appoint Your Spouse as Attorney in Fact?

In most marital situations, there's strong reason for one spouse to select the other to be his attorney in fact.[8] Aside from the emotional sense this makes, there are also powerful legal reasons. In a community property state, each spouse owns one-half of the community property outright—the attorney in fact has no authority at all over the competent spouse's property. And in non-community property states, one spouse has a statutory interest in the other spouse's estate that may conflict with an attorney in fact's management of the incompetent person's affairs. Clearly it's undesirable to risk conflicts between an attorney in fact and a spouse over how marital property should be handled unless it's absolutely necessary.

However, if your spouse is ill, quite elderly, or simply not equipped to manage your affairs, you may have to name someone else as attorney in fact. The wisest course is for you and your spouse to agree on who the attorney in fact should be, perhaps one of your children. It's also prudent for the other spouse to name this same person as his or her attorney in fact.

---

[8] If the attorney in fact designated is your spouse, that designation does not automatically end if your marriage ends in divorce. After a divorce, you must revoke the power of attorney and create a new one, naming someone else as the (new) attorney in fact.

2. Choose a Successor Attorney in Fact

Anyone who establishes a durable power of attorney should name at least one successor attorney in fact in case the original choice can't serve, or needs to resign after serving for a period of time. As a further precaution, you could authorize an attorney in fact to name additional successors to serve if those you named cannot. Certainly it's wise to avoid even the minimal risk that the position might become vacant because of the original attorney in fact's death, disability or resignation. If this occurs, and you haven't named a successor, your durable power of attorney would be useless and there would have to be a court action, such as a full scale conservatorship proceeding. When choosing a successor, take into account the same factors that you did when selecting the attorney in fact.

3. Deciding Whether the Attorney in Fact Should Be Paid

Compensation of an attorney in fact usually depends on the relation of the attorney in fact to the principal, the duties required, and the type of assets subject to the durable power of attorney. In family situations, where the attorney in fact's duties won't be difficult or time-consuming, there's normally no provision for payment. However, if a attorney in fact will be expected to run a business or keep track of complicated financial affairs, payment is appropriate.

Unless the power of attorney document expressly states that the attorney in fact may be paid for services rendered, she has no legal right to payment. So it is important that the principal discuss and work out payment questions with the prospective attorney in fact before finalizing the durable power of attorney. If payment for the attorney in fact is desired, it must be clearly set out in the document.

Example

Martin creates a springing durable power of attorney naming his brother, Andrew, as attorney in fact. Martin has an extensive stock portfolio and other investments. Martin and Andrew agree it's fair that Andrew be paid for his efforts if he has to manage Martin's financial affairs. They consider agreeing on an hourly wage, but decide they don't want to be that definite and limiting now. So Martin inserts a general compensation clause allowing Andrew to pay himself "reasonable" fees for his services.

H. Limitations of Financial Durable Powers of Attorney

A legal tool which is as flexible as a durable power of attorney can involve some complexities. This book doesn't attempt to cover every imaginable problem which can arise with the use of a financial durable power of attorney. However, I do alert you to some possible problems. If you're concerned with one of these areas, it's doubly important to see a knowledgeable attorney to discuss your options and choices and to check your work.

1. Estate Planning

Generally, an attorney in fact doesn't have legal authority to make a will or living trust for the principal. So, if you're preparing a durable power of attorney, be sure you've also arranged for the handling of your property after your death. You can do this by writing a will or, if you want to avoid probate or have complicated desires regarding your property, by engaging in more extensive estate planning such as a living trust.[9]

---

[9]Nolo Press publishes a number of books that can help you with estate planning, including *Nolo's Simple Will Book* and *Plan Your Estate*, both by Denis Clifford. Those with access to computers may want to use *WillMaker* by Nolo/Legisoft, a computer program designed to help you make your own will.

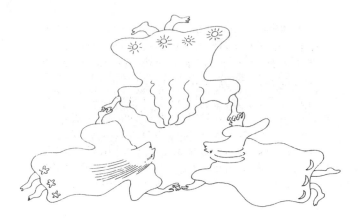

2. Death Taxes

If the attorney in fact's authority over the principal's property is extremely broad, there's a minor risk that the value of that property can be included in the attorney in fact's taxable estate, if the attorney in fact dies before the principal (not likely, but it could happen). The simplest way to eliminate the possibility of a problem in this area is to state in the durable power of attorney that the attorney in fact has no authority to transfer the principal's property to himself (the forms in this book contain such a clause). If you might want the attorney in fact to have authority to give your property to himself, see a lawyer.

3. Out-of-State Property

If you own property which is located in another state, you have to be sure that the power of attorney you prepare is valid in that state. Normally, property located in another state means real estate (real property). But other property, such as bank accounts or physical items, may also be located in a state other than where the principal resides. If you own property in another state, my most cautious advice is to check with an attorney in that state to see what's required. However, I'm aware this may not be easy to do—it would entail the hassle and expense of finding an attorney in a state where you don't live. You can start

by checking the lists in Section B(1) of this chapter to find out that state's rules for financial durable powers. If the state is listed on Chart 1 or 2, a durable power of attorney prepared from the forms in this book is valid and will do the job. But if the state is listed on Chart 3, you must see a lawyer.

4. Court Review of a Financial Durable Power of Attorney

In California, a statute authorizes certain people to petition a court to resolve questions relating to the durable power of attorney. While there are not similar statutes in most other states, under traditional legal rules, the same sorts of petitions can be filed by close relatives and friends of the principal.[10]

Here's how the California law works. Certain people—the principal, the attorney in fact, a spouse or child of the principal, and any person who would inherit property of the principal under intestate laws (close family members who would inherit from the principal if he or she died with no will or other valid method of transferring property)—can petition the court. The petition can be filed to determine whether the power of attorney is still effective, to pass on the acts or proposed acts of the attorney in fact, to compel the attorney in fact to submit an accounting, or to declare the power of attorney terminated.

The power of attorney will be terminated by the court if it decides that the attorney in fact has violated or is unfit to perform his duties or that at the time the durable power of attorney was made, the principal lacked the capacity to make a valid one.

A California durable power of attorney may eliminate the authority of any person to petition the court, except the conservator of the principal's estate, if one has been appointed. To so restrict the

---

[10]In reality, this type of petition, no matter what the state, is very rare.

durable power of attorney the principal must, by law, have been advised of his rights by an attorney, who must then sign a statement to that effect (this clause is presented in Chapter 4, Section E(2)(u)). It isn't hard to imagine situations where a principal would desire to restrict someone's access to court.

Example: Peter is sadly estranged from his son, Ken. Peter appoints his other child, Sue, to act as his attorney in fact if he becomes incapacitated. He's aware that Ken is also angry at Sue and fears he might litigate over the validity of the power of attorney. So he restricts the authority of Ken to do that, by expressly so stating in the durable power of attorney, and consulting with a lawyer and having the lawyer sign the appropriate form.

Unfortunately, however, restricting the power of relatives and friends to petition a court under the California Durable Power of Attorney Act probably doesn't accomplish much. There are many ways to litigate, and although Peter has prevented Ken from suing under the authority of the California durable power of attorney statute, Ken could surely find another method for getting to court. Or, phrased more precisely, Ken can surely find a lawyer who'll get to court, if the lawyer is paid well enough.

CHAPTER 4

SAMPLE FORMS AND CLAUSES FOR FINANCIAL DURABLE POWERS OF ATTORNEY

A. How to Use This Chapter

This chapter contains two sample financial durable power of attorney forms. One form is designed to take effect immediately; the other is "springing," meaning it only takes effect if the principal becomes incapacitated. The chapter also contains a number of sample clauses for use in drafting your own customized financial durable power of attorney.

Note: If you live in Alaska, California, Connecticut, Illinois, Minnesota, New York or North Carolina, also read Chapter 5, "Statutory Financial Durable Powers of Attorney," before deciding which financial durable power of attorney form is best for you.

As you read this chapter, you can use the samples as you would a workbook. Make entries in pencil, erase when needed, and even cut and paste if that makes things easier. Once you complete a rough draft, it should be checked for accuracy, then edited and revised where necessary.

You'll find tear-out, fill-in-the-blanks durable power of attorney forms in the Appendix. Because there are many different forms in the Appendix, be careful that you get the exact one you need. When a sample form is presented in the book, the form number at the top identifies it in the Appendix.

After you've prepared your draft document, reviewed and discussed it with the person you've chosen attorney in fact (and, if need be, a lawyer), you're ready to prepare your final version. You can do this either with the appropriate tear-out form or, if you wish to make additions or subtractions, you can create a customized form and have it typed up on high quality non-erasable bond paper. (See the guidelines for preparing powers of attorney in Chapter 1, Section G).

The "Warnings": All durable power of attorney forms presented in this chapter begin with certain "Warnings" which state how powerful a financial durable power of attorney is. These warnings must be printed in bold type or typed in capital letters, and

are required by California law. While these warnings are not mandatory in other states, I believe it's wise to include them no matter what your state of residence, because they tend to promote acceptability of your document. The people or institutions to whom the durable power of attorney may ultimately be presented will clearly see that you had notice as to the importance of the document you created.

B. Notarization and Witnesses

As previously stated, all durable powers of attorney must be notarized. In many states, notarization is required by law. Even if it isn't, any durable power of attorney which isn't notarized may face serious acceptability problems. Notarization means the principal signs the document in a notary's presence. This, of course, may pose a problem if the principal is gravely ill. In this situation, you'll need to have a notary come to where the principal is, whether home, hospital room, or elsewhere. If the notary needs to come to a hospital or home, find out the charge ahead of time. Locating a notary shouldn't be a problem, as many notaries advertise in the yellow pages. Or you might check with your bank, local real estate office or even an attorney's office.

Witnesses usually aren't required by states' durable power of attorney laws. Nevertheless, the forms presented here provide space for witnessing by two people. The reason is that witnessing can promote acceptability. It makes the document look more official, probably because wills generally require witnesses. In borderline cases, where the principal's capacity to execute a valid durable power of attorney may be subsequently questioned, it's prudent to have witnesses who can testify that in their judgment the principal was competent and knew what he was doing when he signed the document. The witnesses must be competent adults, preferably who reside in your state. The person chosen as attorney in fact should not be a witness.

The major drawback to having witnesses is that they should be present when the principal signs the document before the notary, because the witnesses must state they saw the principal sign. It can be a hassle to arrange three people's schedules to get them all to a notary's office at the same time. If the witnesses appear in front of the notary, their signature should be notarized too.

Remember, witnessing is generally not legally required (with certain exceptions noted in subsequent chapters). If it's too inconvenient to arrange for witnesses to appear before a notary, you can eliminate that. Simply omit the space for witnesses' signatures and addresses from the final document you prepare.

C. Sample Durable Power of Attorney Effective When Principal Signs

This is a basic financial durable power of attorney form. It is generally effective upon signing by the principal unless a later date is specified. This sample form is not completed, but an explanation of the information you need is filled in. (A tear-out, fill-in-the-blanks version of this form is contained in the Appendix as Form 1.)

Form 1

Recording requested by and when recorded mail to

[principal's name]

[principal's address]

Financial Durable Power of Attorney

WARNING TO PERSON EXECUTING THIS DOCUMENT

THIS IS AN IMPORTANT LEGAL DOCUMENT. IT CREATES A DURABLE POWER OF ATTORNEY. BEFORE EXECUTING THIS DOCUMENT, YOU SHOULD KNOW THESE IMPORTANT FACTS:

1. THIS DOCUMENT MAY PROVIDE THE PERSON YOU DESIGNATE AS YOUR ATTORNEY IN FACT WITH BROAD POWERS TO MANAGE, DISPOSE, SELL, AND CONVEY YOUR REAL AND PERSONAL PROPERTY AND TO BORROW MONEY USING YOUR PROPERTY AS SECURITY FOR THE LOAN.

2. THESE POWERS WILL EXIST FOR AN INDEFINITE PERIOD OF TIME UNLESS YOU LIMIT THEIR DURATION IN THIS DOCUMENT. THESE POWERS WILL CONTINUE TO EXIST NOTWITHSTANDING YOUR SUBSEQUENT DISABILITY OR INCAPACITY.

3. YOU HAVE THE RIGHT TO REVOKE OR TERMINATE THIS DURABLE POWER OF ATTORNEY.

IF THERE IS ANYTHING ABOUT THIS FORM THAT YOU DO NOT UNDERSTAND, YOU SHOULD ASK A LAWYER TO EXPLAIN IT TO YOU.

Durable Power of Attorney

1. Creation of Durable Power of Attorney

By signing this document, I, __[principal's name]__,

name

intend to create a durable power of attorney. This durable power of attorney shall not be affected

by my subsequent disability or incapacity, and shall remain effective until my death, or until

revoked by me in writing.

2. Effective Date

This durable power of attorney shall become effective as of the date of my signing it.

[A later date can be specified]

3. Designation of Attorney in Fact

I, ___[principal's name]_____, hereby appoint
name

___[attorney in fact's name]_____ of
name

___[attorney in fact's address]_____ as my
address

attorney in fact, to act for me and in my name and for my use and benefit. Should

___[attorney in fact's name]_____
name

for any reasons fail to serve or cease to serve as my attorney in fact, I appoint

___[successor attorney in fact's name]_____ of
name

___[successor attorney in fact's address]_____
address

to be my attorney in fact.

4. Authority of Attorney in Fact

(A) Except as specified in Paragraph 4(B), I grant my attorney in fact full power and authority over all my property, real and personal, and authorize _____ to do and perform
him/her
all and every act which I as an owner of said property could do or perform and I hereby ratify and confirm all that my attorney in fact shall do or cause to be done under this durable power of attorney.

(B) My attorney in fact has no authority to give any of my property to, or use any of my property for the benefit of _____.
himself/herself

(C) Provisions or Limitations. *[Add any specific limitations, restrictions, directions, etc., you want. Examples of these are discussed in Section E of this chapter.]*

5. Reliance by Third Parties

The powers conferred on my attorney in fact by this durable power of attorney may be exercisable by my attorney in fact alone, and my attorney in fact's signature or act under the authority granted in this durable power of attorney may be accepted by any third person or organization as fully authorized by me and with the same force and effect as if I were personally present, competent and acting on my own behalf.

No person or organization who relies on this durable power of attorney or any representation

my attorney in fact makes regarding _____ authority, including, but not limited to:

his/her

   (i)   the fact that this durable power of attorney has not been revoked;

   (ii)   that I, _____ [principal's name] _____ was competent

name

       to execute this power of attorney;

  (iii)   the authority of my attorney in fact under this durable power of attorney;

shall incur any liability to me, my estate, heirs, successors or assigns because of such reliance on

this durable power of attorney or on any such representation by my attorney in fact.

   Executed this _____ day of _____, 19___, at

_____.

_____

Principal

Witnesses

_____ [signature] _____ of _____ [address] _____

_____

_____ [signature] _____ of _____ [address] _____

_____

Notarization

State of _____

County of _____

On this _____ day of _____ in the year 19___,

before me a Notary Public, State of _____, duly commissioned

and sworn, personally appeared _____,

personally known to me (or proved to me on the basis of satisfactory evidence) to be the person

whose name is subscribed to in this instrument, and acknowledged to me that _____
                                                                            he/she

executed the same.

IN WITNESS WHEREOF, I have hereunto set my hand and affixed my official seal in the

State of _____, County of _____

on the date set forth above in this certificate.

_____
Notary Public

[Notary Seal]   State of _____

My commission expires _____

D. Sample Springing Durable Power of Attorney

This section contains a completed springing financial durable power of attorney. This one is filled in because it can be helpful to see a completed sample form based on a real fact situation. (A tear-out, fill-in-the-blanks version of this form is contained in the Appendix as Form 2.)

Facts: Steven is a widower with three grown children. He's financially comfortable, though not wealthy. He owns his home, a small lakeside summer cottage, some stocks and a money market account. He also receives retirement benefits and social security income. Steven plans to leave his property equally to his three children. To ensure his wishes will be followed after he dies, he also prepares a will for the transfer of his property upon death.

Steven has one son, Jim, who lives out of state. One of his daughters, Maria, is a doctor, divorced and a single parent. His other daughter, Carol, works part-time and has one child, age 22. All of Steven's children are competent people he is close to and trusts. After a family meeting he decides to appoint Carol as his initial attorney in fact, with Maria as her successor (if need be). This makes sense to everyone, considering Maria's greater responsibilities and time pressures, and the fact that Jim resides out of state.

Steven loves both his summer cottage and his home, which he's lived in for 30 years. Steven's son, Jim, and Maria both are fond of the summer home, although Carol isn't much interested in it. He tells Carol he doesn't want either sold unless it's absolutely necessary, and she readily agrees. Still, to be doubly sure his desires will be honored, Steven writes into his durable power of attorney provisions restricting the authority of his attorney in fact to sell either residence.

Form 2

Recording requested by and when recorded mail to

Steven H. Mazzoli

24 Alberton Way

Panache PA

Springing Financial Durable Power of Attorney

WARNING TO PERSON EXECUTING THIS DOCUMENT

THIS IS AN IMPORTANT LEGAL DOCUMENT. IT CREATES A DURABLE POWER OF ATTORNEY. BEFORE EXECUTING THIS DOCUMENT, YOU SHOULD KNOW THESE IMPORTANT FACTS:

1. THIS DOCUMENT MAY PROVIDE THE PERSON YOU DESIGNATE AS YOUR ATTORNEY IN FACT WITH BROAD POWERS TO MANAGE, DISPOSE, SELL, AND CONVEY YOUR REAL AND PERSONAL PROPERTY AND TO BORROW MONEY USING YOUR PROPERTY AS SECURITY FOR THE LOAN.

2. THESE POWERS WILL EXIST FOR AN INDEFINITE PERIOD OF TIME UNLESS YOU LIMIT THEIR DURATION IN THIS DOCUMENT. THESE POWERS WILL CONTINUE TO EXIST NOTWITHSTANDING YOUR SUBSEQUENT DISABILITY OR INCAPACITY.

3. YOU HAVE THE RIGHT TO REVOKE OR TERMINATE THIS DURABLE POWER OF ATTORNEY.

IF THERE IS ANYTHING ABOUT THIS FORM THAT YOU DO NOT UNDERSTAND, YOU SHOULD ASK A LAWYER TO EXPLAIN IT TO YOU.

Durable Power of Attorney

1. Creation of Durable Power of Attorney

By signing this document, I, _____ STEVEN H. MAZZOLI _____,

name

intend to create a durable power of attorney. This durable power of attorney shall not be affected

by my subsequent disability or incapacity, and shall remain effective until my death, or until

revoked by me in writing.

2. Effective Date

This durable power of attorney shall become effective only in the event that I become

incapacitated or disabled so that I am not able to manage my financial affairs in which case it

shall become effective as of the date of the written statement by a physician, as provided in

Paragraph 3. If the durable power of attorney becomes effective, it shall remain effective during any period when I am incapacitated or disabled until my death, or until revoked by me.

3. Determination of Incapacity

The determination of whether I have become incapacitated or disabled so that I am not able to manage my financial affairs shall be made in writing by a licensed physician; if possible, the physician shall be ___DR. JOSEPH BRITEN_____ of

name

___577 Market St., Panache PA_____.

address

In the event that a licensed physician has made a written determination that I have become incapacitated or disabled and am not able to manage my own financial affairs, that written statement shall be attached to the original of this durable power of attorney.

4. Designation of Attorney in Fact

If I become incapacitated or disabled so that I am not able to manage my financial affairs, I,

_____STEVEN H. MAZZOLI_____, hereby appoint

name

__my daughter, CAROL FILLON_____ of

name

__37 North White St., Wilstead PA_____

address

as my attorney in fact, to act for me and in my name and for my use and benefit. Should

_____CAROL FILLON_____ for any reasons fail to serve or cease

name

to serve as my attorney in fact, I appoint _____my daughter, MARIA MAZZOLI_____ of

name

__400 Pine St., Carleton PA_____

address

to be my attorney in fact.

5. Authority of Attorney in Fact

(A) Except as specified in Paragraph 5(B), I grant my attorney in fact full power and authority over all my property, real and personal, and authorize _____her_____ to do and perform

him/her

all and every act which I as an owner of said property could do or perform and I hereby ratify and confirm all that my attorney in fact shall do or cause to be done under this durable power of attorney.

(B) My attorney in fact has no authority to give any of my property to, or use any of my

property for the benefit of _____ herself _____ .

_{himself/herself}

(C) My attorney in fact has no authority to sell my home at 24 Alberton Way, Panache PA, or my summer cottage at Lakeshore Road, Blue Lake PA, unless all my other assets have been depleted or are insufficient to pay for my living expenses and needs.

6. Reliance by Third Parties

The powers conferred on my attorney in fact by this durable power of attorney may be

exercisable by my attorney in fact alone, and my attorney in fact's signature or act under the

authority granted in this durable power of attorney may be accepted by any third person or

organization as fully authorized by me and with the same force and effect as if I were personally

present, competent and acting on my own behalf.

No person or organization who relies on this durable power of attorney or any representation

my attorney in fact makes regarding _____ her _____ authority, including, but not limited to:

_{his/her}

(i)   the fact that this durable power of attorney has not been revoked;

(ii)   that I, _____ STEVEN H. MAZZOLI _____ was competent

_{name}

to execute this power of attorney;

(iii)   the authority of my attorney in fact under this durable power of attorney;

shall incur any liability to me, my estate, heirs, successors or assigns because of such reliance on

this durable power of attorney or on any such representation by my attorney in fact.

Executed this _Tenth_ day of _August_ , 19_91_, at

_____ Panache, Pennsylvania _____ .

_____

Principal   STEVEN H. MAZZOLI

Witnesses

_____ of _5771 Wildwood Road_____

_Panache, Pennsylvania_____

_____ of _8101 Allen Court_____

_Panache, Pennsylvania_____

Notarization

State of _____Pennsylvania_____

County of __Cork_____

On this _____10th_____ day of ___August_____ in the year 19_91_,

before me a Notary Public, State of ___Pennsylvania_____, duly commissioned

and sworn, personally appeared _STEVEN H. MAZZOLI_____,

personally known to me (or proved to me on the basis of satisfactory evidence) to be the person

whose name is subscribed to in this instrument, and acknowledged to me that _____he_____
                                                                                he/she

executed the same.

IN WITNESS WHEREOF, I have hereunto set my hand and affixed my official seal in the

State of _____Pennnsylvania_____ County of ___Cork_____ on

the date set forth above in this certificate.

_____

Notary Public

[Notary Seal]   State of _____Pennsylvania_____

My commission expires _____

E. Customizing Your Financial Durable Power of Attorney

For a variety of reasons, you may want to cover different issues in your durable power of attorney, or treat a covered subject differently from what the basic form provides. This section provides sample clauses for various subjects and, when appropriate, brief discussions of those subjects as well. These clauses may be added to your financial durable power of attorney in the appropriate sections or substituted for clauses you wish to change.

This section provides a number of clauses that are sometimes used in financial durable powers of attorney. Before adopting any, I suggest you read through all the clauses in this section at least once to consider whether any are useful for your needs. Understand that these clauses are not exhaustive. There's a near-infinite number of options when it comes to clauses that can be included in a financial durable power of attorney. If the clauses provided don't meet your needs, you can—within the limits of common sense and the law of your state—create your own. (Since it's unlikely you'll know your state's laws on this matter, if you draft any provision substantially different from those presented in this book, you should check out the legality of your clause. You can either do your own legal research or hire a lawyer—see Chapter 11.) If you do decide to draft your own clauses, explain your intentions in your own words as clearly and specifically as possible.

1. How to Insert Clauses In Your Durable Power of Attorney

If you decide to use or adapt one or more of the clauses in this section for your durable power of attorney, simply substitute or insert them in the appropriate section of your draft. For example, if you want to specify additional powers and limits for your attorney in fact, you'd put these clauses in the paragraph entitled "Authority of Attorney in Fact."

There really are no mysteries or esoteric legal skills involved in adding clauses to your draft. Basic common sense will tell you under which headings the clauses you want to insert should go.

2. Sample Clauses

The sample clauses in this section are designed to present you with options for many situations which can be covered in financial durable powers of attorney. The clauses may be modified as necessary to suit your particular situation.

a. Determination of Incapacity

If you create a springing durable power of attorney, you should specify a reasonable method to determine whether or not you've become incapacitated. This is accomplished in Paragraph 3 in the sample Form 2 set out in Section D of this chapter. A common method is to have the determination made by at least one doctor. Often the doctor you desire to make the determination is specified.

i: Two Physicians Required

A modification is the requirement that two doctors concur on the finding of incapacity. Your doctor may desire that a second opinion be obtained, so check with her before deciding on this matter. This clause also contains a provision excluding the doctors from liability (an "exculpatory" provision).

My incapacity or disability for purposes of this durable power of attorney shall be determined by written statements by two licensed physicians, one of whom shall be, if possible, my personal physician. The written statements shall state that in the physician's opinion I am substantially unable to manage my own financial affairs.

At the date of creation of this durable power of attorney, my personal physician is ____[physician's name]____.

Any licensed physicians or psychiatrists who act under this paragraph shall not be liable to me for any actions taken by them under this paragraph which are done in good faith.

ii: Form for Determining Incapacity

You can include a specific form in your durable power of attorney for a doctor to sign to determine incapacity. That form can include any specifications you desire. It's generally wise to make this a recommended form, not mandatory, because it's hard to be sure now what form a doctor would prefer to use if you become incapacitated. Following is one version of a doctor's form.

DETERMINATION OF INCAPACITY

I, ____[doctor's name]____, declare:

I am a physician licensed to practice in the State of ____[state]____. I have examined ____[principal's name]____. It is my professional opinion that ____[principal's name]____ is incapacitated and is therefore unable to handle __[his/her]__ own financial affairs.

Date: _____

____[signature of physician]____

b. Attorneys in Fact and Successor Attorneys in Fact

In Paragraph 3 of the sample durable power of attorney (Section C) and in Paragraph 4 of the sample springing durable power of attorney (Section D), there is a clause in which you appoint your attorney in fact. Here are some alternatives.

Option 1: Additional Successors Can Be Appointed by Attorney in Fact

You can authorize your attorney in fact to appoint additional successors. Some people may want to include this clause to ensure that the position of the attorney in fact couldn't become vacant.

Each attorney in fact can appoint additional successor attorneys in fact, to serve in the order nominated, by nomination in writing of such additional successor attorneys in fact.

Option 2: Appointment of More Than On Attorney in Fact

Although my preference is generally for a single attorney in fact, there are situations where it makes sense to appoint two or more joint attorneys in fact. Sometimes this is the wisest way to keep domestic and family peace. Or perhaps the burden of serving as attorney in fact needs to be shared.

(a) The attorneys in fact shall be _____[name]_____ of _____[address]_____ and _____[name]_____ of _____[address]_____.

(b) Both attorneys in fact must agree on all actions taken under this durable power of attorney. Both must sign any appropriate documents.

However, if one resigns, or is unable to act because of incapacity, the other may thereafter act alone.

(c) If disputes between the attorneys in fact arise which they're unable to resolve promptly, they shall be settled by:

[Provide for any means you want—you could state that one attorney in fact prevails over the other. Or you could provide for binding arbitration (see Option 3 below) and even name the arbitrator. Or, if there are an uneven number of attorneys in fact, you could state that the majority prevails.]

[As you can see, providing for more than one attorney in fact does raise potentially serious problems of conflicts between them.]

(d) If one of my attorneys in fact cannot serve, or ceases to serve, my successor attorney in fact shall be _____[name]_____ of _____[address]_____ . If both my attorneys in fact cannot serve, or cease to serve, my successor attorneys in fact shall be _____[name]_____ of _____[address]_____ and _____[name]_____ of _____[address]_____ .

Option 3: Compulsory Arbitration if Co-Attorneys in Fact Disagree

If my attorneys in fact cannot agree on a decision or action under the authority delegated to them in this durable power of attorney, that dispute shall be resolved by binding arbitration. The arbitration shall be carried out by a single arbitrator, who shall be _____[name]_____ , if available.

The arbitration shall commence within five days of written notice by any attorney in fact to the arbitrator that a dispute between the attorneys in fact has arisen and has not been resolved.

The details of the arbitration shall be determined by the arbitrator. The written decision of the arbitrator shall be binding on all my attorneys in fact.

c. Specifying Powers of Attorney in Fact

There can be important reasons to include detailed provisions regarding the attorney in fact's powers. Sometimes the specific granting of authority over certain property can increase acceptability of the attorney in fact's authority or reduce the chances of litigation. And some people are by nature cautious, and want to state with precision what their attorney in fact has authority to do.

Option 1: Broad Financial Powers

My attorney in fact has authority over all my property, real and personal, for collections and payment, handling pensions and benefits, acquisitions and sales, management and repairs, banking activities and use of safe deposit boxes, insurance, tax returns, motor vehicles, and business interest, and authority to determine the conditions, provisions, and covenants of any instrument or document which may be executed by my attorney in fact concerning my financial affairs. In the acquisition or disposition of my real or personal property, my attorney in fact shall have exclusive power to fix the terms thereof for cash, credit and/or property and if on credit with or without security.

Option 2: Specific Powers

There are many specific powers listed in this option. You may insert any that are relevant. Make sure you begin with the following sentence, then include whichever powers you wish to designate.

My attorney in fact has the following specific powers, aside from the general powers granted in this durable power of attorney:

• Power to Manage Solely-Owned Business

To manage, control, and take charge of my business of ____[specify nature of business]____ located at _____[address]_____, City of _____, County of _____, State of _____ and to do everything necessary to carry on and continue the affairs of such business including the purchase of materials and supplies, the hiring and firing of personnel, the acceptance of orders for and delivery of merchandise and goods produced, either in cash or for credit, and all transactions of the business, including the authority to sign, execute, acknowledge and deliver any deed, lease, assignment of lease, covenant, indenture, indemnity, agreement, mortgage, deed of trust, assignment of mortgage or of the beneficial interest under deed of trust, extension or renewal of any obligation, subordination or waiver of priority, hypothecation, bill of lading, bill of sale, bill, bond, note, whether negotiable or non-negotiable, receipt, evidence of debt, full or partial release or satisfaction of mortgage, judgment and other debt, request for partial or full reconveyance of deed of trust and such other instruments in writing or any kind or class as may be necessary, and to compound, compromise, adjust, settle and satisfy any obligation, secured or unsecured, owing by or to me and to give or accept any property and/or money whether or not equal to or less in value than the amount owing in payment, settlement or satisfaction thereof.

• Power to Vote Stock

To represent and vote stock, exercise stock rights, accept and deal with any dividend, distribution or bonus, join in any corporate financing, reorganization, merger, liquidation, consolidation or other action and the extension, compromise, conversion, adjustment, enforcement or foreclosure, singly or in conjunction with others of any corporate stock, bond, note, debenture or other security.

• Power to Borrow Money

To borrow money from such sources and on such terms as my attorney in fact may deem fit and proper [to an amount not to exceed $_____], and to execute in conjunction with any such loan of money a security agreement covering any of my real or personal property and to execute, sign, acknowledge, and deliver in such form as may be required any promissory note or any other instrument that may be required in conjunction with such transaction.

• Power to Sell or Convey Specific Real Property

To grant, bargain, sell and convey my real property or any part thereof, located at ____[street address]____, City of _____, County of _____, State of _____, more particularly described as __[insert full legal description]__ for such price and on such terms and conditions as he/she shall deem proper, with or without the taking back of a purchase money mortgage or deed of trust, and to collect and receive the proceeds from any such sale.

To enter into any contract or contracts for the sale of said premises, or any part thereof, with such persons and upon such terms as he/she shall in his/her discretion elect and to execute, acknowledge, and deliver in my name such deeds or conveyances, with such covenants or conditions as he/she may deem proper, that may be required for the transfer of said property or any part thereof or of any interest therein.

• **Power to Manage Real Property**

As to any real property, including time shared interests, condominiums and cooperatives: to collect rents, disburse funds, hire professional property managers, lease to tenants, negotiate and renew leases, borrow against, renew any loan, sell any of the property, and sign any documents needed to carry out the sale or to carry out any transaction for such real property.

• **General Power Over Real Property**

To exercise any or all of the following powers as to real property, any interest therein and/or any building thereon: to contract for, purchase, receive and take possession thereof and of evidence of title thereto; to lease the same for any term or purpose, including leases for business, residence, and oil and/or mineral development, to sell, exchange, grant or convey the same with or without warranty, and to mortgage, transfer in trust, or otherwise encumber or hypothecate the same to secure payment of a negotiable or non-negotiable note or performance of any obligation or agreement.

• **Power to Change Title to Real Property**

To sign and deliver a deed that changes my property interest from or to any of these designations: Joint Tenancy, Community Property, Tenants-in-Common, and Separate Property.

• **Power to Collect Rents**

To demand, sue for, collect, and receive all rents now due or which shall at any time hereafter become due to me from past, present, or future tenants or occupants of the lands, buildings, or other structures, or any parts thereof located at [street address or location, including city and state] and on payment thereof to give receipts in my name and discharges in full satisfaction of said rents.

• **Power to Sell Personal Property**

To sell and to enter into a contract or contracts for the sale of all or any part of my personal property, effects, and belongings of every kind and nature wherever situated, with full power to deliver possession of said personal property, and to execute in my name any documents necessary to transfer title to said personal property, including bills of sale or other documents of title, and to take any security interest for any unpaid balance which my attorney in fact, in her/his discretion, may deem necessary and proper.

• **Promissory Notes, etc.**

To demand, collect, compromise, endorse, borrow against, hypothecate, release, or reconvey any promissory note, debt, interest belonging to or claimed by me, and to use and take any lawful means for the recovery thereof by legal process or otherwise, and to execute and deliver a satisfaction or release therefor, together with the right and power to compromise or compound any claim or demand.

• **Shares of Stock, etc.**

To open accounts with stock brokers, cash or on margin, and to buy, sell, endorse, transfer, hypothecate, or borrow against them, any shares of stock, treasury bills, treasury notes, bonds, or any documents or instruments defined as securities under state law.

• **Money Accounts, etc.**

To open, withdraw from, deposit into, or close any bank or savings and loan checking, savings, credit union or money market accounts, or other money market fund, and to

negotiate, endorse, or transfer any instrument affecting those accounts or items.

To enter, establish, close or maintain my safe deposit box(es).

• **Power to Hire Professional Advisors**

To hire and to pay for from my funds the services of professional advisors, including physicians, accountants, lawyers, and investment counselors, for my welfare.

• **Power to Make Gifts**

To make gifts of my assets at any time or from time to time to: (a) ___[specify, such as "my spouse" or "my children"]___, and (b) gifts to charitable, scientific, religious or educational institutions according to my pattern of charitable giving over the past years.

To have the right to make payments or gifts to my spouse or my descendants provided that the effect of these payments or gifts does not materially alter the ultimate disposition of my estate under my existing estate plan.

Caution: Substantial gifts over $10,000 to any one person per year can be considered a substitute for transferring your property after your death. If so, gifts made by your attorney in fact may be subject to challenge as an improper substitute for a will. If you expect your attorney in fact to make substantial gifts, see an attorney.

- **Authority to Manage Trusts**

To create, amend, supplement or terminate any trust and to instruct and advise the trustee of any trust of which I am or may be trustor or beneficiary and to transfer to any revocable trust of which I am a settlor any or all of my assets.

- **Authority to Exercise Powers of Appointment**

To exercise any special or general power of appointment I may hold, except that my attorney in fact may not give any of my assets, including those subject to such powers of appointment to ___[himself/herself]___.

MY ATTORNEY IN FACT SHALL HAVE NO AUTHORITY TO SELL, ENCUMBER OR TRANSFER MY PAL MOSS.

d. Other Clauses Concerning Authority of Attorney in Fact

You can insert clauses that pertain to the attorney in fact's authority to act on your behalf.

Option 1: Delegating Authority or Appointing Temporary Attorney in Fact

If the attorney in fact may be absent for periods of time, the wisest method for handling this can be to allow the attorney in fact to temporarily delegate her authority—in other words, permit the attorney in fact to create a secondary power of attorney for you.

My attorney in fact has authority to appoint, in writing, any other person as temporary attorney in fact, or to delegate in writing any authority granted under this durable power of attorney. Any such appointment of temporary attorney in fact or delegation of authority shall set forth the period for which it is valid, and specify the limits, if any, of such appointment or delegation during such period.

Option 2: Requirement that Attorney in Fact Post Bond

A bond is basically an insurance policy, generally issued by a surety company. In exchange for the payment of an annual premium (paid by the principal), the surety company agrees to reimburse the principal for any damages caused by the attorney in fact's improper actions. Normally, there's no reason to require the attorney in fact to post a bond. If you don't trust the attorney in fact, a durable power of attorney doesn't make sense. And if you do trust your attorney in fact, why add the expense of a bond? A bond is not required unless it's expressly set out in the durable power of attorney. If for some reason you want a bond, perhaps because the attorney in fact will be handling a large amount of money, here's an appropriate clause:

The authority of my attorney in fact under this durable power of attorney shall become effective only upon his/her posting of a bond for faithful performance of his/her duties in the amount of $_____.

e. Compensating the Attorney in Fact

Often, the attorney in fact is not compensated. This is particularly, but not always, done when family members are appointed. In the basic forms set out in Sections C and D of this chapter, there are no provisions provided for compensation of the attorney in fact. Without express authority, the attorney in fact has no right to use any of the principal's assets to pay herself for services rendered.

If you decide that your attorney in fact is to be compensated, state that in the durable power of attorney document. Also, if she's to be compensated, it's wise to define how. There is a variety of possible methods of compensation. The following are some major options:

Option 1: Compensation Decided by Attorney in Fact

The attorney in fact shall be entitled to reasonable compensation for his or her services. Reasonable compensation shall be determined exclusively by the attorney in fact.

Option 2: Compensation at Designated Rate

The attorney in fact shall be entitled to reasonable compensation for his or her services. The attorney in fact shall receive compensation of: $_____ per hour [or $_____ per year, etc.].

Option 3: Compensation Determined by Percentage

The attorney in fact shall be entitled to reasonable compensation for his or her services. The attorney in fact shall receive compensation of: _____% of the net assets of the principal subject to this durable power of attorney [or _____% of net income of assets subject to this durable power of attorney, etc.].

f. Standard of Care By Attorney in Fact

Legally, an attorney in fact is a "fiduciary" for the principal, which means the attorney in fact must act in the highest good faith. There can be no conflict of interest. The competence required in managing the principal's affairs is the care and diligence expected of a reasonable person.

The attorney in fact is normally liable to the principal, or his or her heirs, for damages caused by any negligence committed while acting as attorney in fact. Obviously this is a high standard. You may wish to lower it because you don't want your attorney in fact to be subject to punishment for a good faith mistake. Following is an example of lessening the attorney in fact's standard of responsibility, in this case to liability, only for willful misconduct or gross negligence. This basically means that the attorney in fact can be held liable only for intentional wrongdoing or truly reckless, irresponsible behavior.

Neither my attorney in fact nor any successor attorney in fact shall incur any liability to me, my estate, my heirs, successors, or assigns for acting or refraining from acting hereunder, except for willful misconduct or gross negligence. Neither my attorney in fact nor any successor substitutes shall have responsibility to make my assets productive of income, to increase the value of my estate, to diversify my investments, or to enter into transactions authorized by this document, as long as my attorney in fact or successor believes such actions are in my best interests or in the best interests of my estate and those interested in my estate.

g. Permitting Self-Dealing by Attorney in Fact

Legally, an attorney in fact is normally not permitted to profit or benefit personally from any transaction she engages in as the principal's representative. However, there can be instances where this limitation is not desirable. For example, if the attorney in fact is co-owner of a business with the principal, it may well be better to have the attorney in fact have authority to run the business as a single entity, not split with half the business run as a fiduciary for the principal. Or perhaps the principal wants to permit the attorney in fact to purchase certain of the principal's assets, if the attorney in fact desires to do so.

Option 1: General Self-Dealing Clause

My attorney in fact shall be permitted to purchase any assets of mine, or to engage in any transaction he/she deems in good faith to be in my interest, no matter what the interest of, or benefit to, my attorney in fact.

Option 2: Limited Self-Dealing Permitted Clause

My attorney in fact shall not be permitted to be personally involved in or to benefit personally from any transaction he/she engages in for me as principal, except that my attorney in fact shall [add whatever is desired, e.g., "be able to purchase my 1953 T-Bird if he deems the sale necessary for my interest" or "be able to purchase, at fair market value, my house at 21 Third Street, Philadelphia, Pennsylvania," etc.].

h. Record Keeping by Attorney in Fact

The attorney in fact is legally required to keep detailed records of the principal's financial affairs. If you don't want to impose this obligation on the attorney in fact, use or adapt the following clause. (The attorney in fact must keep sufficient records, of course, to file appropriate tax returns for the principal.)

Option 1: Record Keeping Determined by Attorney in Fact

My attorney in fact shall keep only those financial records he/she deems advisable.

Option 2: Bank Accounts Required

My attorney in fact shall maintain separate checking and/or savings accounts for all my finances and transactions, but no other record keeping shall be required.

i. Permitting Commingling by Attorney in Fact

Legally, the attorney in fact cannot commingle the principal's monies with his own. However, sometimes the funds of the principal and attorney in fact actually have been commingled for some time. This is true often for spouses and long-term lovers. If commingling is likely to exist, it specifically should be authorized:

My attorney in fact may commingle any of my funds with any funds of his/hers and maintaining separate accounts is not required.

j. Paying Expenses of Principal's Children

As discussed in Chapter 3, Section D(3), if the principal has minor children, there may be a need to authorize the attorney in fact to use some of the principal's assets to pay for the children's living expenses. If so, use or adapt the following clauses:

Option 1: General Clause

My attorney in fact has authority to use any of my income or assets as he/she deems necessary to pay any reasonable expense of (each of) my child(ren), ___[name each child]___ until each child becomes a legal adult.

Option 2: Clause Providing for Payment of Basic Needs

My attorney in fact has authority to use any of the following assets: [define] _____ _____ _____ _____ for my children _____ [name each child] _____ for each such child's support and maintenance, health care or educational expenses until such child becomes a legal adult. Education includes, but is not limited to, grade school, high school, college or vocational studies.

Caution: Be sure to update your financial durable power of attorney if you have children born after its execution, since the children are specifically named in these clauses.

k. Reporting Requirements by Attorney in Fact

The principal can require any reporting by the attorney in fact desired. Sometimes, the reason for reporting is for business reasons—i.e., an annual financial statement regarding a business owned by the principal is to be sent to investors. Sometimes the reason for reporting is personal—perhaps the principal wants a check on the attorney in fact, so requires quarterly financial reporting to another trusted person. Or perhaps the principal wants to diffuse a potentially explosive personal conflict by reassuring people mistrustful of the attorney in fact that they'll receive regular financial reports regarding the handling of the principal's affairs by the attorney in fact.

Option 1: Semi-Annual Reports

My attorney in fact shall prepare semi-annual financial reports regarding my finances, including the income and expenses received and incurred by my attorney in fact for me during the previous six-month period. These reports shall be mailed within 30 days of the end of each such six-month period to: ____[list names and addresses]____ .

Option 2: Annual Reports

My attorney in fact shall prepare an annual report including a balance sheet, a statement of profits or losses, regarding any purchase or sale he/she made of my assets, and such reports shall be sent within a reasonable time to: ____[list names and addresses]____ .

l.   Limiting Authority of Attorney in Fact

As previously discussed, you can impose any limitation you want to on the authority of your attorney in fact. Following are some sample clauses regarding certain restrictions.

Option 1: Restricting Sale or Encumbrance of Home

During any period of my disability or incapacity my attorney in fact shall have no authority to engage in any transaction to sell, convey, exchange, transfer, partition, lease or encumber my home, the real property, or any rights or security interest therein, of my principal place of residence located at ____[street address, city, state, zip]____ more particularly described as ____[insert full legal description]____ .

Option 2: Restrictions Regarding Sale of Business

My attorney in fact shall have no authority to sell, transfer, or otherwise exchange or encumber my business at ____[street address, city, state, zip]____ , ____[describe in detail]____ .

Option 3: Notice Required

In the event my attorney in fact deems it necessary to sell ____[whatever you specify]____ , he shall give written notice of that intent to sell, as soon as reasonably possible, to: ____[list names and addresses]____ .

m. Separate Property if Attorney in Fact Dies First

This clause is designed to prevent the IRS from claiming that the attorney in fact "owned" any of the principal's property if the attorney in fact dies before the principal.

My attorney in fact: (a) shall have no incidents of ownership over any life insurance policy in which I may own an interest and which insures his/her life; (b) is prohibited from (i) appointing, assigning, or designating any of my assets, interests, or rights having a value in excess of the federal gift tax annual exclusion amount in any one calendar year directly or indirectly to himself/herself, or estate, creditors, or the creditors of his/her estate, (ii) disclaiming assets to which I would otherwise be entitled if the effect of such disclaimer is to cause such assets to pass directly or indirectly to my attorney in fact or his/her estate in excess of the federal gift tax annual exclusion amount in any one calendar year, or (iii) using my assets to discharge any of his/her legal obligations, including any obligation of support which he/she may owe to others (excluding me and those whom I am legally obligated to support), and the annual right to appoint, assign, designate or disclaim assets, interests, or rights to him/her or his/her benefit within the federal gift tax annual exclusion amount shall be non-cumulative and shall lapse at the end of each calendar year; and (c) my attorney in fact shall not hold or exercise any powers which I may have over assets he/she has given to me or over assets held in an irrevocable trust of which he/she is a grantor.

n. Formal Acceptance by Attorney in Fact

Though not legally required, you may be comforted by a written acceptance by the attorney in fact of that role. This written acceptance may aid in acceptability.

ACCEPTANCE BY ATTORNEY IN FACT

I, ___[attorney in fact's name]___, hereby accept my nomination as attorney in fact for ___[principal's name]___.

Dated:

_____

_____

Attorney in Fact

o. Limited Duration of Durable Power of Attorney

If, for some unusual reason, you don't want the durable power of attorney to last until your death, you may add a clause limiting its duration.

This power of attorney is granted for the period of _____. It shall become effective on _____, 19___ and shall terminate on _____, 19___.

p. Principal's Right to Revoke Durable Power of Attorney

Legally, a principal can revoke a durable power of attorney at any time (see Chapter 10). If you feel more comfortable restating that right in your durable power of attorney, include:

I retain the right to revoke or terminate this durable power of attorney at any time or to substitute another attorney in fact in place of my present attorney in fact.

q. Nominating Conservator

It's possible, though highly unlikely, that a court proceeding could be brought to set aside, or override, the durable power of attorney. Grounds for this include incompetence of the principal at the time of execution of the durable power of attorney, fraud, technical error in the durable power of attorney, or breach of duty by the attorney in fact. If such a court proceeding ever arises, and the durable power of attorney is declared invalid, you can protect yourself by naming the person whom the court should appoint to handle your financial affairs. There is no guarantee that a court will follow this nomination, but it will generally be honored. (See Chapter 1, Sections E and F for more information on conservatorships and court proceedings.)

If, in a court proceeding, it's ever resolved that I need a "conservator" (or other name for a person appointed to administer and supervise either my estate or person), I nominate for conservator _____[name]_____ of _____[address]_____. If _____[name]_____ cannot, for any reason, act as my conservator, I nominate _____[name]_____ of _____[address]_____ to be my conservator.

r. Selecting Guardian of Minor Children

If you have minor children, and you become incapacitated, there may be a need for a personal and property guardian for the children. This is discussed in detail in Chapter 3, Section D(3). Be sure you also nominate the same guardian in your will.

In the event a guardian is required for the person(s) and/or property of my minor children _____[names of minor children]_____, I nominate ___[proposed guardian's name]___ of _____[address]_____. I believe ____[proposed guardian's name]____ is the person best suited to be guardian of my minor children because: _____[enumerate your reasons]_____.

s. Encouraging Acceptability of Durable Power of Attorney

Though not legally required, you can insert clauses which may help promote the acceptability of your durable power of attorney.

i: Recital of Intent Clause

You can insert a recital before you sign your durable power of attorney showing you understood and intended to create a durable power of attorney. For example:

I understand the importance of the powers I delegate to my attorney in fact in this document, and I recognize that the document gives my attorney in fact broad powers over my assets, and that these powers shall become effective as of the date of my incapacity (or sooner if specified in this document) and shall continue indefinitely thereafter unless or until I revoke or terminate this durable power of attorney.

ii: Exculpation Clauses

The financial durable power of attorney forms in this book contain standard clauses designed to encourage people and institutions to accept them. If you feel a need to use more language to further promote acceptability, following are additional clauses you can use or adapt. These clauses don't change the legality of your durable power of attorney. They're simply designed to reassure cautious types who are made secure by legalese.

Option 1: Some Verbiage

All acts done by my attorney in fact pursuant to this durable power of attorney have the same effect and inure to the benefit of and bind me, as principal, and my successors in interest or heirs, as if I were competent and did those acts myself.

I specifically authorize that all acts of my attorney in fact, or successor attorney in fact, be given full effect without inquiry by any relying party or organization concerning the authority of my attorney in fact.

Option 2: Still More Verbiage

A. For the purpose of inducing any physician, hospital, bank, broker, insurer, lender, taxing authority, governmental agency, or other organization or party to act in accordance with the powers granted in this document, I hereby represent, warrant, and agree that:

1. If this document is revoked or amended, for any reason, I, my estate, my heirs, successors, and assigns will hold such party or parties harmless from any loss suffered, or liability incurred, by such party or parties in acting in accordance with this document prior to that party's receipt of written notice of any such revocation or amendment.

2. The powers conferred on my attorney in fact by this durable power of attorney may be exercised by my attorney in fact alone, and his/her signature or act under the authority granted in this durable power of attorney may be accepted by third parties as fully authorized by me and with the same force and effect as if I were personally

present, competent, and acting on my own behalf.

3. No person who relies upon any representation my attorney in fact may make regarding (a) the fact that his/her powers are then in effect, (b) the scope of his/her authority under this document, (c) my competency at the time this document was executed, (d) the fact that this document has not been revoked, shall incur any liability to me, my estate, my heirs, successors, or assigns for permitting my attorney in fact to exercise any power granted to him/her, nor shall any person who deals with him/her be responsible to determine or insure the proper application of funds or property.

4. All third parties from whom my attorney in fact may request information regarding my personal affairs are hereby authorized to provide such information to him/her without limitation and are released from any legal liability whatsoever to me, my estate, my heirs, successors, or assigns for complying with his/her requests.

5. My attorney in fact shall have the right to seek appropriate court orders requiring acts which he/she deems appropriate if a third party refuses to comply with actions taken by my attorney in fact which are authorized by this document or forbidding acts by third parties which he/she has not authorized. If I have the capacity to confirm this authorization at the time of the request, third parties may seek such confirmation from me if they so desire. In addition, my attorney in fact may sue a third party who fails to comply with actions I have authorized him/her to take and demand damages, including punitive damages, on my behalf for such noncompliance.

B. For the purpose of inducing my lawyer(s) to act in accordance with the powers granted in this document, I hereby represent, warrant, and agree that:

1. All the exculpatory clauses relating to those who provide information or records to my attorney in fact shall apply, also, to my lawyer or lawyers who provide information or records to my attorney in fact.

2. I authorize in advance any lawyer or lawyers of whom I am or have been a client to release to my attorney in fact all information or photocopies of any records which he/she may request.

3. I hereby waive all privileges which may be applicable to such information and records, and to any communication pertaining to me and

made in the course of a lawyer-client relationship.

t. Making Durable Power of Attorney Binding on Heirs

My heirs, successors, and assigns shall be bound by my attorney in fact's acts under this durable power of attorney.

u. Restricting Court Proceedings (for California Durable Powers of Attorney Only)

See Chapter 3, Section H(4) for a discussion of why you might want to restrict the right of people to petition a court regarding your durable power of attorney. The following is an example of as severe a restriction on the right to petition a court as is possible in California. A lawyer must sign her approval to the restriction.

I hereby restrict to the fullest extent possible the authority of anyone (except me or the conservator of my estate) to petition any court for any of the purposes enumerated in Section 2412 of the California Civil Code, or successor sections thereto. This power of attorney has been reviewed and approved on my behalf by a lawyer licensed to practice law in the State of California where it has been executed by me. My attorney's approval is set forth at the end of this document and is incorporated herein by reference. I have also told my lawyer of my decision to limit to the fullest extent possible the authority of anyone to petition any court regarding this durable power of attorney.

_____[signature of principal]_____

APPROVAL BY LAWYER OF
RESTRICTION OF COURT

I am an attorney licensed to practice in California where the foregoing durable power of attorney has been executed. I reviewed the foregoing durable power of attorney with ____[name]____ before he/she signed it and advised him/her regarding the effect of restricting the right to petition a court as set forth above, and he/she communicated that he/she desired such a restriction in this durable power of attorney and I therefore approved this durable power of attorney and supervised _____[name]_____'s signing of it.

I declare under penalty of perjury under the laws of the State of California that the foregoing is true and correct.

_____[signature]_____

(Type or Print Name)
Attorney at Law

CHAPTER 5

STATUTORY FINANCIAL DURABLE POWERS OF ATTORNEY

A. Introduction

Several state legislatures have adopted some version of what's called a statutory "short form" financial durable power of attorney. These forms have been approved in Alaska, California, Connecticut, Illinois, Minnesota, New York and North Carolina. They're called "short forms" because many provisions of the state's statutes, such as lengthy sections defining the authority of the attorney in fact to conduct specific transactions, are not included in the form itself. Rather, when you complete the actual form you simply accept these statutory definitions (even if you don't know what they are), unless you strike out the summary caption for that type of authority. For example, the New York statutory form provides that the attorney in fact has authority to conduct "(A) real estate transactions." Another section of the statute not included in the actual durable power of attorney form defines, at some length (indeed, nearly ad nauseum), what "real estate transaction" means.

Use of a statutory short form durable power of attorney is not mandatory in states which have passed these laws. The other financial durable power of attorney forms set out in Chapter 4 offer legal, and often sensible, alternatives.

If you live in a state which has adopted a statutory short form, you have a choice of which type of durable power of attorney form to use. Though either the statutory short form or the forms presented in this book in Chapter 4 are legal, the statutory short form can be preferable if your attorney in fact may likely be engaged in complex financial transactions, such as real estate investments, or managing an active stock account. This is because there should be absolutely no acceptability problems from financial institutions for a specifically approved form. Also, the legislation that authorizes the statutory short form conveys the kind of detailed legalese authority to the attorney in fact that some stuffy financial institutions find comforting.

The Appendix contains the statutory short form for California (Form 3) and New York (Form 4).

More and more states will be passing statutory short form durable powers, so it isn't possible, for space reasons, to include all those states' forms in this book. If you live in one of the states which has adopted a statutory short form not included in this book, and want to use your state's form, you can locate it yourself by doing your own legal research or by seeing an attorney (see Chapter 11).

If you live in California or New York and decide to use your state's short form, you can modify and change that form as long as those changes are not inconsistent with the statute itself. As a practical matter, any reasonable addition you want to make can legally be inserted in the statutory form. So, even if you decide to use the statutory form, review Chapter 4, Section E, for additional clauses which may suit your needs.

There are minor variations between various states' statutory short form financial durable power of attorney laws, but essentially they all work as I've just described. The heart of each statutory form is its "authority granted" clause, which lists over a dozen different types of financial transactions the attorney in fact is authorized to perform. For example, the first type of transaction listed is for "real estate transactions;" a later type is for "bond, share, and commodity transactions." For each of the types of transactions specified, the legislatures of the respective states have provided an extensive statutory definition of what that transaction means. As indicated, these definitions are not printed out in the durable power of attorney form itself, but are made a part of it by operation of law. In others words, in the states which have adopted these laws, by simply using a statutory short form durable power of attorney, you adopt a very thorough body of definitions of what authority is conveyed to the attorney in fact.[1]

---

[1] The statutory definitions of the "authority granted" in California are set forth in Civil Code §§2450-2473. New York statutory definitions are contained in New York General Obligation Law §§5-1502.

This book advises that it's often desirable to make broad general grants of authority to your attorney in fact, with such specific limits and restrictions as you choose. The statutory short form durable power of attorney essentially works the other way. It spells out, in extensive detail, what the authority conveyed means, without the necessity of having these wordy definitions included in your specific form. Frankly, either approach—the extensive definition approach or the broad delegation approach—usually works well. Which approach is best for you depends on your personal preference and an assessment of your situation.

B. Can Residents of Other States Use the Statutory Short Form?

Even if your state legislature hasn't specifically adopted a statutory short form durable power of attorney, technically, you could use or adopt the statutory forms presented in this book, but not with the confidence that you'd have using a form specifically validated by your state's laws. This means your use of a statutory short form durable power of attorney will not promote its acceptability in your state. So, realistically, there's no sensible reason for readers who live in a state which hasn't adopted a statutory short form to use one from another state.

C. For California or New York Residents: Using a 'Short Form' Contained in the Appendix

Begin by locating the correct form for your state. Tear-out, fill-in-the-blanks short forms for California and New York are contained in the Appendix, as Forms 3 and 4. Before you begin completing the form, carefully read it, including the section on authority granted. It may be helpful to look at the sample completed statutory short form provided in Section E of this chapter. Prepare your own statutory short form as follows.

- *Delegating Authority*. Delete any types of authority listed which you determine you don't want your attorney in fact to handle. For example, suppose you only want your attorney in fact to have authority to handle your personal property, not your real estate. You can eliminate the authority to handle real estate by simply drawing a line through the specification of that type of authority in the statutory short form durable power of attorney (or omitting it in a retyped draft). For the New York form, you must also write your initials in the box opposite the authority you want deleted.

- *Modifying the Form*. You may make any other modification, limit or change in the statutory short form durable power of attorney you desire, as long as that change isn't inconsistent with the statutory form itself. This is usually not a particularly significant restriction, as most changes you're likely to want to make would not be inconsistent with the form language. (Sample clauses are contained in Chapter 4, Section E.)

- *Making the Short Form a "Springing" Durable Power of Attorney*. The California and New York statutory short forms provide that they're effective and operational upon signature of the principal. If you want to create a "springing" form, which doesn't become operational unless you become incapacitated, you must add the following language to the form:

  "This durable power of attorney shall become effective only if I become so incapacitated or disabled that I am not able to manage my financial affairs."

  [You can also provide that the determination of your incapacity be made by a physician of your choosing.]

Making this change means you'll have to retype the statutory form provided in this book and can't just fill in the blanks. See the example in Section E below.

D. Special California Requirements

The statutory short form durable power of attorney for California must meet all of these requirements:

- It must contain the full text of the "Warning" which precedes the actual form (if retyped, the "warnings" must be in capital letters);

- It must be signed and dated by the principal;

- It must both be signed by two witnesses, and signed by the principal before a notary public (i.e., it must be notarized).[2]

The California statute doesn't expressly require the witnesses signatures to be notarized. But if you can have the witnesses' signatures notarized readily, do so.

E. Sample Statutory Short Form Durable Power of Attorney

This sample form is completed, so you can see how a finished one looks. I use California in this example, but New York is very similar. Form 13 in the Appendix was re-typed by the principal, and the warnings in bold print were typed in capitals.

Facts: John O'Leary appoints his brother, Timothy, as his attorney in fact. John wants Timothy to have all possible powers, so he doesn't delete any of the types of transactions listed in Section 3, "Statement of Authority Granted." John adds a sentence in Section 2, making the durable power of attorney effective only if he becomes incapacitated. He re-types his final durable power of attorney.

---

[2]The general California durable power of attorney law provides that the document must *either* be witnessed by two witnesses *or* notarized. It's not clear why the legislature required both for the statutory short form, but, for some reason, it did.

CALIFORNIA STATUTORY SHORT FORM DURABLE POWER OF ATTORNEY

WARNING! UNLESS YOU LIMIT THE POWER IN THIS DOCUMENT, THIS DOCUMENT GIVES YOUR AGENT THE POWER TO ACT FOR YOU IN ANY WAY YOU COULD ACT FOR YOURSELF. FOR EXAMPLE, YOUR AGENT CAN:
* BUY, SELL, AND MANAGE REAL AND PERSONAL PROPERTY FOR YOU. THIS MEANS THAT YOUR AGENT CAN SELL YOUR HOME, YOUR SECURITIES AND YOUR OTHER PROPERTY.
* DEPOSIT AND WITHDRAW MONEY FROM YOUR CHECKING AND SAVINGS ACCOUNTS.
* BORROW MONEY USING YOUR PROPERTY AS SECURITY FOR THE LOAN.
* PUT THINGS IN AND TAKE THINGS OUT OF YOUR SAFETY DEPOSIT BOX.
* OPERATE YOUR BUSINESS FOR YOU.
* PREPARE AND FILE TAX RETURNS FOR YOU AND ACT FOR YOU IN TAX MATTERS.
* ESTABLISH TRUSTS FOR YOU AND TAKE OTHER ACTIONS FOR YOU IN CONNECTION WITH PROBATE AND ESTATE PLANNING MATTERS.
* PROVIDE FOR THE SUPPORT AND WELFARE OF YOUR SPOUSE, CHILDREN, AND DEPENDENTS.
* CONTINUE PAYMENTS TO THE CHURCH AND OTHER ORGANIZATIONS OF WHICH YOU ARE A MEMBER AND MAKE GIFTS TO YOUR SPOUSE, DESCENDANTS, AND CHARITIES.

THIS DOCUMENT DOES NOT AUTHORIZE YOUR AGENT TO MAKE MEDICAL AND OTHER HEALTH CARE DECISIONS FOR YOU. YOU CAN DESIGNATE AN AGENT TO MAKE HEALTH CARE DECISIONS FOR YOU ONLY BY A SEPARATE DOCUMENT.

IT MAY BE IN YOUR BEST INTEREST TO CONSULT WITH A CALIFORNIA LAWYER BECAUSE THE POWERS GRANTED BY THIS DOCUMENT ARE BROAD AND SWEEPING. THEY ARE DEFINED IN SECTIONS 2460 TO 2473, INCLUSIVE, OF THE CALIFORNIA CIVIL CODE.

THE POWERS GRANTED BY THIS DOCUMENT WILL EXIST FOR AN INDEFINITE PERIOD OF TIME UNLESS YOU LIMIT THEIR DURATION IN THIS DOCUMENT. THESE POWERS WILL CONTINUE TO EXIST NOTWITHSTANDING YOUR SUBSEQUENT DISABILITY OR INCAPACITY UNLESS YOU INDICATE OTHERWISE IN THIS DOCUMENT.

YOU CAN ELIMINATE POWERS OF YOUR AGENT BY CROSSING OUT ANY ONE OR MORE OF THE POWERS LISTED IN PARAGRAPH 3 OF THIS FORM. YOU CAN WRITE OTHER LIMITATIONS AND SPECIAL PROVISIONS IN PARAGRAPH 4 OF THIS FORM. HOWEVER, IF YOU DO NOT WANT TO GRANT YOUR AGENT THE POWER TO ACT FOR YOU IN ANY WAY YOU COULD ACT FOR YOURSELF, IT MAY BE IN YOUR BEST INTEREST TO CONSULT WITH A LAWYER INSTEAD OF USING THIS FORM.

THIS DOCUMENT MUST BE SIGNED BY TWO WITNESSES AND BE NOTARIZED TO BE VALID.

YOU HAVE THE RIGHT TO REVOKE OR TERMINATE THIS POWER OF ATTORNEY.

YOU ARE NOT REQUIRED TO USE THIS FORM; YOU MAY USE A DIFFERENT POWER OF ATTORNEY IF THAT IS DESIRED BY THE PARTIES CONCERNED.

IF THERE IS ANYTHING ABOUT THIS FORM THAT YOU DO NOT UNDERSTAND, YOU SHOULD ASK A LAWYER TO EXPLAIN IT TO YOU.

1. DESIGNATION OF AGENT

I, JOHN O'LEARY, 14 Sea Bright Avenue, San Francisco, California do hereby appoint TIMOTHY O'LEARY, 104 Hill Road, San Francisco, California, as my attorney in fact (agent) to act for me and in my name as authorized in this document.

2. CREATION OF DURABLE POWER OF ATTORNEY

By this document I intend to create a general power of attorney under Sections 2450 to 2473, inclusive, of the California Civil Code. This durable power of attorney shall become effective only if I become so incapacitated or disabled that I am not able to manage my financial affairs. Subject to any limitations in this document, this power of attorney is a durable power of attorney and shall not be affected by my subsequent incapacity.

[If you want this power of attorney to terminate automatically when you lack capacity, you must so state in paragraph 4 ("Special Provisions and Limitations") below.]

3. STATEMENT OF AUTHORITY GRANTED

Subject to any limitations in this document, I hereby grant to my agent(s) full power and authority to act for me and in my name, in any way which I myself could act, if I were personally present and able to act, with respect to the following matters as each of them is defined in Chapter 3 (commencing with Section 2450) of Title 9 of Part 4 of Division 3 of the California Civil Code to the extent that I am permitted by law to act through an agent.

(1) Real estate transactions.
(2) Tangible personal property transactions.
(3) Bond, share, and commodity transactions.
(4) Financial institution transactions.
(5) Business operating transactions.
(6) Insurance transactions.
(7) Retirement plan transactions.
(8) Estate transactions.
(9) Claims and litigation.
(10) Tax matters.
(11) Personal relationships and affairs.
(12) Benefits from military service.
(13) Records, reports, and statements.
(14) Full and unqualified authority to my agent(s) to delegate any or all of the foregoing powers to any person or persons whom my agent(s) shall select.
(15) All other matters.

[Strike out any one or more of the items above to which you do not desire to give your agent authority. Such elimination of any one or more of items (1) to (14), inclusive, automatically constitutes an elimination of item (15). TO STRIKE OUT AN ITEM, YOU MUST DRAW A LINE THROUGH THE TEXT OF THAT ITEM.]

4. SPECIAL PROVISIONS AND LIMITATIONS

In exercising the authority under this power of attorney, my agent(s) is subject to the following special provisions and limitations:

_____

_____

_____

_____

[Special provisions and limitations may be included in the statutory short form power of attorney only if they conform to the requirements of Section 2455 of the California Civil Code.]

5. EXERCISE OF POWER OF ATTORNEY WHERE MORE THAN ONE AGENT DESIGNATED

If I have designated more than one agent, the agents are to act

_____.

[If you designate more than one agent and wish each agent alone to be able to exercise this power, insert in this blank the word "severally." Failure to make an insertion or the insertion of the word "jointly" will require that the agents act jointly.]

6. DURATION

[The powers granted by this document will exist for an indefinite period of time unless you limit their duration below.]

This power of attorney expires on _____.

[Fill in this space ONLY if you want the authority of your agent to terminate before your death.]

7. NOMINATION OF A CONSERVATOR OF ESTATE

[A conservator of the estate may be appointed for you if a court decides that one should be appointed. The conservator is responsible for the management of your financial affairs and your property. You are not required to nominate a conservator but you may do so. The court will appoint the person you nominate unless that would be contrary to your best interests. You may, but are not required to, nominate as your conservator the same person you named in paragraph 1 as your agent. You may nominate a person as your conservator by completing the space below.]

If conservator of the estate is to be appointed for me, I nominate the following person to serve as conservator of the estate: TIMOTHY O'LEARY, 104 Hill Road, San Francisco, California.

DATE AND SIGNATURE OF PRINCIPAL

[YOU MUST DATE AND SIGN THIS POWER OF ATTORNEY]
I sign my name to this Statutory Short Form Power of Attorney on November 1, 1992 at San Francisco, California.

_____

[THIS POWER OF ATTORNEY WILL NOT BE VALID UNLESS IT IS BOTH (1) SIGNED BY TWO ADULT WITNESSES WHO ARE PRESENT WHEN YOU SIGN OR ACKNOWLEDGE YOUR SIGNATURE; AND (2) ACKNOWLEDGED BEFORE A NOTARY PUBLIC IN CALIFORNIA.]

STATEMENT OF WITNESSES

[READ CAREFULLY BEFORE SIGNING. You can sign as a witness only if you personally know the principal or the identity of the principal is proved to you by convincing evidence.]

[To have convincing evidence of the identity of the principal, you must be presented with and reasonably rely on any one or more of the following:

(1) An identification card or driver's license issued by the California Department of Motor Vehicles that is current or has been issued within five years.

(2) A passport issued by the Department of State of the United States that is current or has been issued within five years.

(3) Any of the following documents if the document is current or has been issued within five years and contains a photograph and description of the person named on it, is signed by the person, and bears a serial or other identifying number:

(a) A passport issued by a foreign government that has been stamped by the United States Immigration and Naturalization Service.

(b) A driver's license issued by a state other than California or by a Canadian or Mexican public agency authorized to issue driver's licenses.

(c) An identification card issued by a state other than California.

(d) An identification card issued by any branch of the armed forces of the United States.]

(Other kinds of proof of identity are not allowed.)

I declare under penalty of perjury under the laws of California that the person who signed or acknowledged this document is personally known to me (or proved to me on the basis of convincing evidence) to be the principal, that the principal signed or acknowledged this power of attorney in my presence, and that the principal appears to be of sound mind and under no duress, fraud, or undue influence.

Signature:_____   Residence Address:_____

Print Name:_____   _____

Date:_____   _____

Signature:_____   Residence Address:_____

Print Name:_____   _____

Date:_____   _____

NOTARIZATION

State of California   )
) ss.
County of San Francisco   )

    On this first day of November, in the year 1992, before me, _____ personally appeared JOHN O'LEARY, personally known to me (or proved to me on the basis of satisfactory evidence) to be the person whose name is subscribed to this instrument, and acknowledged that he executed it.

[Notary Seal]   _____

CHAPTER 6

DURABLE POWERS OF ATTORNEY

FOR HEALTH CARE

A. Introduction

This chapter discusses using a durable power of attorney to enforce health decisions you've already made, including the refusal of medical treatment under specified conditions. It also discusses how you may authorize your attorney in fact to make health care decisions that you haven't already made.

The first question some readers may have is: Will my durable power of attorney for health care be legal? The answer is "yes." In my opinion, the laws of each of the 50 states and the District of Columbia authorize residents to use durable powers of attorney for health care. However, as discussed in Section B, you may need to review your durable power of attorney for health care with a lawyer before finalizing it.

1. Acceptability

A related question is: Will my durable power of attorney for health care be accepted in the real world by doctors, nurses, hospitals and other medical personnel and institutions? In many states and areas of the country, the answer is clearly "yes." For example, the California Medical Association has published a brochure and form, sent to all hospitals, explaining that a durable power of attorney for health care is fully legal in the state. However, durable powers of attorney for health care are a relatively recent legal development, and in some places, medical people are less familiar with these documents. If medical officials refuse to accept the authority of your attorney in fact, she'll have to try to persuade them to accept her authority. If that fails, she may need to see a lawyer. After they talk with their own lawyers, hospitals and doctors are unlikely to want to defend a lawsuit challenging their refusal to honor an attorney in fact's authority.

Obviously, you'd prefer that your attorney in fact not become enmeshed in these kinds of struggles. So it's sensible to do all you can to insure that your durable power of attorney for health care will be accepted if you become incapacitated. You can take these steps to promote the acceptability of your durable power of attorney for health care:

- *Carefully draft your document.* If you live in a state that requires a specific statutory form, use that form. Unless you use a fill-in-the-blanks form in the Appendix, type or word process your document on high quality, nonerasable white bond paper.

- *Sign the document and have it notarized and witnessed.* Have the witnessing done by two competent adults who are not entitled to inherit your property and who do not own or work for any health care facility.

- *Check with the doctor, hospital and any health care facility you or your attorney in fact are likely to deal with.* Determine if they're familiar with durable powers of attorney for health care. Assuming they are, ask if they have any procedural requirements of their own. If they do, work with them to be sure your durable power of attorney for health care conforms to their rules. If you encounter people who are unfamiliar with how durable powers of attorney work, consider providing them with some basic legal education on the subject (e.g., showing them a copy of this book).

- *Store the original durable power of attorney for health care in a safe place.* It should be easily accessible to the attorney in fact in the event you become incapacitated. Review and prepare a new one at least every seven years.

- *Place a copy of your durable power of attorney for health care in your medical records with your regular doctor.* If you have medical insurance which keeps records, place another copy there. And put copies in any other medical records maintained for you (e.g., by veteran's officials or medical institutions).

2. What Is 'Health Care'?

As a matter of common sense, most people—including medical personnel—probably have a working notion of what "health care" and "health care decisions" mean. Sensible definitions of these terms are found in California law. Health care is defined as: "any care treatment, service or procedure to maintain, diagnose, or treat an individual's physical or mental condition." Health care decision is similarly defined as "consent, refusal of consent or withdrawal of consent to health care." However, some states are more restrictive and do not permit an attorney in fact to refuse or withdraw consent for medical treatment.

3. How to Proceed

Before you plunge into actually drafting your own document, it's important that you gain a more thorough understanding of how durable powers of attorney for health care work. Read this entire chapter and carefully consider the information provided. You may want to review the general discussion of durable powers of attorneys in Chapter 1 before proceeding to the appropriate chapter to draft your own durable power of attorney for health care. Then turn to Chapter 7 unless you live in California, where you should turn to Chapter 8. Those chapters provide you with specific sample forms and clauses you can use, adapt, or modify to design your own durable power of attorney for health care.

Note on Financial Management: Incapacity obviously raises problems concerning finances as well as health care decisions. Unless yours are unusual circumstances, you'll also want to authorize someone to make financial decisions. If is often simplest and wisest to authorize the same person to handle decision-making in both areas, even though you create two separate documents. Turn to Chapter 3 for an overview of durable powers of attorney for

finances, and then Chapters 4 or 5 for instructions on drafting one.

B. Legal Status of Durable Powers of Attorney for Health Care

Each state has its own laws concerning durable powers of attorney for health care, and these laws are changing rapidly. A number of states have expressly authorized durable powers of attorney for health care. In most other states, you can safely prepare one using this book. Only in a minority of states is it absolutely essential that your draft be checked by a knowledgeable lawyer.

The charts in Section B(1) below present four different categories of states' legal basis for durable powers of attorney for health care:

- *Chart 1:* These states expressly authorize, either by statute or court decision, durable powers of attorney for health care. A few states authorize the attorney in fact to consent to medical treatment, but do not mention authority to withhold or terminate life sustaining procedures. The Appendix contains specific statutory forms that were created by some of these states' legislatures.

- *Chart 2:* In these states, there have been no problems using durable powers of attorney for health care. They have authorized appointment of an agent for health care in their Living Will or Natural Death Acts, or there is some other official basis for appointing an attorney in fact, such as an Attorney General's opinion. They have also adopted either the Uniform Durable Power of Attorney Act or the Uniform Probate Code provisions for Durable Powers of Attorney.

- *Chart 3:* States listed here have adopted the Uniform Durable Power of Attorney Act or the Uniform Probate Code provisions for durable powers of attorney, and have evidenced no problems allowing durable powers of attorney to be used for health care.

- *Chart 4:* In states listed on Chart 4, there are some uncertainties, special requirements or limits regarding the legal scope of durable powers of attorney for health care. For example, there may be statutory restrictions on the authority of the attorney in fact or only specified relatives may serve in that capacity. *If you live in a state listed in Chart 4, you must see a lawyer before preparing your durable power of attorney for health care.*

1. Charts Summarizing State Laws

Set out below are Charts 1-4. When you've found your state, make sure you understand the consequences of its categorization as explained above.

CHART 1: STATES WHICH EXPRESSLY AUTHORIZE DURABLE POWERS OF ATTORNEY FOR HEALTH CARE

Alaska*	Kansas	Rhode Island
California	Maine	South Dakota
Colorado*	Nevada	Texas
District of Columbia	New Mexico	Vermont
Idaho	North Carolina*	Washington
Illinois	Pennsylvania*	West Virginia

*State laws authorize an attorney in fact to consent to medical treatment, but are silent on authority to withhold or terminate life sustaining procedures.

CHART 2: STATES WHICH AUTHORIZE AN AGENT FOR HEALTH CARE AND HAVE ADOPTED DURABLE POWER OF ATTORNEY PROVISIONS

Arizona	Iowa	New York
Delaware	Maryland	Utah
Hawaii	Minnesota	Virginia
Indiana	New Jersey	Wyoming

CHART 3: STATES WHICH ADOPTED DURABLE POWERS OF ATTORNEY PROVISIONS IN THE UNIFORM DURABLE POWER OF ATTORNEY ACT OR UNIFORM PROBATE CODE

Kentucky	Missouri	Tennessee
Massachusetts	Montana	Wisconsin
Michigan	Nebraska	

CHART 4: STATES WHERE YOU MUST SEE A LAWYER BEFORE COMPLETING YOUR DURABLE POWER OF ATTORNEY FOR HEALTH CARE

Alabama	Louisiana	Ohio
Arkansas	Mississippi	Oklahoma
Connecticut	New Hampshire	Oregon
Florida	North Dakota	South Carolina
Georgia		

WARNING: CHANGING LAWS

These charts are accurate as of the last printing of this book. But this area of the law changes frequently, and bills are pending before many state legislatures to adopt new laws or revise existing laws. As soon as possible, changes will be noted in the quarterly Nolo News (available from Nolo Press—see information at the back of this book). To be absolutely sure your form is up-to-date and the best to use in your state, you can check your form with a lawyer familiar with durable powers of attorney for health care.

2. Be Specific In Your Durable Power of Attorney

No matter where you live, be as clear and specific in your durable power of attorney for health care as possible. Examples of specific clauses to specify your desires and intentions for your health care and medical treatment are found in Chapter 7, Section F. Defining your intentions and stating the authority of attorney in fact is important because:

- Specific provisions defining your desires for health care treatment remove all doubt as to your intent.

- Acceptability of your attorney in fact's decisions by doctors and other health care professionals is more likely.

- For major medical decisions, a hospital or other facility might be reluctant, or refuse to accept, a broad delegation of power to the attorney in fact. This is especially true for vital matters like use of life sustaining procedures (see Section F of this chapter). But that institution will be more likely to accept the decision of the attorney in fact if you specifically gave her authority to make those important health care decisions.

C. Durable Powers of Attorney for Health Care and Alternatives

By definition, incapacity means someone has a health problem. However, not all serious health problems render a person unable to make his own health care decisions. A person may be able to competently decide whether he wants to risk major surgery even if he can't remember to take his medication every day or is unable to make business decisions. But incapacity can be so serious that a person cannot competently make health care decisions. Or the incapacity can involve a degenerative disease, which means a likelihood of losing competence to make health care decisions sometime in the near future.

If a person cannot make her own medical/health care decisions, someone else must gain legal authority to make them. These decisions can range from relatively minor concerns to matters of utmost gravity—choices concerning physicians, methods of treatment and major surgery. Particularly important for many people are issues regarding the use of life sustaining procedures. If a person has an incurable illness and lacks capacity to make health care decisions, must life support equipment be used, no matter how hopeless the medical condition, even if the person's family and friends know she is opposed to the concept of being kept alive artificially? How can permission to make decisions about life support equipment be delegated to someone else?

Normally, the most efficient method of establishing authority to make medical/health care decisions for an incapacitated person is by use of a durable power of attorney. Any competent adult can create her own durable power of attorney for health care. Even married people are well advised to prepare a durable power of attorney for health care, since it can't hurt and may prove essential. As with financial durable powers of attorney, one for health care can become effective on signing by the principal, or can be designed to become effective only if the principal becomes incapacitated (i.e., "springing"). Most people who aren't likely to become incapacitated in the near future prefer the "springing" type.

There are various other methods you can use to delegate authority for health care decisions. Let's look at them.

1. Informal Authorization

In some situations, health care providers—doctors, hospitals, nursing homes—will accept the "inherent" authority of family members, especially a spouse, to make decisions for someone who is incapacitated. However, for serious matters such as a decision to terminate life support equipment, health care providers are often unwilling, or legally unable, to accept the authority of a family member—including a spouse— without prior written permission from the incapacitated person.

2. 'Living Wills'

In a majority of states, you can use a document called a "living will" to record and enforce your decisions regarding life support systems. (Living wills are discussed in more detail in Section G of this chapter and Chapter 7, Section D.) However, use of living wills is often seriously restricted. First, they're not

valid in all states. Second, they only apply to use of life sustaining procedures, not all medical care decisions. Third, a living will is addressed directly to doctors and medical personnel, but you don't appoint anyone to be sure your instructions are carried out. Finally, there are often other limits imposed on living wills by state law which further restrict their effectiveness. However, as I subsequently discuss, it may be prudent to prepare both a living will and a durable power of attorney for health care.

3. Court Proceedings ('Conservatorships')

Another method for establishing authority to make medical/health care decisions for an incapacitated person is through court (conservatorship) proceedings. If no advance legal work has been done, this is probably the route you will have to follow. However, for the reasons discussed earlier (see Chapter 1, Section E), court proceedings for incapacitated persons are generally best avoided.

D. Decisions About Your Durable Power of Attorney for Health Care

This section provides a discussion of the basic decisions you must make to draft your own durable power of attorney for health care.

1. Which Type of Durable Power of Attorney Fits Your Situation

The first choice that must be made by anyone preparing a durable power of attorney for health care is whether it should be:

- A *standard durable power of attorney for health care*, effective upon your signing (or on some other specific date you specify); or

- A *"springing" durable power of attorney for health care*, effective only if you become incapacitated and are unable to make health care decisions.

The choice is properly dictated by circumstances. A person who's close to an incapacitated state, or facing a serious operation when the durable power is prepared, will choose the first type. Someone who is healthy now but wants to prepare a durable power of attorney for health care as a kind of insurance will want a "springing" durable power of attorney.

2. What Health Care Decisions Can Be Conveyed

By using a durable power of attorney for health care, a principal can accomplish two things, if the need arises. First, the principal can set out certain health care decisions she's made and wants her attorney in fact to enforce for her. Second, the principal can convey broad powers to her attorney in fact to make health care decisions for her.

There are only a few limits of the health care authority that can be delegated. By law in California, authority to authorize several sensitive medical procedures or operations, such as lobotomies and abortion, cannot be delegated. In other states, similar limits should be observed as a matter of common sense, even though there's no statutory law on the subject. Also, some decisions regarding use of life sustaining procedures may be restricted by state law. For example, some states don't allow either a principal or attorney in fact to authorize termination of artificial feeding. But otherwise, an attorney in fact can be authorized to make any medical or health care decision she deems necessary for any illness or problems afflicting the incapacitated principal.

One important point that bears repeating is that even though state law allows an extremely broad delegation of authority for health care, the principal can also limit, restrict or define the authority of the attorney in fact over health care decisions however

she desires. So, by use of a durable power of attorney for health care, the principal can maintain control over medical care, treatment and decisions, even if she's incapacitated. Probably the most significant area where people want to retain control concerns use—or non-use—of life support systems. A durable power of attorney for health care is generally the most reliable legal method to insure your desires in this area are followed. (See the discussion in Section F.)

3. Some Advice on Selecting an Attorney in Fact

To repeat what's been stressed already, it's vitally important that you choose an attorney in fact you totally trust (see discussion in Chapter 3, Section G). It's generally, but by no means always, wise to have the same person be the attorney in fact for health care decisions and finance. However, if you have compelling reasons why you believe you should have two separate attorneys in fact, do so. For example, you might want your spouse to make health care decisions, but believe someone else—your business partner, say—is much better equipped to manage your finances.

In California and a few other states, statutory restrictions prohibit certain classes of people from being named as attorney in fact for health care decisions. Even though these restrictions don't legally apply in most states, it is wise to observe them. First of all, they seem sensible. Secondly, authorities in other states could prove to be reluctant to accept the authority of a person from a class prohibited by California law. As you'll see, it's unlikely you'd want to name a person from one of these prohibited classes as your attorney in fact:

- The owner, operator or employee of a health care provider (hospital, nursing home, etc.); or

- The owner, operator or employee of a health care facility (nursing homes, board and care homes, etc.).

Should you wish someone who's in one of these groups to serve as your attorney in fact, see a lawyer.

In deciding upon the choice of your attorney in fact for health care decisions, it's important to consider the realities of your situation, and take whatever steps you can to insure that the person you've chosen to be your attorney in fact will not be challenged.

Example

Simon creates a "springing" durable power of attorney for health care, authorizing his friend, Herman, to be his attorney in fact. Simon knows that his son, Ben, has orthodox religious beliefs which involve rigid opinions regarding what medical treatment Simon should and should not receive if he is sick, especially if he becomes incapacitated. Simon doesn't agree with his son's religious views. Simon informs his son that he has chosen Herman to be his attorney in fact to make health care decisions, and requests that his son honor Herman's decisions and not put any pressure on Herman to adhere to Ben's medical views. In his durable power of attorney document, Simon states that Ben is not to have any authority whatsoever to decide or affect Simon's medical treatment. Simon discusses this matter with his personal doctor, who promises to adhere to Simon's expressed desires.

4. How Incapacity Will Be Determined

Many people want any determination of incapacity to be made by the doctor or medical facility they're most familiar with and trust. This can be specified in the durable power of attorney document. Of course, the matter should be discussed with the involved doctor or medical facility to be sure they'll accept the responsibility.

Example

Alan's personal physician is Dr. Jean Rice. He has also been treated extensively by Dr. Alice Jones of the Whitefield Medical Clinic. Alan trusts his personal doctors, and also respects the other doctors at the clinic. He puts the following clause in his durable power of attorney for health care: "The determination that I have become incapacitated and am unable to make health care decisions for myself shall be made in writing by Dr. Jean Rice, [address], if possible. If Dr. Rice is unavailable to make this determination, it shall be made, in writing, by Dr. Alice Jones [provide address], or, if she is unavailable to do so, it shall be made, in writing, by any other physician of the Whitefield Medical Clinic, if possible."

5. Reviewing, Revoking or Amending a Durable Power of Attorney for Health Care

At a minimum, you should review your durable power of attorney every seven years. Even if your desires haven't changed, it's wise to prepare a new document every seven years. In California there is a legal seven-year limit (after the date of signing) on the validity of durable powers of attorney for health care, unless the principal is incapacitated at the expiration of that seven years.

As long as you're competent, you can revoke a durable power of attorney for health care at any time. If you wish to revoke yours, read Chapter 10 and use or adapt the revocation form provided in the Appendix. Make sure your doctor and any other concerned health care provider or financial institutions receive a copy of any Notice of Revocation.

There's no generally accepted method for amending a durable power of attorney for health care. Rather than trying to invent an amendment form, and hope it will be accepted, I feel it's prudent to offer this conservative advice: If you want to revise or amend your document, revoke it completely and prepare a new one.

6. Which Form Should You Use?

In the Appendix you'll find tear-out, fill-in-the-blanks durable power of attorney for health care forms. Forms 5 and 6 may be used by residents of states that don't require statutory forms.

You must use statutory forms if you live in these states:

* California (Forms 13-15);
* Idaho (Form 7);
* Nevada (Form 8);
* Rhode Island (Form 9); and
* Vermont (Form 10).

Although not required by law, residents of these states would be wise to use their state's specific form:

* District of Columbia (Form 11); and
* Illinois (Form 12).

a. Other Sources for Forms

If you reside in a state with statutorily required forms—or live in Kansas, Maine, Maryland, New Jersey, New Mexico, New York, Ohio, Oregon, Texas or Utah—you can obtain a durable power of attorney for health care from the Society for the Right to Die. I mention this for thoroughness, in case you want to check a form you've drafted using this book with someone else's. The address and additional information about the Society for the Right to Die are contained in Section G(1) of this chapter. There is no charge for the forms, although a donation is suggested.

E. Authority of Your Attorney in Fact

As discussed in Section D(2) of this chapter, there are very few limits on the authority a principal can grant an attorney in fact. If you want to restrict the power of your attorney in fact, or direct that certain acts are required or forbidden, you need to state that in your durable power of attorney document. Commonly, the principal makes specific provisions regarding life support systems. In addition, the principal can impose any reasonable directions or restrictions she wants.

Example 1
Sara is seriously ill, faces major surgery, and knows she will soon be unable to make all her own medical and health care decisions. She prepares a durable power of attorney, delegating to her sister, Kendell, the authority to make health care decisions for her. To make sure that her own wishes are followed, she inserts clauses restricting Kendell's power. Specifically, Sara wants to be operated on by Dr. June Lee at Mattan Hospital. So, in defining the attorney in fact's authority powers, she includes the restriction that all surgery performed on her is to be done Dr. June Lee, unless Dr. Lee is unable to perform such surgery.

Example 2
Janette doesn't want to be removed from her home unless that's absolutely necessary. She therefore states in her durable power of attorney that her attorney in fact has no authority to have her removed from her home to any medical or health care facility, unless a doctor has certified in writing that, in his opinion, such removal is essential in order to provide Janette with proper medical care.

Jot down now, if you haven't already, specific concerns you have or restrictions you might want to impose, so that later on you'll be sure to draft provisions covering each concern for inclusion in your document. And be sure to review all the clauses provided in Chapter 7 carefully, to check that you haven't overlooked something.

If no restrictions are imposed, your attorney in fact is authorized to make all health care decisions that you could make yourself while competent. Because this area is so important, let's take the time to examine the general authority of the attorney in fact.

1. Authority of Attorney in Fact Unless Restricted by the Principal

Under a general delegation of authority to the attorney in fact to make health care decisions for the principal, the attorney in fact's broad authority includes—but is by no means limited to—the following:

- Authority to consent, refuse to consent or withdraw consent as to the choice of doctors, hospitals and/or treatment, including medication and surgery;

- Power to make anatomical gifts before the principal dies. All states have adopted the Uniform Anatomical Gift Act, and allow a person to make anatomical gifts (i.e., body parts used for heart, kidney or eye transplants, etc.). Under a general delegation of authority for health care an attorney in fact can authorize the donation of bodily parts and organs from a dying principal to another person;

- Right to information and reports from all treating doctors, hospitals and medical facilities regarding proposed health care, surgery, or any other aspect of the principal's treatment, including the right to receive, review and disclose the principal's medical records;

- Right to hire and fire all medical personnel and professionals treating the principal;

- Authority to execute any and all medical consent, insurance or other benefit forms on behalf of the principal;

- Right to consent, or refuse to consent, to psychiatric care to be given to the principal;

- Right to refuse or require that life prolonging procedures and technologies be used for the principal (discussed further in Section F below); and

- Power to control visitation rights to the principal, to the extent the hospital or other medical facility allows any outside person control over visitation rights.

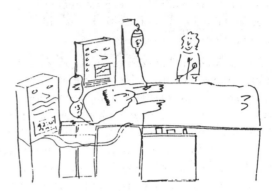

F. Life Sustaining Procedures and Technologies

The issue of life sustaining procedures, including use of life support systems, is one of the most vital concerns of many people preparing a durable power of attorney for health care. This section contains information about this important issue, and helps you understand your choices.

Modern medical technology often has the ability to keep an incurably ill person alive for an extended period of time, even when there's no chance the person will ever recover. Currently, over 80% of all deaths in the United states occur in institutions (hospitals, nursing facilities, etc.) whereas only a generation ago it was less than 50%. To many, the possibility of being institutionalized and hooked up to a tangle of wire and tubes, helplessly dependent, with no hope of recovering normal life, is a nightmare. Increasingly, many people feel this kind of "living" isn't life, and isn't worth it. If they have an irreversible disease, they want to die a "natural" death, rather than prolong life artificially by the use of medical technology or treatment.

If a patient is conscious, she has the right to refuse or terminate any medical treatment, including use of life support systems. No institution or person has the legal right to force treatment on a competent adult who doesn't want it. But serious problems can arise if a person is mentally incapacitated, unconscious, or otherwise unable to express her own desires, and the question of whether to use life sustaining procedures arises.

Several well-publicized court decisions have held that life support systems couldn't be cut off for a comatose or unconscious patient, no matter how hopeless her condition, since she had not left legally binding instructions on this matter. Although other cases have decided the opposite, it is risky and uncertain to leave the issue of use and termination of life sustaining procedures, including life support systems, up to a court. You can use a durable power of attorney for health care to insure this fate doesn't befall you. You can specify, in advance, what you want done regarding life sustaining procedures in the event you become incapacitated and unable to express your own desires.

Traditionally, family members have made important medical decisions for an incapacitated person. However, this custom seems to be changing. Some people want a lover or friend—rather than family—to have authority to make medical decisions for them. Naturally, most doctors would rather administer medical care than mediate a dispute among a patient's family and friends over who has the right to make medical decisions. Moreover, physicians are increasingly concerned with being protected from legal liability. Durable powers of attorney for health care cover all these issues, resulting in their increasing popularity with doctors and hospital authorities.

Because durable powers of attorney are so recent, there is no well-established legal precedent validating their authority for termination of life support systems. However, I know of no instance where any hospital or medical authority has refused to follow the directions of an attorney in fact clearly appointed in a valid durable power of attorney document. Use of a durable power of attorney to specify one's desires

regarding use of life sustaining procedures answers a clear social need and so will be honored.

The realities of life sustaining procedures are at the forefront of contemporary medicine. The issues being raised can be deep and complex.[1] What are the ethical, practical and legal realities involved in terminating, or continuing, life support systems? What types of procedures and technologies can a patient end? Is a diagnosis of Alzheimer's disease an "irreversible condition" that can justify the withdrawal of life support systems? I raise these questions here to remind you to proceed carefully when preparing a clause concerning life support systems in your durable power of attorney. Because this area is so new, there's little technical, legal language that has become settled and clear. For example, you can state in your durable power of attorney, "I don't want any life support systems used." But what, as a practical, and legal, matter would this mean? What are "life support systems"? Moreover, when should they not be used? Any time you're ill? Or only if you have a fatal illness with no chance of recovery? Who can say what amounts to "no chance" of recovery?

These issues don't mean that you can't draft a clear provision regarding your desires concerning use of life support systems. You can. What they do demonstrate is that you need to give the matter some serious thought. It's unwise to simply plug a vague general phrase about use of life sustaining procedures into your durable power of attorney for health care.

---

[1] Books on the subject include: *Intensive Care: Facing the Critical Choices*, by Thomas A. Rafkin, Joel N. Shurkin and Warton Sinkler (W.H. Freeman, 1989); *Emerging Legal Issues of Death and Dying*, by Norman L. Cantor (Indiana University Press, 1987); and *By No Extraordinary Means: The Choice to Forgo Life-Sustaining Food and Water*, Joanne Lynn, Editor (Indiana University Press, 1987). Updated information can be obtained from the Society for the Right to Die, 250 West 57th St., NY, NY 10107, telephone (212) 246-6973.

1. Defining 'Life Sustaining Procedures' and 'Life Support Systems'

Any treatment which artificially extends someone's life is a "life sustaining procedure." Initially, this referred only to "life support systems" such as heart, kidney or other machines that artificially maintained a vital body organ. Discontinuance of life support systems meant, in the vernacular, "pulling the plug."

Now, however, the term "life sustaining procedure" includes artificial hydration and feeding—i.e., being fed water and food through tubes. It includes resuscitating a patient who has stopped breathing. The current trend in medical and legal practice is to reject any distinction between "extraordinary" and "ordinary" treatment. Basically, any medical treatment can be considered a "life sustaining procedure" or a "life support system" if it is used to artificially maintain a life.

2. Deciding About Life Sustaining Procedures

Your first decision is to resolve how you feel about life sustaining procedures. Do you want them used no matter what? Do you want to prohibit the use of life sustaining procedures to the maximum extent possible? Or do you want to draw a more specific line—maybe requiring that life sustaining procedures be discontinued if you're diagnosed as having a fatal illness and you're comatose? In the event you have irreparable brain damage, do you want to be kept alive by being fed with a tube? Or—to phrase it bluntly—would you prefer to starve to death?

In Chapter 7, Section F(1), you'll find a number of different clauses regarding life sustaining procedures which you can use verbatim or adapt to your own language. But to do that, you need to be clear about your personal position on the use of such methods.

I suggest you resolve this matter yourself, rather than leaving decisions regarding use of life sustaining procedures to your attorney in fact. As a practical matter, many hospitals and doctors would be unwilling, or at best reluctant, to accept the authority of your attorney in fact to make such a basic decision for you. Also, thrusting such a grave decision on your attorney in fact seems unnecessarily burdensome. If the issue of life sustaining procedures arises, she'll have responsibility enough trying to see that your express directions are carried out.

3. When Life Sustaining Procedures Can Be Discontinued

The basic purpose of refusing or discontinuing life sustaining procedures is to allow a "natural" death and prevent the pointless extension of a form of life by artificial means. Thus a person must have some type of fatal, irreversible disease or condition before any discontinuance of any life support systems can be allowed. Functionally, this generally works. Most people, including doctors, seem to know what's meant by having a "fatal" or "terminal" condition, but logically things aren't clear. After all, from one perspective, we all have a "fatal" and "terminal" condition.

At times, a number of other words or phrases are used to indicate the condition a person must be in to permit discontinuance of life support systems. The American Medical Association refers to "imminently dying," or "irreversibly comatose" patients. Other definitions refer to "terminally ill," "permanently unconscious," "irrevocable and fatal disease," or "artificially prolonging the moment of death." A Wall Street Journal editorial used the words "...incurable condition leaving you...unable to relate to life in a meaningful way."

In sum, there are no magic legal words to define the condition one must be in to permit discontinuance of life support systems. Whatever definition or conditions you use, there must be a medical decision that you're in that condition before your directions regarding life sustaining procedures will be honored. If you're in a coma, will you recover? Sometimes, doctors are unable to determine this. However you've defined that condition that justifies termination of life support systems in your durable power of attorney —"fatal," "irreversible," etc.—a doctor must conclude you're in that condition. I reiterate this point here to emphasize once again that, to the extent you can, you shouldn't rely solely on the wording in your durable power of attorney for health care to be sure your intent is carried out. Making sure you have a sympathetic doctor and hospital can be crucial.

4. Limits on Authority to Refuse or Terminate Life Sustaining Procedures

Different states have differing laws regarding what types of life sustaining procedures you can or cannot prohibit in your durable power of attorney for health care. Many states' laws don't present any problem here; they allow you to authorize termination of any type of support system, from heart machines to artificial feeding. Some states' laws only specifically regulate certain types of life support systems. For example, New York has a special law authorizing you to appoint a proxy (i.e., an attorney in fact) to enforce your condition regarding "do not resuscitate" orders.

However, a few states laws severely restrict your authority to order termination of life support systems. For example, in Arkansas, your attorney in fact cannot authorize termination of life support procedures at all. All states which significantly restrict your authority regarding life support systems are on the list in Chart 4 of Section B(1) of this chapter. If your state is on this list, check with a lawyer if you want to authorize termination of life support systems in your durable power of attorney.

a. Artificial Feeding and Hydration

One controversial area is termination of artificial feeding or hydration. The American Medical Association has stated that it is medically ethical to terminate artificial feeding when a patient is in a "persistent vegetative state" and the feeding is futile and only prolongs the dying process. States such as Illinois, Alaska and Ohio, specifically authorize termination of artificial feeding. Other states, such as Missouri, North Dakota and Oklahoma, have passed laws forbidding anyone from the termination of artificial feeding. And still other state laws are silent on the question.

If this issue concerns you, it's wise to check the current law in your state with an attorney. You can also check with the Society for the Right to Die, which maintains updated information on "tube feeding" laws for all states. (See Section G of this chapter.)

If you determine that termination of artificial feeding is permitted in your state, and you decide to authorize or require that in your durable power of attorney, check your local hospital's practices and discuss the matter with your attorney in fact. If artificial feeding is actually ended, powerful realities are involved, since it means that the patient will starve to death. A hospital may say: "Okay, if that's what he wants—but not here. Take him home—or to a different hospital." Particularly if you can't find a hospital willing to accept a patient under these conditions, handling this problem can be, candidly, a disturbing and even dreadful reality.

Questions of artificial feeding can touch on an even larger issue: what are the outer limits of one's authority over medical treatment; what can you authorize or prohibit another from doing? For example, what treatments and procedures can be withheld from Alzheimer's patients? Don't they have a hopeless, terminal condition? Also, it's been estimated that at least 10,000 people in the U.S. hover between life and death in a condition that cannot, medically, be described as hopeless or necessarily imminently terminal, even though it's close. These all point to a troubling general question: at what point does termination of life sustaining procedures become euthanasia?

Fortunately, most people who are concerned about life sustaining procedures don't have to bother with these difficult questions. They want to prevent the futile prolongation of the process of dying. All they really seek is to prevent the tragedy of spending weeks, months, even years of being kept technically alive when they're unconscious, comatose, or otherwise incapable of living anything that resembles authentic life. For these purposes, a durable power of attorney works fine (with the reminder caveat that in states listed on Chart 4 of Section B(1), you need to check the law with a lawyer).

G. Living Wills

A "living will" is a document you can use, in a majority of states, to express your desires regarding use of life sustaining procedures, including life support systems. A living will is not a form of a conventional will, designating how property should be distributed after a person's death. A living will is also distinct from a "living trust," which is an estate planning device used to transfer property outside of probate.

Most states and the District of Columbia have adopted some form of living will law. The substance of these laws varies significantly from state to state. Similarly, the title of the law varies widely (e.g., "Natural Death Act," "Living Will Statute," "Right to Death with Dignity Act," "Life Sustaining Procedures Act," etc.). Also, the document itself can go by other names than a living will, such as a "Directive to Physicians."

STATES WITH LIVING WILL STATUTES

Living wills may be used in:

Alabama, Alaska, Arizona, Arkansas, California, Colorado, Connecticut, Delaware, District of Columbia, Florida, Georgia, Hawaii, Idaho, Illinois, Indiana, Iowa, Kansas, Kentucky, Louisiana, Maine, Maryland, Minnesota, Mississippi, Missouri, Montana, Nevada, New Hampshire, New Mexico, North Carolina, North Dakota, Oklahoma, Oregon, South Carolina, Tennessee, Texas, Utah, Vermont, Virginia, Washington, West Virginia, Wisconsin, Wyoming.[2]

Living wills were the initial legal device for handling the problems of life sustaining procedures being used to artificially extend a life. Now these problems can also be handled by a durable power of attorney for health care. However, in a number of states, the living will statute is far more specific than the durable power of attorney law regarding use and termination of life sustaining procedures. Because the issue of life sustaining procedures is so vital to many people, and because it's such a new area of law and medicine, it can be prudent to express your desires in both legal forms—a durable power of attorney and a living will. Certainly, this can't hurt, assuming, of course, that the two documents are consistent.

In my opinion, a living will shouldn't be the exclusive document you use to express your decisions regarding life sustaining procedures. You should always express those desires in a durable power of attorney for health care as well.[3] The reasons for this are:

- A living will is normally addressed only to physicians. In most states, you cannot use a living will to appoint someone to see to it that your

---

[2]Those states that have not adapted living will statutes include Massachusetts, Michigan, Nebraska, New Jersey, New York, Ohio, Pennsylvania, Rhode Island, South Dakota.

[3]The American Medical Association agrees with this recommendation.

decisions regarding life sustaining procedures are carried out.

- In some states, living wills are restricted so that they're binding only if executed after you have been informed you have a "terminal condition."

- In a number of states, to prepare a living will, you usually must use a statutory-required form, and cannot make significant changes in it. You generally cannot specify in your own words what you mean by "life sustaining procedures" or "life support systems," or otherwise express your own detailed desires in the document.

- Living wills cover only life sustaining procedures for the terminally ill. You cannot use one to handle other health care decisions. So you need to prepare a durable power of attorney for health care anyway.

1. How to Obtain a Living Will Form

The actual form required for a valid living will varies widely from state to state, and space limitations do not allow this book to include forms for all states. A California living will form is contained in the Appendix, as Form 16. To obtain a living will form for all other states with living will statutes, contact:

The Society for the Right to Die
250 West 57th Street, Suite 323
New York, NY 10107
(212) 246-6973

This excellent non-profit organization is on the forefront of the efforts to allow each person the right to decide what medical treatment she wants in a life-threatening condition. The Society welcomes (tax-deductible) donations, but free of charge will send you an up-to-date living will form for your state. Requests should be accompanied by a self-addressed, stamped envelope.

TERMINAL ILLNESSES AND HOSPICES

In recent years, hospice programs have been set up throughout the country to help terminally ill people maintain their right to control how they live and ultimately die. Over 188,000 people nationwide use the services of approximately 1,700 hospices.

Typically, the terminally ill person stays at home, where care is provided by family, close friends and medical professionals. Special counselling is given to the terminally ill person and those close to him. Hospice programs help ensure that a terminally ill person doesn't end up on life support systems, which is likely to happen if he dials 911 or enters a hospital facility.

Information about hospices throughout the country can be obtained from the Hospice Help Line, (800) 658-8898.

CHAPTER 7

SAMPLE DURABLE POWERS OF ATTORNEY FOR HEALTH CARE FORMS AND CLAUSES

A. Introduction

This chapter provides you with two sample forms and a number of clauses you can use to draft a durable power of attorney for health care. A tear-out, fill in the blanks version of each form is contained in the Appendix, as Forms 5 and 6. You can either use the pre-printed forms as is or modify them.

Note: These forms can't be used if you live in California, Idaho, Nevada, Rhode Island or Vermont —but even if you live there, you should still read this chapter to gain a general understanding of how durable powers of attorney for health care work. Then, if you live in California, proceed to Chapter 7, which discusses the specific forms required by law in that state. The form for Idaho is included as Form 7 in the Appendix. The form for Nevada is included as Form 8. The form for Rhode Island is included as Form 9, and for Vermont it is Form 10. Also included in the Appendix are statutory forms for the District of Columbia (Form 11) and Illinois (Form 12), which are suggested but not mandatory.

The "Warnings": Some health care forms in the Appendix begin with "Warnings" which explain the importance of a durable power of attorney for health care. Whenever included on a form, these "Warnings" are required by law. They should be typed in bold type or in capital letters on your final document. The "Warnings" show doctors and institutions to whom the durable power of attorney may be presented that you had notice as to the nature of the powerful document you created.

1. Notarizing and Witnessing Your Durable Power of Attorney

Your durable power of attorney for health care should be notarized, if possible. Notarization means the principal signs the document in a notary's presence. This, of course, may pose a problem if the principal is gravely ill or bedridden. In this situation, it's desirable to have a notary come to where the principal is, such as at home or in a hospital room.

Locating a notary shouldn't be a problem, as many notaries advertise in the yellow pages. Or you might check with your bank, a local real estate office or even an attorney's office. If the notary needs to come to a hospital or home, find out the charge ahead of time. If you can't manage to get the document notarized, consult with a lawyer to learn the best course of action to make your document acceptable in your state.

The durable power of attorney for health care forms provided in this book have space allowing for both witnessing and notarization. Some state laws require witnessing, and it's always a good idea. In borderline cases, where the principal's capacity to execute a valid durable power of attorney may be subsequently questioned or challenged, it's prudent to have witnesses who can testify that in their judgment the principal knew what he was doing and was indeed competent at the time of signing of the document. The witnesses must be competent adults, preferably who reside in your state. If possible, the person you've chosen as attorney in fact should not be a witness.

The major drawback to having witnesses is that they should be present when the principal signs the document before the notary, because the witnesses must state they saw the principal sign. It can be a hassle to arrange three people's schedules to get them all to a notary's office at the same time. If the witnesses do appear at the notary's office, their signature should be notarized too. If it's too inconvenient to arrange for witnesses to appear before a notary, check with an attorney to be sure witnessing isn't required in your state.

B. Sample Springing Durable Power of Attorney for Health Care

This is a basic "springing" form, which only goes into effect if the principal becomes incapacitated.

Facts: The principal, Gail Dannatt, appoints her sister, Cecilia Dannatt, to be her attorney in fact to make health care decisions for her if she becomes incapacitated. The only restriction Gail places on her attorney in fact (in Paragraph 5) is a prohibition against the use of life support systems to artificially prolong her life if she's diagnosed as having a terminal condition.

Form 6

Springing Durable Power of Attorney for Health Care

1. Creation of Durable Power of Attorney

To my family, relatives, friends and my physicians, health care providers, community care facilities and any other person who may have an interest or duty in my medical care or treatment:

I, _____ GAIL DANNATT _____, being of sound
name

mind, willfully and voluntarily intend to create by this document a durable power of attorney for my health care by appointing the person designated as my attorney in fact to make health care decisions for me in the event I become incapacitated and am unable to make health care decisions for myself. This power of attorney shall not be affected by my subsequent incapacity.

2. Designation of Attorney in Fact

The person designated to be my attorney in fact for health care in the event I become

incapacitated is _____ CECILIA DANNATT _____ of
name

2662 Pearl Street, Mayfield, New Jersey _____ . If
address

_____ CECILIA DANNATT _____
name

for any reason shall fail to serve or ceases to serve as my attorney in fact for health care,

_____ RANDY DANNATT _____ of
name

136 South Street, Mayfield, New Jersey _____ shall be
address

my attorney in fact for health care.

3. Effective on Incapacity

This durable power of attorney shall become effective in the event I become incapacitated and am unable to make health care decisions for myself, in which case it shall become effective as of the date of the written statement by a physician, as provided in Paragraph 4.

4. Determination of Incapacity

(a) The determination that I have become incapacitated and am unable to make health care decisions shall be made in writing by a licensed physician. If possible, the determination shall be made by _____DR. WILLIAM SMITH, Faith Hospital, Mayfield,__ ,

name of physician

__New Jersey_____ .

address

(b) In the event that a licensed physician has made a written determination that I have become incapacitated and am not able to make health care decisions for myself, that written statement shall be attached to the original document of this durable power of attorney.

5. Authority of My Attorney in Fact

My attorney in fact shall have all lawful authority permissible to make health care decisions for me, including the authority to consent, or withdraw consent or refuse consent to any care, treatment, service or procedure to maintain, diagnose or treat my physical or mental condition, EXCEPT

```
that in the event I am diagnosed as having a terminal condition,
no life support technology shall be used to artificially prolong
my life and I shall be allowed a natural death.
```

6. Inspection and Disclosure of Information Relating to My Physical or Mental Health

Subject to any limitations in this document, my attorney in fact has the power and authority to do all of the following:

(a) Request, review, and receive any information, verbal or written, regarding my physical or mental health, including, but not limited to, medical and hospital records.

(b) Execute on my behalf any releases or other documents that may be required in order to obtain this information.

(c) Consent to the disclosure of this information.

7. Signing Documents, Waivers, and Releases

Where necessary to implement the health care decisions that my attorney in fact is author-ized by this document to make, my attorney in fact has the power and authority to execute on my behalf all of the following:

(a) Documents titled or purporting to be a "Refusal to Permit Treatment" and "Leaving Hospital Against Medical Advice."

(b) Any necessary waiver or release from liability required by a hospital or physician.

8. Duration

I intend that this Durable Power of Attorney remain effective until my death, or until revoked by me in writing.

Executed this _____9th_____ day of ____December_____,

19 _92_ at ____Mayfield, New Jersey_____.

_____
Principal

Witnesses

I declare that the principal is personally known to me, that the principal signed or acknowl-edged this durable power of attorney in my presence, that the principal appears to be of sound mind and under no duress, fraud, or undue influence.

I further declare that I am not related to the principal by blood, marriage, or adoption, and to the best of my knowledge, I am not entitled to any part of the estate of that principal upon the death of the principal under a Will now existing or by operation of law.

_____ of ____8013 Leon Way,_____

Mayfield, New Jersey
_____

_____ of ____318 Alison Place,_____

Mayfield, New Jersey
_____

Notarization

State of _____ New Jersey _____

County of _____ Mayfield _____

On this ____ 9th _____ day of _____ December _____ in the year 19_92,

before me a Notary Public, State of _____ New Jersey _____, duly commissioned

and sworn, personally appeared ___ GAIL DANNATT _____,

personally known to me (or proved to me on the basis of satisfactory evidence) to be the person

whose name is subscribed to in this instrument, and acknowledged to me that __ she _____
he/she

executed the same.

IN WITNESS WHEREOF, I have hereunto set my hand and affixed my official seal in the

State of _____ New Jersey _____, County of _____ Mayfield _____

on the date set forth above in this certificate.

_____

Notary Public

[Notary Seal]   State of _____ New Jersey _____

My commission expires _____

C. Sample Durable Power of Attorney for Health Care Effective When Signed

In this basic form, the principal, Mark Pierson, authorizes his friend, Justin Clarke, to be his attorney in fact for health care. This power of attorney takes effect on signing, and has no restriction on the attorney in fact's authority.

Form 5

Durable Power of Attorney for Health Care

1. Creation of Durable Power of Attorney

To my family, relatives, friends and my physicians, health care providers, community care facilities and any other person who may have an interest or duty in my medical care or treatment:

I, ____MARK PIERSON_____, being of sound mind,

name

willfully and voluntarily intend to create by this document a durable power of attorney for my health care by appointing the person designated as my attorney in fact to make health care decisions for me. This power of attorney shall not be affected by my subsequent incapacity.

2. Designation of Attorney in Fact

The person designated to be my attorney in fact for health care is

____JUSTIN CLARKE_____ of

name

____112 West Orange Street, Queens, New York____ . If

address

____JUSTIN CLARKE_____ for any

name

reason shall fail to serve or ceases to serve as my attorney in fact for health care,

____PHIL JONES_____ of

name

____418-1/2 Gray Street, Queens, New York____ shall be

address

my attorney in fact for health care.

3. Effective on Signing

This durable power of attorney shall become effective as of the date I sign it [or specify some other specific date].

4. Authority of My Attorney in Fact

My attorney in fact shall have all lawful authority permissible to make health care decisions for me, including the authority to consent, or withdraw consent or refuse consent to any care, treatment, service or procedure to maintain, diagnose or treat my physical or mental condition,

~~EXCEPT~~

5. Inspection and Disclosure of Information Relating to My Physical or Mental Health

Subject to any limitations in this document, my attorney in fact has the power and authority to do all of the following:

(a) Request, review, and receive any information, verbal or written, regarding my physical or mental health, including, but not limited to, medical and hospital records.

(b) Execute on my behalf any releases or other documents that may be required in order to obtain this information.

(c) Consent to the disclosure of this information.

6. Signing Documents, Waivers, and Releases

Where necessary to implement the health care decisions that my attorney in fact is authorized by this document to make, my attorney in fact has the power and authority to execute on my behalf all of the following:

(a) Documents titled or purporting to be a "Refusal to Permit Treatment" and "Leaving Hospital Against Medical Advice."

(b) Any necessary waiver or release from liability required by a hospital or physician.

7. Duration

I intend that this Durable Power of Attorney remain effective until my death, or until revoked by me in writing.

Executed this ____10th____ day of ____February____,
19_92_ at __Queens, New York_____.

_____

MARK PIERSON

Witnesses

I declare that the principal is personally known to me, that the principal signed or acknow-ledged this durable power of attorney in my presence, and that the principal appears to be of sound mind and under no duress, fraud, or undue influence.

I further declare that I am not related to the principal by blood, marriage, or adoption, and to the best of my knowledge, I am not entitled to any part of the estate of the principal upon the death of the principal under a Will now existing or by operation of law.

_____ of _____

_____

_____ of _____

_____

Notarization

State of __New York_____

County of ____Queens_____

On this ____10th____ day of _____February_____ in the year 19_92_,

before me a Notary Public, State of __New York_____, duly commissioned

and sworn, personally appeared ____MARK PIERSON_____,

personally known to me (or proved to me on the basis of satisfactory evidence) to be the person

whose name is subscribed to in this instrument, and acknowledged to me that ___he_____
                                                                              he/she

executed the same.

IN WITNESS WHEREOF, I have hereunto set my hand and affixed my official seal in the

State of __New York_____, County of ____Queens_____ on the date set forth

above in this certificate.

_____
Notary Public

[Notary Seal]   State of __New York_____

My commission expires _____

D. Sample 'Living Will'

Use of a living will or a directive to physicians to prohibit the use of life support equipment is discussed in Chapter 6, Section G. In most states, a "living will" can be used to define your desires regarding use of life sustaining procedures, including life support systems. As was discussed there, a durable power of attorney for health care is generally preferable if you prepare only one document. However, there is no disadvantage to preparing both (as long as they're consistent), and it might prove helpful. In some states, living will statutes are more detailed and precise about your authority to terminate life support systems than those states' durable power of attorney laws.

Space limitations don't permit inclusion of living will forms for all states which allow them. Each state has its own form. Following is an example of a completed California form (Form 16 in the Appendix). If you're not a California resident and are interested in obtaining a living will, see Chapter 6, Section G.

The California living will form is called a "Directive to Physicians." The form provides space in Paragraph 4 for the signer to declare that she has been diagnosed at least 14 days ago as having a terminal illness. If that portion of Paragraph 4 isn't completed, the living will is only "advisory," not legally binding.

Note that in Paragraph 3 of this form is a provision that the directive isn't effective if the signer is diagnosed as being pregnant. Obviously, a male signer should delete this paragraph.

The form must be signed, dated, and witnessed by two people.

Form 16

California Living Will and Directive to My Physicians

Directive made this _____8th_____ day of ____September_____, 19_92_ .

I, _____EDWINA JOHNSTON_____, residing in the County

of __Alameda_____, State of __California_____,
name

being of sound mind, willfully and voluntarily make known my desire that my life shall not be ar-

tificially prolonged under the circumstances set forth below and do hereby declare:

1. If at any time I should have an incurable injury, disease, or illness certified to be a terminal

condition by two physicians, and where the application of life-sustaining procedures would serve

only to artificially prolong the moment of my death and where my physician determines that my

death is imminent whether or not life-sustaining procedures are utilized, I direct that such

procedures be withheld or withdrawn, and that I be permitted to die naturally.

2. In the absence of my ability to give directions regarding the use of such life-sustaining

procedures, it is my intention that this directive shall be honored by my family and physician(s)

as the final expression of my legal right to refuse medical or surgical treatment and accept the

consequences from such refusal.

3. If I have been diagnosed as pregnant and that diagnosis is known to my physician, this

directive shall have no force or effect during the course of my pregnancy.

4. I have been diagnosed and notified at least 14 days ago as having a terminal condition by

_____, M.D., whose address is
physician's name

_____, and whose
address

telephone number is _____. I understand that if I have not filled in the

physician's name and address, it shall be presumed that I did not have a terminal condition when

I made out this directive.

5. This directive shall have no force or effect five years from the date filled in above.

6. I understand the full import of this directive and I am emotionally and mentally competent to make this directive.

Dated: ___September 8_____ , 19 _92_

_____

EDWINA JOHNSTON

Berkeley, Alameda County, California
city, county and state of residence

This declarant has been personally known to me and I believe him or her to be of sound mind.

_____

Residing at ___15 Juanita Way_____

_Berkeley_____ , _California_____

_____

Residing at _____4601 Rose Street_____

_Berkeley_____ , _California_____

E. Sample Form for Determination of Incapacity by Doctor

This form can be used or adapted with a "springing" durable power of attorney in the event you ever become incapacitated. In that case, there must be a written statement by a doctor that you're now incapacitated. This form, once completed by a doctor, can be attached to the durable power of attorney so that the attorney in fact can easily establish that incapacity has occurred.

Form 17

Determination of Incapacity

I, _____, declare: I am a
name

physician licensed to practice in the State of _____.

I have examined _____. It is my
name

professional opinion that _____ is
name

incapacitated and is therefore unable to make health care decisions for _____.
himself/herself

Dated:_____

_____
signature of physician

F. Customizing Your Durable Power of Attorney for Health Care

As discussed in Chapter 6, you can include any reasonable provision in your durable power of attorney for health care which you desire. The following clauses cover some common options that people may wish to use to define the powers of the attorney in fact. You might add clauses if you determine your doctor or hospital would prefer more specificity. If your needs aren't covered here, you'll have to do your own research or see a lawyer (discussed in Chapter 11). Remember, a durable power of attorney is potentially a flexible document that you can personalize to meet all sorts of special needs. (Information on how to insert clauses into a durable power of attorney is covered in Chapter 4, Section E(1)).

1. Clauses Concerning the Use of Life Sustaining Procedures

The following clauses express different choices, and different degrees of specificity, regarding the use of life sustaining procedures. You can use or adapt one of these, and insert it in the paragraph covering authority of the attorney in fact.

Reminder: All of these clauses require a determination of a medical status by a doctor: "terminal condition," "irreversible coma," etc. Having a doctor who's willing to make an honest determination of your status is crucial to the effectiveness of your clause regarding use of life support equipment.

a. Four Broad General Clauses Prohibiting Use of Life Sustaining Procedures

These four clauses show that many different phrases and concepts can be used when prohibiting use of life sustaining procedures. No one is "better" than the others. You can use or adapt whatever you want from

any. You should, though, only have one clause regarding life sustaining procedures in your power of attorney.

Option 1: Prohibit Life Support

If at any time I should be diagnosed by a doctor as being incurably ill or having a terminal condition I direct that all life sustaining procedures, including all life support systems, be withheld or withdrawn, and that I be permitted to die naturally.

Option 2: Specify When Life Support Prohibited

I do not want my life to be artificially or forcibly prolonged unless there is some reasonable hope that my physical and mental health may be restored, and I do not want life sustaining procedures, including life support systems, to be provided or continued if the burdens of the treatment outweigh the expected benefits. I do not want any life sustaining procedures or life support systems if I have a terminal condition (any disease or illness that is incurable or will result in my death) or am in a coma from which there is no significant possibility of my ever regaining consciousness or the higher functions of my brain.

Option 3: When Life Sustaining Procedures Used or Withdrawn

If the extension of my life would result in a mere biological existence, devoid of cognitive function, and with no reasonable hope of normal functioning, then I do not desire any form of life sustaining procedures, including life support systems, or if any have been instituted, I direct that they be withdrawn.

Option 4: Directions Regarding Life Sustaining Procedures and Attorney in Fact's Role

I do not want my life to be artificially or forcibly prolonged, unless there is some hope that both my physical and mental health may be restored. And I do not want life sustaining procedures, including life support systems, or treatment to be provided or continued if the burdens of these outweigh the expected benefits. I want my attorney in fact to consider the relief of suffering and the quality of the possible extension of my life in making decisions concerning life sustaining procedures and life support equipment. At all times, my dignity shall be maintained.

b. Prohibiting Use of Life Sustaining Procedures Unless Terminal Condition

If at any time I should be diagnosed by a doctor as having a terminal condition, and where the application of life sustaining procedures, including life support equipment, would only serve to artificially prolong the moment of my death, I direct that such procedures and equipment be withheld or withdrawn, and that I be permitted to die naturally.

c. Directions for Use of Life Sustaining Procedures if Irreversible Coma

Again, these clauses show different choices you can make regarding use of life sustaining procedures if you're in an irreversible coma. And again, no one choice is "right," or "better." You can select whichever options you want, but don't include more than one clause on this subject in your durable power of attorney.

Option 1: General Clause

If I am in a coma which my doctors have reasonably concluded is irreversible, I direct that life sustaining or prolonging procedures, including life support equipment, not be used.

Option 2: If Coma Lasts Over 15 Days

If I should have been in a coma for at least 15 days and the coma is certified to be irreversible by a

physician, meaning that there is no
reasonable possibility of my ever
regaining consciousness, I direct
that life sustaining procedures,
including life support equipment, be
withdrawn or withheld and that I be
permitted to die naturally.

Option 3: If Coma Lasts Over 30 Days (More Descriptive)

I direct that life sustaining
procedures, including all life
support equipment and artificial
means of providing nourishment, be
withdrawn or withheld so as to allow
the natural process of dying to
occur if I have been in an
irreversible coma for 30 days and if
a physician determines that because
of my irreversible coma I am unable
to experience pain that may result
from nourishment being withheld from
me (whether by naso-gastric tube,
intravenous feeding, or otherwise).

d. Requirement That Life Sustaining Procedures Be Used

I desire that my life be
prolonged to the extent medically
possible, and direct that life
sustaining procedures, including
life support equipment, be used if
necessary and desirable to preserve
my life.

e. Specific Medical Treatment Directions

You can insert any, or all, of these provisions in your
durable power of attorney if you wish.

• Nutrition and Hydration, Generally

This is, as is discussed in Chapter 6, Section F, a
controversial area, and you need to check the law of
your state.

All life sustaining equipment and
procedures, including the providing
of nutrition and hydration
intravenously or by a similar means
are legally equivalent and I regard
them as such when directing that no
life sustaining equipment or
procedures be used under the
conditions I've previously defined.

• Alleviation of Pain

My desire is that pain should be
alleviated to the extent possible,
unless the measures taken to relieve
pain would impair the possibility,
if any, that my health might be
restored. When the circumstances are

appropriate, and in accordance with my wishes as I have expressed them, such pain relief may be authorized even though its use may lead to physical damage, addiction, or even hasten the moment of (but not intentionally cause) my death.

• **Burns**

If I have a serious burn, I do not wish to be resuscitated if any of the following apply: (a) my condition is terminal; (b) after the full course of treatment, the quality of my life would be drastically impaired, tantamount to "social death;" (c) after the full course of treatment, I would be so severely disabled that I couldn't function independently and would require continuous nursing care.

f. Defining When Life Sustaining Procedures Are to Be Withheld

If you want to include broad definitions of "terminal condition" and "comatose condition" in your durable power of attorney, use or adapt the following:

(i) Definition of terminal condition

"Terminal condition" means any disease, illness or other condition that is incurable, terminal and expected to result in my death within six (6) months, and that the use of life sustaining procedures

would only prolong the dying process.

(ii) Definition of comatose condition

"Comatose condition" means a coma or vegetative state that has persisted for at least seven (7) days and from which there is no significant possibility of my ever regaining consciousness or the higher functions of my brain.

g. Granting Authority to Attorney in Fact to Decide Use of Life Sustaining Procedures

My attorney in fact shall determine if life sustaining procedures shall be used, to the extent permitted by law. I do not desire treatment to be provided and/or continued if the burdens of the treatment outweigh the expected benefits. My attorney in fact is to consider the relief of suffering, the preservation or restoration of functioning, and the quality as well as the extent of the possible extension of my life.

h. Terminating Life Sustaining Procedures in Case of Severe Dementia

If I have been diagnosed as having severe irreversible dementia and the degree of dementia is such that I usually lack competence, meaning that I fail to recognize family members or friends, am unable to comprehend most of what I hear or read (if I can read at all) or am unable to relate meaningfully to other people, I absolutely do not wish to have life sustaining procedures used.

2. Clauses Concerning Visitation Rights

If there is any potential for conflict between your attorney in fact and any of your family members, it's wise to state explicitly that your attorney in fact has priority rights to visit you in the hospital.

a. General Clause

I direct that my attorney in fact have first priority to visit me in any medical facility.

b. More Specific Clause

In the event that injury, illness, or incapacity through other cause necessitates my hospitalization or treatment in a medical facility; and in the event that such hospitalization or treatment in a medical facility requires, in the opinion of a physician, surgeon or a dentist, that there be imposed a limit on the visitors admitted to see me; then it is my wish that my attorney in fact be given preference in such visits, notwithstanding that there may be

parties related to me by blood or by law or other parties desiring to visit me, unless and until contrary instructions are freely given by me to competent medical personnel in the facility involved.

3. Clauses Regarding Medical Treatment

a. Authorizing Use of Pain-Relieving Drugs and Procedures

My attorney in fact has authority to consent to and arrange for the administration of pain relieving drugs of any type, or other surgical or medical procedure calculated to relieve my pain even though their use may lead to permanent physical damage, addiction or even hasten the moment of (but not intentionally cause) my death.

b. Authorizing Attorney in Fact to Sign Releases

My attorney in fact has authority to sign on my behalf any documents necessary to carry out the authorization described above, including waivers or releases of liability required by any health care provider.

c. Authorizing Attorney in Fact to Obtain Medical Records

(i) Generally:

My attorney in fact has authority to request, review and receive any information, verbal or written, regarding my physical or mental health, including medical and hospital records, and to execute any releases or other documents that may be required in order to obtain this information.

(ii) Releasing Liability:

All third parties from whom my attorney in fact may request information regarding my health or medical treatment are hereby authorized to provide such information to him/her without limitation and are released from any legal liability whatsoever by me, my estate, my heirs, successors or assigns for complying with his/her requests. With specific reference to medical information, including information about my mental condition, I am authorizing in advance all physicians and psychiatrists who have treated me, and all other providers of health care, including hospitals, to release to my attorney in fact all information or photocopies of any records which he/she may request.

d. Authorizing Attorney in Fact to Hire Medical Personnel

My attorney in fact has authority to employ and discharge physicians, dentists, nurses, therapists and other health care professionals as may be necessary for my physical and mental well-being and to pay them reasonable compensation, to revoke or change any consent previously given or implied by law to any medical care or treatment, and to arrange for my placement in or removal from any hospital, convalescent home or other medical facility.

e. Directions if Attorney in Fact Temporarily Unavailable

If my attorney in fact is temporarily unavailable, I authorize my alternate attorney in fact to serve until my attorney in fact is again available to serve.

f.   Blood Transfusions

If my treating physician(s) determine that a blood transfusion is advisable or necessary, I direct [Insert your specific direction, such as: "any blood used for the transfusion be donated by a family relative, if feasible," or "nevertheless that no blood transfusion be permitted."]

g.   Decision to Die at Home

If at all possible, and the economic and hospital costs are not unduly burdensome, I declare that I want to die at home (or at least remain home as long as possible) with appropriate medical, nursing, social, and emotional support and any necessary medical equipment or treatment needed to keep me comfortable.

h.   Specifying and Restricting Specific Treatment

You can create any provisions which fit your beliefs regarding specific things you want done, or prohibited, including any dietary restrictions you want.

4.   Clauses Concerning Anatomical Gifts

Unless specifically authorized by state law to do so, the attorney in fact has no authority to act for the principal after her death. However, the attorney in fact could make arrangements for anatomical gifts if he does so before the principal's death.

a.   Authorizing Attorney in Fact to Make Anatomical Gifts

My attorney in fact has authority to make arrangements before my death on my behalf with respect to anatomical gifts under the Uniform Anatomical Gift Act.

b.   Prohibiting Attorney in Fact from Making Anatomical Gifts

Neither my attorney in fact nor any other person shall have the right to make arrangements on my behalf before my death with respect to anatomical gifts under the Uniform Anatomical Gift Act.

5.   Clause of General Statement of Intent

If you desire, you can create any statement you wish regarding your intent in establishing your durable power of attorney for health care, and insert that statement in the document. There's no legal requirement that you do this. You might decide to do it simply because you want to make your intent known. Also, if your state isn't one where durable powers of attorney for health care are widely used, such a statement could help promote acceptability. Following is one example of such a statement.

I authorize my attorney in fact to make medical and health care decisions on my behalf because I trust his/her judgment fully. I delegate this authority to my attorney in fact in order that he/she may exercise it promptly on my behalf and in my best interests without having to seek court authority for such decisions or court supervision regarding them.

6. Clause Authorizing Payment of Attorney in Fact

An attorney in fact for a durable power of attorney for health care is normally not compensated, but you can include a clause in your form permitting or requiring compensation. This might be desirable, for instance, if the principal knew it was likely that the attorney in fact would have to spend many hours on the principal's medical problems. (See Chapter 4, Section E(2)(e) for more clauses on compensation.)

My attorney in fact shall be entitled to reasonable compensation for his/her services rendered on my behalf.

[You can define "reasonable compensation" any sensible way you want to: leave it up to the attorney in fact, or set an hourly rate, etc.]

My attorney in fact shall be paid for his/her services from my funds in _____ [specify source] _____.

CHAPTER 8

CALIFORNIA DURABLE POWERS OF ATTORNEY FOR HEALTH CARE

A. Introduction

In California, a durable power of attorney for health care must always be a separate document, meeting specific statutory requirements. This chapter shows Californians how to prepare this type of durable power of attorney. It only covers California laws and information, and should not be used by non-Californians.

The California legislature has adapted a "statutory" durable power of attorney for health care, a modified fill in the blanks form. Use of the statutory form isn't mandatory in California—in other words, you can use either the statutory form or an independently-drafted durable power of attorney for health care form such as the one provided in Section H of this chapter. The advantage to drafting your own form is that it may be more expressive of your needs, or more geared to your situation.

However, there may be an important advantage for Californians in using the statutory form. If a doctor or hospital is unfamiliar with or wary of durable powers of attorney for health care, your attorney in fact easily could demonstrate that the form you used was specifically approved and promulgated by the California legislature. It's difficult to see how a California hospital or doctor could refuse to honor the statutory form.

The California statutory health care form is Form 13 of the Appendix; Forms 14 and 15 are other versions of valid California durable powers of attorney for health care.

B. Legal Requirements and Limitations

California state law imposes a number of specific requirements and limitations on durable powers of attorney for health care. The California forms in this chapter and the Appendix fully comply with these legal conditions. Following is an explanation of the legal requirements.

1. 'Warning' Requirements

"Warnings" must be set forth in any durable power of attorney for health care unless it is prepared by an attorney.[1] These "Warnings" should be read by anyone considering a durable power of attorney for health care. There's a tendency for the prose contained in "Warnings" to make one's eyes glaze over and brain malfunction. Please don't give in to these tendencies. If read carefully, the "Warnings" can increase your understanding of the potency of a durable power of attorney for health care, and what's involved in creating one.

2. Signature and Witness Requirements

California law specifies what is required in signing and witnessing a durable power of attorney for health care:

- It must be signed and dated by the principal.

- If you create your own form, it must be either notarized or signed by two witnesses. However, if you use the "statutory" durable power of attorney for health care discussed in this chapter, witnessing is required.

Certain rules must be followed for the witnessing process. Here is a summary of those requirements:

- The two witnesses must be residents of California, over 18, be mentally competent and know the principal or have the principal's identity proven by specific means (these rules are set out in the printed forms).

---

[1] Durable powers of attorney for health care prepared by a lawyer must include a signed certificate stating that the client was advised of her rights in connection with the durable power of attorney as well as the consequences of signing or not signing, and that the client executed the durable power of attorney after being so advised.

- None of the following people can be a witness:[2]

   — the attorney in fact, or any successor attorney in fact;

   — an owner, operator or employee of a health care provider—unless that person is your relative;

   — an owner, operator or employee of a community care facility—unless that person is your relative; or

   — an owner, operator or employee of a residential care facility for the elderly—unless that person is your relative.

- Each person must actually see the principal either sign the document or hear the principal acknowledge her signature on the document.

- Each witness must sign a declaration listed on the form which states under penalty of perjury that the witnessing requirements were all fulfilled.

- At least one of the witnesses must sign a declaration stating that she is neither a relative of the principal by blood, marriage, or adoption nor, to the best of her knowledge, entitled to inherit any portion of the principal's estate.

- Finally, if the principal is a patient in a skilled nursing facility,[3] one witness must be a patient advocate or ombudsman designated by the State Department of Aging[4] who must sign a special declaration listed on the form.

---

[2]The California statute isn't totally clear or consistent on whether a relative connected with a health care provider, community care facility or residential care facility can serve as a valid witness. If this matters to you, check with a lawyer.

[3]This is defined in California law as "a health care facility which provides skilled nursing and supportive care to patients whose primary need is for availability of skilled nursing care on an extended basis."

[4]Contact the local office of the State Department of Aging to learn more about the ombudsman patent advocate program.

Practical Note on Choice of Witnesses: You want witnesses who are likely to be around in the future, in case there's any question or challenge regarding your execution of the durable power of attorney. So try to choose witnesses likely to stay nearby and remain healthy.

3. Statutory Limitations

A California durable power of attorney for health care is generally valid for seven years after the date of execution. However, if the principal is incapacitated when this seven-year period expires, the durable power of attorney lasts until the principal regains competence or dies. This is true whether or not the statutory form is used.

California law specifically states that any restriction, limit or direction expressly set forth by the principal in the durable power of attorney document is binding and must be followed by the attorney in fact. In addition, the attorney in fact must act in "a manner consistent with the known desires of the principal," even if those desires aren't expressly contained in the durable power of attorney document itself. When the principal's desires aren't known, the attorney in fact must act "in the best interests" of the principal.

An attorney in fact must follow the principal's wishes regarding obtaining, withholding or withdrawing the health care necessary to keep the principal alive. In other words, the principal always retains the final word concerning use of life sustaining procedures and life support systems.

An attorney in fact cannot be authorized in a durable power of attorney document to consent to certain medical procedures. These include:

- committing or placing the principal in a mental health treatment facility;

- authorizing convulsive treatment (i.e., shock therapy) or psychosurgery (i.e., lobotomy, psychiatric surgery, behavioral surgery and all other forms of brain surgery, for modification/control of thoughts/feelings);

- sterilization; or

- abortion.

4. Information About the Attorney in Fact

A principal cannot name an employee or operator of a treating health care provider, community health care facility or residential care facility as his attorney in fact, unless that person is a relative by blood, marriage or adoption.

Unless a durable power of attorney expressly provides the contrary, if the principal has designated his or her spouse as attorney in fact to make health care decisions, the subsequent dissolution or annulment of the marriage automatically revokes the durable power of attorney for health care.[5]

5. Adding Clauses to the Statutory Form

You may add to the statutory form as long as your changes aren't inconsistent with it. In general, a competent principal can delegate authority for almost all health care decisions to an attorney in fact (see limitations in Section B(3) just above). The principal may provide any reasonable restrictions or limitations desired on the authority of the attorney in fact. Before completing any forms, check the additional sample clauses provided in Chapter 7, Section F.

C. California Law and Life Sustaining Procedures

As previously discussed, whether to use life sustaining procedures, including life support systems, to "artificially" prolong life is an issue of prime importance to many people (see Chapter 6, Sections F and G). Under California law, the principal's direction in the power of attorney document is binding regarding use of life sustaining procedures and life support systems.

When preparing a durable power of attorney for health care, it's important to resolve how you feel about use of life sustaining procedures, and incorporate your directions in your document. Review the discussion of life sustaining procedures in Chapter 6, Section F, and the sample clauses in Chapter 7, Section F(1).

California law allows the principal to change his mind at any time regarding life sustaining procedures. If the principal objects to the attorney in fact's decision—even if that decision was previously authorized or required by the principal—this situation is treated as if no durable power of attorney existed.[6]

By law, nothing in the Durable Power of Attorney for Health Care Statute may be "...construed to condone, authorize, or approve mercy killing, or to permit any affirmative or deliberate act or omission to end life other than the withholding or withdrawal of health care pursuant to a durable power of attorney so as to permit the natural process of dying."

In other words, all that a principal can require is the withdrawal of life sustaining procedures. However, the statute itself doesn't specify when this can be done. Under California case law a person has the right to require withdrawal of life sustaining proce-

---

[5]This is not true in California for a financial durable power of attorney.

[6]Theoretically, there could still be a conflict if the attorney in fact asserted that the principal wasn't competent to change her mind. In reality, a hospital or doctors are most unlikely to go against the expressed wishes of a patient on such a crucial matter as use of life support systems.

dures when he has (been diagnosed of having) an "incurable illness." Life sustaining procedures can be terminated even though the person's condition is (not yet) diagnosed as terminal. Unfortunately, neither the term "incurable illness" nor "terminal condition" is very clear. They can mean anything from the first diagnosis of a condition for which there is no known cure, but where the patient can live for years, or it can mean where the patient may die in days. As a practical matter, using broad language requiring termination of life sustaining procedures to allow a natural death should prevent you from being kept artificially alive in a comatose, vegetative state, which is what most people fear.

If you choose to restrict the use of life sustaining procedures, doctors and/or hospitals will be involved in making your decision effective. A California doctor must certify that a patient has an "incurable illness," or a "terminal condition," or that the "burdens of life sustaining treatments outweigh the expected benefits," before the power of attorney provisions are enforceable, both legally and practically.

So a seriously ill principal, or the attorney in fact if the principal is already incapacitated, should check with doctors and hospital policies regarding termination of life sustaining procedures and life support systems to be sure the hospital selected has a policy compatible with the desires expressed in the durable power of attorney.

In addition to a durable power of attorney for health care, California law also allows you to request or require a "natural death" by preparing a "Directive to Physicians," which is often called a "living will." (This is discussed in Chapter 6, Section G. A blank, tear-out California living will form is contained in the Appendix as Form 16 and a sample is provided in Chapter 7, Section D.) The directive is your statement that you don't want life sustaining technologies to be used if you've been diagnosed as having a terminal condition, and where the application of life support equipment will only artificially prolong the moment of death. As was discussed earlier, it can be

prudent to prepare a living will, as well as a durable power of attorney for health care.

1. Sample Clauses Regarding Life Sustaining Procedures

Clauses regarding use of life sustaining procedures are set out in Chapter 7, Section F(1). If you want to cover the subject in your durable power of attorney for health care, be sure to review those clauses. Also, the California Medical Association has developed its own clauses regarding use of life sustaining procedures.[7] You can use, or adapt, any of the CMA clauses printed below into your durable power of attorney. The advantage in doing so is that these clauses should be familiar and acceptable to most California doctors and hospitals.

Option 1: Life Sustaining Procedures Determined by Attorney in Fact

I don't want my life to be prolonged, and I don't want life-sustaining treatment to be provided or continued if the burdens of the treatment outweigh the expected benefits. I want my agent [i.e., attorney in fact] to consider the relief of suffering and the quality as well as the extent of the possible extension of my life in making decisions concerning life-sustaining treatment.

---

[7]The California Medical Association has issued a bulletin on sample forms for a Durable Power of Attorney for Health Care (available for $1.60 apiece from the CMA by writing to: Sutter Publications, P.O. Box 7690, San Francisco, CA 94120). Most hospitals and many doctors are familiar with these materials.

Option 2: No Life Support if Terminal Illness

I don't want my life to be prolonged, and I don't want life support equipment or procedures to be used if I have an incurable illness, or a terminal condition.

Option 3: Life Support Unless an Irreversible Coma

I want my life to be prolonged and I want life-sustaining treatment to be provided unless I am in a coma which my doctors reasonably believe to be irreversible. Once my doctors have reasonably concluded I am in an irreversible coma, I don't want life-sustaining treatment to be provided or continued.

Option 4: Life Support Required

I want my life to be prolonged to the greatest extent possible without regard to my condition, the chances I have for recovery or the cost of the procedures.

D. California Requirements Applicable to Health Care Providers

California law contains specific provisions designed to insure that responsibilities and duties of "health care providers" (hospitals, doctors, etc.) are clear. Because of these provisions, there should be little trouble having a durable power of attorney for health care accepted in California. In fact, most hospitals and other medical facilities are well aware of durable powers of attorney for health care, and have their own internal legal memoranda regarding them.

Following is a summary of the statutory provisions.

- *Authority of Attorney in Fact.* Unless a durable power of attorney for health care provides otherwise, an attorney in fact who is known to the health care provider to be available and willing to make health care decisions has priority over any other person to act for the principal in all matters of health care decisions. However, the attorney in fact doesn't have authority to make a particular health care decision if the principal is able to give informed consent with respect to that decision. This means that the health care provider may require both the attorney in fact and the principal to agree to health care decisions if the provider is uncertain whether the principal has the capacity to give informed consent.

- *Durable Power of Attorney Cannot be Mandatory.* No health care provider, health care service plan, insurer issuing disability insurance, self-insured employee welfare plan, or nonprofit hospital plan or similar insurance plan, may condition admission to a facility, or the providing of treatment, or insurance, on the requirement that a patient execute a durable power of attorney for health care.

- *Revocation, Notification of Attorney in Fact.* If a principal notifies a health care provider that the attorney in fact's authority has been revoked, the health care provider must make the notification part of the principal's health care record and make a reasonable effort to notify the attorney in fact of the revocation.

- *Determine Principal's Wishes.* If an attorney in fact makes a decision to withhold or withdraw health care necessary to keep a principal alive, the law requires the health care provider to also make a good faith effort to determine the desires of the principal and make the results of that effort part of the medical record.

- *Liability*. The law states that no health care provider will be subject to criminal liability or professional disciplinary action for failing to withdraw health care necessary to keep a principal alive.

- *Negligence Standards*. If the health care provider complies with the restrictions of California law, and any specific restrictions in the durable power of attorney for health care, the health care provider is subject to the same standards of negligence for medical malpractice as it would be if there were no durable power of attorney. In order for these protections to apply to a California health care provider, it must have acted reasonably and in good faith, as defined by law.

E. Revocation of Durable Power of Attorney

As with any durable power of attorney, a competent principal can revoke a California durable power of attorney for health care at any time, for any reason. (See the discussion and sample forms concerning revocation in Chapter 10. Tear-out, fill-in-the-blanks revocation forms are also contained in the Appendix, as Forms 21 and 22.)

Under California law, a principal is presumed by law to have the capacity to revoke a durable power of attorney for health care. The effect of this presumption is that if the attorney in fact contests the revocation in a legal proceeding, the burden of proof is on the attorney in fact to establish the principal's incapacity.

By statute, revocation of a durable power of attorney for health care can be made by the principal either by notifying the attorney in fact or the concerned health care provider. Legally, the revocation is valid whether made orally (verbally) or in writing. However, because oral revocation is so risky, it should only be used as a last resort. The safest and best way to revoke any durable power of attorney for health care is by written notice to the attorney in

fact, with a copy sent to any involved health care provider.

Important: Remember that a durable power of attorney for health care expires, as a matter of law in California, seven years after it was adopted (unless the principal is incapacitated at the end of that seven-year period). So, every seven years or sooner you must prepare a new durable power of attorney for health care. Usually you can simply re-copy your old one. But you do have to get the new one signed, witnessed and notarized again.

F. Prohibiting Court Proceedings in California

Unless specifically prohibited in a durable power of attorney for health care, certain court proceedings can be filed in California to determine whether the durable power of attorney is in effect, the authority of the attorney in fact, and whether she is acting properly. Generally, a court proceeding may be brought by:

- the principal;

- the attorney in fact;

- a treating health care provider;

- the principal's spouse, child, parent, legal heir or the court investigator of the county where the principal resides.

However, the principal may expressly eliminate the authority of any of these people (except the attorney in fact) to petition a court if: (1) the durable power of attorney for health care is executed by the principal at a time when the principal has the advice of a California lawyer, and (2) the attorney signs a declaration to that effect.

This means that people who are likely to be most concerned about the principal and what's happening under the durable power of attorney for health care have the right to go to court if a concern arises. This is in fact a very infrequent occurrence. It also means that you can restrict this right if you wish. This might be something you would want to attempt, for example, if someone in your family had very different ideas (perhaps religious ones) as to proper standards of health care.

Is it a good idea to see a lawyer and restrict the authority of people to petition a court? In my experience it is a most unusual case where this would make sense. If a close family member is so upset about your durable power of attorney for health care that he would petition a court under these legal provisions, he would almost surely get to court by another route even if you adopted a restriction in your document. In other words, there are a number of other legal theories that could be used to get past your restriction if the situation was serious enough. In any event, in California if you want to investigate this matter further, it is a statutory requirement that you must see a lawyer.

G. Sample California Statutory Durable Power of Attorney for Health Care (Effective Upon Signing)

1. Introduction

Facts: In this filled-in version of the California Statutory Durable Power of Attorney for Health Care form, the principal, Duane Barnett, who is quite ill, has designated his best friend, Jim Edmonds, to be his attorney in fact. Duane has also provided that life sustaining procedures not be used, and that if he needs to be hospitalized, he be placed in a specific hospital. He does this by filling in the blanks provided for that purpose in Paragraph 4 of the statutory form (Form 13 in the Appendix).

Notice that this power of attorney becomes effective upon signing. If Duane wanted to create a "springing" statutory durable power of attorney, he would substitute the following language for that contained in Paragraph 2 of the form:

2. CREATION OF DURABLE POWER OF ATTORNEY FOR HEALTH CARE. By this document I intend to create a durable power of attorney for health care under Sections 2430 to 2443, inclusive, of the California Civil Code. This power of attorney is authorized by the Keene Health Care Agent Act and shall be construed in accordance with the provisions of Sections 2500 to 2506, inclusive, of the California Civil Code. This power of attorney shall not be affected by my subsequent incapacity.

This durable power of attorney shall become effective in the event I become incapacitated and am unable to make health care decisions for myself, in which case it shall become effective as of the date of the written statement by a physician that I have become incapacitated and am unable to make health care decisions. If possible, the determination shall be made by ___[name of physician]___.

Duane could also create a "springing" durable power of attorney for health care by using a non-statutory form (e.g., Form 14 in the Appendix). However, as I've discussed, some Californians may prefer to use the statutory form because it has been specifically created and approved by the legislature. If you do want to use the statutory form, you should know how to make it into a "springing" durable power of attorney, if that's what you want.

Form 13

Statutory Form Durable Power of Attorney for Health Care
(California Civil Code Section 2500)

WARNING TO PERSON EXECUTING THIS DOCUMENT

THIS IS AN IMPORTANT LEGAL DOCUMENT WHICH IS AUTHORIZED BY THE KEENE HEALTH CARE AGENT ACT. BEFORE EXECUTING THIS DOCUMENT, YOU SHOULD KNOW THESE IMPORTANT FACTS:

THIS DOCUMENT GIVES THE PERSON YOU DESIGNATE AS YOUR AGENT (THE ATTORNEY IN FACT) THE POWER TO MAKE HEALTH CARE DECISIONS FOR YOU. YOUR AGENT MUST ACT CONSISTENTLY WITH YOUR DESIRES AS STATED IN THIS DOCUMENT OR OTHERWISE MADE KNOWN.

EXCEPT AS YOU OTHERWISE SPECIFY IN THIS DOCUMENT, THIS DOCUMENT GIVES YOUR AGENT THE POWER TO CONSENT TO YOUR DOCTOR NOT GIVING TREATMENT OR STOPPING TREATMENT NECESSARY TO KEEP YOU ALIVE.

NOTWITHSTANDING THIS DOCUMENT, YOU HAVE THE RIGHT TO MAKE MEDICAL AND OTHER HEALTH CARE DECISIONS FOR YOURSELF SO LONG AS YOU CAN GIVE INFORMED CONSENT WITH RESPECT TO THE PARTICULAR DECISION. IN ADDITION, NO TREATMENT MAY BE GIVEN TO YOU OVER YOUR OBJECTION AT THE TIME, AND HEALTH CARE NECESSARY TO KEEP YOU ALIVE MAY NOT BE STOPPED OR WITHHELD IF YOU OBJECT AT THE TIME.

THIS DOCUMENT GIVES YOUR AGENT AUTHORITY TO CONSENT, TO REFUSE TO CONSENT, OR TO WITHDRAW CONSENT TO ANY CARE, TREATMENT, SERVICE, OR PROCEDURE TO MAINTAIN, DIAGNOSE, OR TREAT A PHYSICAL OR MENTAL CONDITION. THIS POWER IS SUBJECT TO ANY STATEMENT OF YOUR DESIRES AND ANY LIMITATIONS THAT YOU INCLUDE IN THIS DOCUMENT. YOU MAY STATE IN THIS DOCUMENT ANY TYPES OF TREATMENT THAT YOU DO NOT DESIRE. IN ADDITION, A COURT CAN TAKE AWAY THE POWER OF YOUR AGENT TO MAKE HEALTH CARE DECISIONS FOR YOU IF YOUR AGENT (1) AUTHORIZES ANYTHING THAT IS ILLEGAL, (2) ACTS CONTRARY TO YOUR KNOWN DESIRES, OR (3) WHERE YOUR DESIRES ARE NOT KNOWN, DOES ANYTHING THAT IS CLEARLY CONTRARY TO YOUR BEST INTERESTS.

UNLESS YOU SPECIFY A SHORTER PERIOD IN THIS DOCUMENT, THIS POWER WILL EXIST FOR SEVEN YEARS FROM THE DATE YOU EXECUTE THIS DOCUMENT AND, IF YOU ARE UNABLE TO MAKE HEALTH CARE DECISIONS FOR YOURSELF AT THE TIME WHEN THIS SEVEN-YEAR PERIOD ENDS, THE POWER WILL CONTINUE TO EXIST UNTIL THE TIME WHEN YOU BECOME ABLE TO MAKE HEALTH CARE DECISIONS FOR YOURSELF.

YOU HAVE THE RIGHT TO REVOKE THE AUTHORITY OF YOUR AGENT BY NOTIFYING YOUR AGENT OR YOUR TREATING DOCTOR, HOSPITAL, OR OTHER HEALTH CARE PROVIDER ORALLY OR IN WRITING OF THE REVOCATION.

YOUR AGENT HAS THE RIGHT TO EXAMINE YOUR MEDICAL RECORDS AND TO CONSENT TO THEIR DISCLOSURE UNLESS YOU LIMIT THIS RIGHT IN THIS DOCUMENT.

UNLESS YOU OTHERWISE SPECIFY IN THIS DOCUMENT, THIS DOCUMENT GIVES YOUR AGENT THE POWER AFTER YOU DIE TO (1) AUTHORIZE AN AUTOPSY, (2) DONATE YOUR BODY OR PARTS THEREOF FOR TRANSPLANT OR THERAPEUTIC OR EDUCATIONAL OR SCIENTIFIC PURPOSES, AND (3) DIRECT THE DISPOSITION OF YOUR REMAINS.

THIS DOCUMENT REVOKES ANY PRIOR DURABLE POWER OF ATTORNEY FOR HEALTH CARE.

YOU SHOULD CAREFULLY READ AND FOLLOW THE WITNESSING PROCEDURE DESCRIBED AT THE END OF THIS FORM. THIS DOCUMENT WILL NOT BE VALID UNLESS YOU COMPLY WITH THE WITNESSING PROCEDURE.

IF THERE IS ANYTHING IN THIS DOCUMENT THAT YOU DO NOT UNDERSTAND, YOU SHOULD ASK A LAWYER TO EXPLAIN IT TO YOU.

YOUR AGENT MAY NEED THIS DOCUMENT IMMEDIATELY IN CASE OF AN EMERGENCY THAT REQUIRES A DECISION CONCERNING YOUR HEALTH CARE. EITHER KEEP THIS DOCUMENT WHERE IT IS IMMEDIATELY AVAILABLE TO YOUR AGENT AND ALTERNATE AGENTS OR GIVE EACH OF THEM AN EXECUTED COPY OF THIS DOCUMENT. YOU MAY ALSO WANT TO GIVE YOUR DOCTOR AN EXECUTED COPY OF THIS DOCUMENT.

DO NOT USE THIS FORM IF YOU ARE A CONSERVATEE UNDER THE LANTERMAN-PETRIS-SHORT ACT AND YOU WANT TO APPOINT YOUR CONSERVATOR AS YOUR AGENT. YOU CAN DO THAT ONLY IF THE APPOINTMENT DOCUMENT INCLUDES A CERTIFICATE OF YOUR ATTORNEY.

1. Designation of Health Care Agent. I, _DUANE BARNETT, 14 Ocean Rd.,_
insert your name and address
Los Angeles, CA

do hereby designate and appoint _JIM EDMONDS, 1 View Terrace, Los Angeles,_
_CA, 213/841-0022_ .

[Insert name, address, and telephone number of one individual only as your agent to make

health care decisions for you. None of the following may be designated as your agent: (1)

your treating health care provider, (2) a nonrelative employee of your treating health care

provider, (3) an operator of a community care facility, (4) a nonrelative employee of an

operator of a community care facility, (5) an operator of a residential care facility for the

elderly, or (6) a nonrelative employee of an operator of a residential care facility for the

elderly.]

as my attorney in fact (agent) to make health care decisions for me as authorized in this docu-

ment. For the purposes of this document, "health care decision" means consent, refusal of

consent, or withdrawal of consent to any care, treatment, service, or procedure to maintain,

diagnose, or treat an individual's physical or mental condition.

2. Creation of Durable Power of Attorney For Health Care. By this document I intend to

create a durable power of attorney for health care under Sections 2430 to 2443, inclusive, of the

California Civil Code. This power of attorney is authorized by the Keene Health Care Agent Act and shall be construed in accordance with the provisions of Sections 2500 to 2506, inclusive, of the California Civil Code. This power of attorney shall not be affected by my subsequent incapacity.

3. General Statement of Authority Granted. Subject to any limitations in this document, I hereby grant to my agent full power and authority to make health care decisions for me to the same extent that I could make such decisions for myself if I had the capacity to do so. In exercising this authority, my agent shall make health care decisions that are consistent with my desires as stated in this document or otherwise made known to my agent, including, but not limited to, my desires concerning obtaining or refusing or withdrawing life-prolonging care, treatment, services, and procedures.

[If you want to limit the authority of your agent to make health care decisions for you, you can state the limitation in paragraph 4 ("Statement of Desires, Special Provisions, and Limitations") below. You can indicate your desires by including a statement of your desires in the same paragraph.]

4. Statement of Desires, Special Provisions, and Limitations. (Your agent must make health care decisions that are consistent with your known desires. You can, but are not required to, state your desires in the space provided below. You should consider whether you want to include a statement of your desires concerning life-prolonging care, treatment, services, and procedures. You can also include a statement of your desires concerning other matters relating to your health care. You can also make your desires known to your agent by discussing your desires with your agent or by some other means. If there are any types of treatment that you do not want to be used, you should state them in the space below. If you want to limit in any other way the authority given your agent by this document, you should state the limits in the space below. If you do not state any limits, your agent will have broad powers to make health care decisions for you, except to the extent that there are limits provided by law.)

In exercising the authority under this durable power of attorney for health care, my agent shall act consistently with my desires as stated below and is subject to the special provisions and limitations stated below:

(a) Statement of desire concerning life-prolonging care, treatment, service, and procedures: <u>If I am diagnosed as having an incurable disease or illness or terminal condition, I direct that no life-prolonging care, treatment, services and life sustaining procedures be used.</u>

_____

_____

_____

_____

_____

(b) Additional statement of desires, special provisions, and limitations:

If I need to be hospitalized, I direct that I be placed in St.

Mary's Hospital, Los Angeles, CA if possible.

_____

_____

_____

_____

_____

[You may attach additional pages if you need more space to complete your statement. If you attach additional pages, you must date and sign each of the additional pages at the same time you date and sign this document.]

5. Inspection and Disclosure of Information Relating To My Physical Or Mental Health. Subject to any limitation in this document, my agent has the power and authority to do all of the following:

(a) Request, review, and receive any information, verbal or written, regarding my physical or mental health, including, but not limited to, medical and hospital records.

(b) Execute on my behalf any releases or other documents that may be required in order to obtain this information.

(c) Consent to the disclosure of this information.

[If you want to limit the authority of your agent to receive and disclose information relating to your health, you must state the limitations in paragraph 4 ("Statement of Desires, Special Provisions, and Limitations") above.]

6. Signing Documents, Waivers, and Releases. Where necessary to implement the health care decisions that my agent is authorized by this document to make, my agent has the power and authority to execute on my behalf all of the following:

(a) Documents titled or purporting to be a "Refusal to Permit Treatment" and "Leaving Hospital Against Medical Advice."

(b) Any necessary waiver or release from liability required by a hospital or physician.

7. Autopsy; Anatomical Gifts; Disposition of Remains. Subject to any limitations in this document, my agent has the power and authority to do all of the following:

(a) Authorize an autopsy under Section 7113 of the Health and Safety Code.

(b) Make a disposition of a part or parts of my body under the Uniform Anatomical Gift Act (Chapter 3.5 (commencing with Section 7150) of Part 1 of Division 7 of the Health and Safety Code).

(c) Direct the disposition of my remains under Section 7100 of the Health and Safety Code.

[If you want to limit the authority of your agent to consent to an autopsy, make an anatomical gift, or direct the disposition of your remains, you must state the limitations in paragraph 4 ("Statement of Desires, Special Provisions, and Limitations") above.]

8. Duration. (Unless you specify a shorter period in the space below, this power of attorney will exist for seven years from the date you execute this document and, if you are unable to make health care decisions for yourself at the time when this seven-year period ends, the power will continue to exist until the time when you become able to make health care decisions for yourself.)

This durable power of attorney for health care expires on

_____
fill in this space only if you want the authority of your agent to end earlier than the seven-year period described above

9. Designation of Alternate Agents. (You are not required to designate any alternate agent but you may do so. Any alternate agent you designate will be able to make the same health care decisions as the agent you designated in paragraph 1, above, in the event that agent is unable or ineligible to act as your agent. If the agent you designated is your spouse, he or she becomes ineligible to act as your agent if your marriage is dissolved.)

If the person designated as my agent in paragraph 1 is not available or becomes ineligible to act as my agent to make a health care decision for me or loses the mental capacity to make health care decisions for me, or if I revoke that person's appointment or authority to act as my agent to make health care decisions for me, then I designate and appoint the following persons to serve as my agent to make health care decisions for me as authorized in this document, such persons to serve in the order listed below:

A. First Alternate Agent ___MARY EDMONDS, 1 View Terrace, Los Angeles,___
insert name, address, and telephone number of first alternate agent
CA, 213/841-0022

B. Second Alternate Agent _____

_____
insert name, address, and telephone number of second alternate agent

_____

10. Nomination of Conservator of Person. (A conservator of the person may be appointed for you if a court decides that one should be appointed. The conservator is responsible for your physical care, which under some circumstances includes making health care decisions for you. You are not required to nominate a conservator but you may do so. The court will appoint the person you nominate unless that would be contrary to your best interests. You may, but are not required to, nominate as your conservator the same person you named in paragraph 1 as your health care agent. You can nominate an individual as your conservator by completing the space below.)

If a conservator of the person is to be appointed for me, I nominate the following individual to serve as conservator of the person   TIM EDMONDS, 1 View Terrace, Los
Angeles, CA
insert name and address of person nominated as conservator of the person
_____.

11. Prior Designations Revoked. I revoke any prior durable power of attorney for health care.

Date and Signature of Principal

(YOU MUST DATE AND SIGN THIS POWER OF ATTORNEY)

I sign my name to this Statutory Form Durable Power of Attorney for Health Care

on   May 1, 1992 _____ at _____ Los Angeles _____,
date   city
California
_____.
state

_____
you sign here

(THIS POWER OF ATTORNEY WILL NOT BE VALID UNLESS IT IS SIGNED BY TWO QUALIFIED WITNESSES WHO ARE PRESENT WHEN YOU SIGN OR ACKNOWLEDGE YOUR SIGNATURE. IF YOU HAVE ATTACHED ANY ADDITIONAL PAGES TO THIS FORM, YOU MUST DATE AND SIGN EACH OF THE ADDITIONAL PAGES AT THE SAME TIME YOU DATE AND SIGN THIS POWER OF ATTORNEY.)

Statement of Witnesses

(This document must be witnessed by two qualified adult witnesses. None of the following may be used as a witness: (1) a person you designate as your agent or alternate agent, (2) a health care provider, (3) an employee of a health care provider, (4) the operator of a community care facility, (5) an employee of an operator of a community care facility, (6) the operator of a residential care facility for the elderly, or (7) an employee of an operator of a residential care facility for the elderly. At least one of the witnesses must make the additional declaration set out following the place where the witnesses sign.)

(READ CAREFULLY BEFORE SIGNING. You can sign as a witness only if you personally know the principal or the identity of the principal is proved to you by convincing evidence.)

(To have convincing evidence of the identity of the principal, you must be presented with and reasonably rely on any one or more of the following:

(1) An identification card or driver's license issued by the California Department of Motor Vehicles that is current or has been issued within five years.

(2) A passport issued by the Department of State of the United States that is current or has been issued within five years.

(3) Any of the following documents if the document is current or has been issued within five years and contains a photograph and description of the person named on it, is signed by the person, and bears a serial or other identifying number:

(a) A passport issued by a foreign government that has been stamped by the United States Immigration and Naturalization Service.

(b) A driver's license issued by a state other than California or by a Canadian or Mexican public agency authorized to issue driver's licenses.

(c) An identification card issued by a state other than California.

(d) An identification card issued by any branch of the armed forces of the United States.)

(Other kinds of proof of identity are not allowed.)

I declare under penalty of perjury under the laws of California that the person who signed or acknowledged this document is personally known to me (or proved to me on the basis of convincing evidence) to be the principal, that the principal signed or acknowledged this durable power of attorney in my presence, that the principal appears to be of sound mind and under no duress, fraud, or undue influence, that I am not the person appointed as attorney in fact by this document, and that I am not a health care provider, an employee of a health care provider, the operator of a community care facility, an employee of an operator of a community care facility, the operator of a residential care facility for the elderly, nor an employee of an operator of a residential care facility for the elderly.

Signature: _____   Residence Address: _____

Print Name: _____   _____

Date: _____   _____

Signature: _____   Residence Address: _____

Print Name: _____   _____

Date: _____   _____

(AT LEAST ONE OF THE ABOVE WITNESSES MUST ALSO SIGN THE FOLLOWING DECLARATION.)

I further declare under penalty of perjury under the laws of California that I am not related to the principal by blood, marriage, or adoption, and, to the best of my knowledge, I am not entitled to any part of the estate of the principal upon the death of the principal under a will now existing or by operation of law.

Signature: _____

Signature: _____

Statement of Patient Advocate or Ombudsman

(If you are a patient in a skilled nursing facility, one of the witnesses must be a patient advocate or ombudsman. The following statement is required only if you are a patient in a skilled nursing facility—a health care facility that provides the following basic services: skilled nursing care and supportive care to patients whose primary need is for availability of skilled nursing care on an extended basis. The patient advocate or ombudsman must sign both parts of the "Statement of Witnesses" above and must also sign the following statement.)

I further declare under penalty of perjury under the laws of California that I am a patient advocate or ombudsman as designated by the State Department of Aging and that I am serving as a witness as required by subdivision (f) of Section 2432 of the Civil Code.

Signature: _____

H. Sample California Springing Durable Power of Attorney for Health Care

Following is an example of a completed California springing durable power of attorney prepared using Form 14 from the Appendix. This document is not a statutory form, but one authorized by the general California law governing durable powers of attorney for health care (Section 2430 of the Civil Code).

1. Introduction

Facts: The principal is Juanita Smith, a widow, elderly and ill. Though still competent to handle her own medical (and financial) affairs, she worries that her health may deteriorate in a few months or years so that she can no longer manage either. Accordingly, she creates a financial springing durable power of attorney and a separate springing durable power of attorney for health care.

Juanita has one son, Phillip, whom she wishes to be her attorney in fact for health care. The only drawback is that Phillip travels extensively on business. Juanita and Phillip talk, and he agrees to be her attorney in fact for health care, as long as she will name another attorney in fact who can act, if need be, when Phillip is out of town and can't be reached. The two agree that Juanita's best choice for her second attorney in fact is her good friend, Eileen Jones. Eileen is healthy and active, feels she can take on this responsibility, and agrees to serve as (co-) attorney in fact. Although it's most unlikely her two attorneys in fact would disagree, Juanita has covered that remote contingency by providing that if there is a conflict, Phillip's decision will prevail.

Juanita also adds several specific provisions to her durable power of attorney for health care as follows:

- that her personal physician determine, if possible, if she has become incapacitated;

- that no life sustaining procedures be used if she is diagnosed as having a terminal illness; and

- that her attorneys in fact comply with her funeral and burial instructions in her will.

Following is the draft document Juanita prepared modifying Form 14 from the Appendix.

Form 14

California Springing Durable Power of Attorney (Health Care)

WARNING TO PERSON EXECUTING THIS DOCUMENT

THIS IS AN IMPORTANT LEGAL DOCUMENT. IT CREATES A DURABLE POWER OF ATTORNEY FOR HEALTH CARE. BEFORE EXECUTING THIS DOCUMENT, YOU SHOULD KNOW THESE IMPORTANT FACTS.

THIS DOCUMENT GIVES THE PERSON YOU DESIGNATE AS YOUR AGENT (THE ATTORNEY IN FACT) THE POWER TO MAKE HEALTH CARE DECISIONS FOR YOU. YOUR AGENT MUST ACT CONSISTENTLY WITH YOUR DESIRES AS STATED IN THIS DOCUMENT OR OTHERWISE MADE KNOWN.

EXCEPT AS YOU OTHERWISE SPECIFY IN THIS DOCUMENT, THIS DOCUMENT GIVES YOUR AGENT THE POWER TO CONSENT TO YOUR DOCTOR NOT GIVING TREATMENT OR STOPPING TREATMENT NECESSARY TO KEEP YOU ALIVE.

NOTWITHSTANDING THIS DOCUMENT, YOU HAVE THE RIGHT TO MAKE MEDICAL AND OTHER HEALTH CARE DECISIONS FOR YOURSELF SO LONG AS YOU CAN GIVE INFORMED CONSENT WITH RESPECT TO THE PARTICULAR DECISION. IN ADDITION, NO TREATMENT MAY BE GIVEN TO YOU OVER YOUR OBJECTION, AND HEALTH CARE NECESSARY TO KEEP YOU ALIVE MAY NOT BE STOPPED OR WITHHELD IF YOU OBJECT AT THE TIME.

THIS DOCUMENT GIVES YOUR AGENT AUTHORITY TO CONSENT, TO REFUSE TO CONSENT, OR TO WITHDRAW CONSENT TO ANY CARE, TREATMENT, SERVICE, OR PROCEDURE TO MAINTAIN, DIAGNOSE, OR TREAT A PHYSICAL OR MENTAL CONDITION. THIS POWER IS SUBJECT TO ANY STATEMENT OF YOUR DESIRES AND ANY LIMITATIONS THAT YOU INCLUDE IN THIS DOCUMENT. YOU MAY STATE IN THIS DOCUMENT ANY TYPES OF TREATMENT THAT YOU DO NOT DESIRE. IN ADDITION, A COURT CAN TAKE AWAY THE POWER OF YOUR AGENT TO MAKE HEALTH CARE DECISIONS FOR YOU IF YOUR AGENT (1) AUTHORIZES ANYTHING THAT IS ILLEGAL, (2) ACTS CONTRARY TO YOUR KNOWN DESIRES, OR (3) WHERE YOUR DESIRES ARE NOT KNOWN, DOES ANYTHING THAT IS CLEARLY CONTRARY TO YOUR BEST INTERESTS.

UNLESS YOU SPECIFY A SHORTER PERIOD IN THIS DOCUMENT, THIS POWER WILL EXIST FOR SEVEN YEARS FROM THE DATE YOU EXECUTE THIS DOCUMENT AND, IF YOU ARE UNABLE TO MAKE HEALTH CARE DECISIONS FOR YOURSELF AT THE TIME WHEN THIS SEVEN-YEAR PERIOD ENDS, THIS POWER WILL CONTINUE TO EXIST UNTIL THE TIME WHEN YOU BECOME ABLE TO MAKE HEALTH CARE DECISIONS FOR YOURSELF.

YOU HAVE THE RIGHT TO REVOKE THE AUTHORITY OF YOUR AGENT BY NOTIFYING YOUR AGENT OR YOUR TREATING DOCTOR, HOSPITAL, OR OTHER HEALTH CARE PROVIDER ORALLY OR IN WRITING OF THE REVOCATION.

YOUR AGENT HAS THE RIGHT TO EXAMINE YOUR MEDICAL RECORDS AND TO CONSENT TO THEIR DISCLOSURE UNLESS YOU LIMIT THIS RIGHT IN THIS DOCUMENT.

UNLESS YOU OTHERWISE SPECIFY IN THIS DOCUMENT, THIS DOCUMENT GIVES YOUR AGENT THE POWER AFTER YOU DIE TO (1) AUTHORIZE AN AUTOPSY, (2) DONATE YOUR BODY OR PARTS THEREOF FOR TRANSPLANT OR THERAPEUTIC OR EDUCATIONAL OR SCIENTIFIC PURPOSES, AND (3) DIRECT THE DISPOSITION OF YOUR REMAINS.

IF THERE IS ANYTHING IN THIS DOCUMENT THAT YOU DO NOT UNDERSTAND, YOU SHOULD ASK A LAWYER TO EXPLAIN IT TO YOU.

THIS POWER OF ATTORNEY WILL NOT BE VALID FOR MAKING HEALTH CARE DECISIONS UNLESS IT IS EITHER (1) SIGNED BY TWO QUALIFIED ADULT WITNESSES WHO PERSONALLY KNOW YOU AND WHO ARE PRESENT WHEN YOU SIGN OR ACKNOWLEDGE YOUR SIGNATURE OR (2) ACKNOWLEDGED BEFORE A NOTARY PUBLIC IN CALIFORNIA.

Durable Power of Attorney for Health Care

1. Creation of Durable Power of Attorney

To my family, relatives, friends and my physicians, health care providers, community care facilities and any other person who may have an interest or duty in my medical care or treatment:

I, ___JUANITA SMITH_____, being of sound

           name

mind, willfully and voluntarily intend to create by this document a durable power of attorney for

my health care by appointing the person designated as my attorney in fact to make health care

decisions for me in the event I become incapacitated and am unable to make health care deci-

sions for myself. This power of attorney shall not be affected by my subsequent incapacity.

2. Designation of Attorney in Fact

(A) The persons designated to be my attorney in fact for health care in the event I become incapacitated are my son, PHILIP SMITH, of 8 Lee St., Marysville CA, and EILEEN JONES, of 23 Overlook Road, Winton, CA.

(B) In the event of medical emergency or necessity, if I have become incapacitated, any one of my attorneys in fact is authorized to act for me and make any permitted medical decision under this durable power of attorney, if the other named attorney in fact is unavailable or unable to act as attorney in fact during such medical emergency or necessity. To the extent possible, the attorneys in fact shall confer and agree on any medical decision permitted under this durable power of attorney.

(C) In the event of any conflict between my attorneys in fact, the decision of my son, PHILLIP SMITH, shall be final.

3. Effective on Incapacity

This durable power of attorney shall become effective in the event I become incapacitated and am unable to make health care decisions for myself, in which case it shall become effective as of the date of the written statement by a physician, as provided in Paragraph 4.

4. Determination of Incapacity

The determination that I have become incapacitated and am unable to make health care decisions shall be made in writing by a licensed physician. If possible, the determination shall be made by <u>my regular physician, Dr. Jim Goldberg of the Springtown</u>,
<small>name of physician</small>
<u>Medical Clinic, 1010 Wyland Avenue, Springtown, CA</u>.
<small>address</small>

5. Authority of My Attorney in Fact

My attorney in fact shall have all lawful authority permissible to make health care decisions for me, including the authority to consent, or withdraw consent or refuse consent to any care, treatment, service or procedure to maintain, diagnose or treat my physical or mental condition, EXCEPT as limited in Paragraph 5(b). Subject to the limitations in Paragraph 5(b), my attorneys in fact are granted full power and authority to make health care decisions for me to the same extent that I could make such decisions for myself if I had the capacity to do so. In exercising this authority, my attorneys in fact shall make health care deisions that are consistent with my desires as stated in this document or otherwise made known to my attorneys in fact. My attorneys in fact shall do all acts necessary to insure that I am made comfortable and receive the best possible health care and day-to-day care, including hiring any nurses or other person-nel necessary and advisable to provide such care.

(b) (i) If at any time I should have an incurable injury, disease or illness which is a terminal condition, or am in a coma which is irreversible, meaning there is no possibility of my ever regaining consciousness, and where the application of life sustaining procedures or technology would serve only to artificially prolong the moment of my death, I direct that no life sustaining procedures or technology be used, and that I be permitted to die naturally.

(ii) If I suffer a loss of mental powers or a paralysis sets in, I direct that no treatment be done to extend my life, and that I be permitted to die naturally.

(iii) My attorneys in fact shall follow the funeral and burial instructions I have written and authorized in Paragraph 11 of my Will.

6. Inspection and Disclosure of Information Relating to My Physical or Mental Health

Subject to any limitations in this document, my attorney in fact has the power and authority to do all of the following:

(a) Request, review, and receive any information, verbal or written, regarding my physical or mental health, including, but not limited to, medical and hospital records.

(b) Execute on my behalf any releases or other documents that may be required in order to obtain this information.

(c) Consent to the disclosure of this information.

7. Signing Documents, Waivers, and Releases

Where necessary to implement the health care decisions that my attorney in fact is authorized by this document to make, my attorney in fact has the power and authority to execute on my behalf all of the following:

(a) Documents titled or purporting to be a "Refusal to Permit Treatment" and "Leaving Hospital Against Medical Advice."

(b) Any necessary waiver or release from liability required by a hospital or physician.

8. Duration

I intend that this Durable Power of Attorney remain effective until my death, or until revoked by me in writing.

Executed this _____1st_____ day of _____July_____,

19 _92_ at _____Springtown, California_____.

_____
Principal   JUANITA SMITH

Statement of Witnesses

(This document must be witnessed by two qualified adult witnesses. None of the following may be used as a witness: (1) a person you designate as your agent or alternate agent, (2) a health care provider, (3) an employee of a health care provider, (4) the operator of a community care facility, (5) an employee of an operator of a community care facility, (6) the operator of a residential care facility for the elderly, (7) an employee of an operator of a residential care facility for the elderly. At least one of the witnesses must make the additional declaration set out following the place where the witnesses sign.)

(READ CAREFULLY BEFORE SIGNING. You can sign as a witness only if you personally know the principal or the identity of the principal is proved to you by convincing evidence.)

(To have convincing evidence of the identity of the principal, you must be presented with and reasonably rely on any one or more of the following:

(1) An identification card or driver's license issued by the California Department of Motor Vehicles that is current or has been issued within five years.

(2) A passport issued by the Department of State of the United States that is current or has been issued within five years.

(3) Any of the following documents if the document is current or has been issued within five

years and contains a photograph and description of the person named on it, is signed by the person, and bears a serial or other identifying number:

(a) A passport issued by a foreign government that has been stamped by the United States Immigration and Naturalization Service.

(b) A driver's license issued by a state other than California or by a Canadian or Mexican public agency authorized to issue driver's licenses.

(c) An identification card issued by a state other than California.

(d) An identification card issued by any branch of the armed forces of the United States.)

(Other kinds of proof of identity are not allowed.)

I declare under penalty of perjury under the laws of California that the person who signed or acknowledged this document is personally known to me (or proved to me on the basis of convincing evidence) to be the principal, that the principal signed or acknowledged this Durable Power of Attorney in my presence, that the principal appears to be of sound mind and under no duress, fraud, or undue influence, that I am not the person appointed as attorney-in-fact by this document, and that I am not a health care provider, an employee of a health care provider, the operator of a community care facility, nor an employee of an operator of a community care facility, an operator of a residential care facility for the elderly, nor an employee of an operator of a residential care facility for the elderly.

Signature: _____ Print Name: _____

Residence Address: _____ _____ _____

Date: _____

Signature: _____ Print Name: _____

Residence Address: _____ _____

Date: _____

(AT LEAST ONE OF THE ABOVE WITNESSES MUST ALSO SIGN THE FOLLOWING DECLARATION.)

I further declare under penalty of perjury under the laws of California that I am not related to the principal by blood, marriage, or adoption, and to the best of my knowledge, I am not entitled to any part of the estate of the principal upon the death of the principal under a will now existing or by operation of law.

Signature: _____

Signature: _____

Statement of Patient Advocate or Ombudsman

(If you are a patient in a skilled nursing facility, one of the witnesses must be a patient advocate or ombudsman. The following statement is required only if you are a patient in a skilled nursing facility—a health care facility that provides the following basic services: skilled nursing care and supportive care to patients whose primary need is for availability of skilled nursing care on an extended basis. The patient advocate or ombudsman must sign both parts of the "Statement of Witnesses" above AND must also sign the following statement.)

I further declare under penalty of perjury under the laws of California that I am a patient advocate or ombudsman as designated by the State Department of Aging and that I am serving as a witness as required by subdivision (f) of Section 2432 of the Civil Code.

Signature:_____

Notarization

State of California   )
) ss
County of _____   )

On this _____1st_____ day of _____July_____, in the year 19_92,

before me, a Notary Public, State of California, duly commissioned and sworn, personally ap-

peared ___JUANITA SMITH_____, personally known
                        name of principal

to me (or proved to me on the basis of satisfactory evidence) to be the person whose name is

subscribed to this instrument, and acknowledged that __she_____ executed it. I declare under
                                                          he/she

penalty of perjury that the person whose name is subscribed to this instrument appears to be of

sound mind and under no duress, fraud, or undue influence.

_____
                                            signature of notary public

[Notary Seal]   Notary Public for the State of California

                           My commission expires:_____, 19_____

CHAPTER 9

'CONVENTIONAL' POWERS OF ATTORNEY

A. The Nature of a 'Conventional' Power of Attorney

This book uses the term "conventional" power of attorney to help differentiate that form from "durable" powers of attorney. Traditionally, the word "conventional" wasn't used, as there was no such thing as a durable power of attorney, and thus no need for the distinction. The major difference between the two is that conventional powers of attorney must terminate if the principal becomes incapacitated. However, the very purpose of a durable power of attorney is that it remains effective (or becomes effective if it is the "springing" variety) if the principal is incapacitated.

Conventional powers of attorney are used to authorize someone to handle finances or property, often for a limited period of time, while the principal is competent. Conventional powers of attorney are valid in all states. Because a conventional power of attorney terminates upon incapacity of the principal, it is never appropriate for handling health or medical care decisions.[1]

In form, a conventional power of attorney is simple. The principal signs a document appointing the attorney in fact and defining his power and authority. Appropriate institutions and people are given copies, and the attorney in fact takes on responsibility for handling whatever is specified in the document. The conventional power of attorney must be notarized.

B. Uses of Conventional Powers of Attorney

There are a variety of reasons why it can make sense to authorize someone to handle certain of your financial/property affairs even though you're not incapacitated. Among the common ones are:

- Going on vacation and needing to have business transacted in your absence;

- Authorizing an expert to make business decisions for you and carry them out;

- Being in the military service or involved in some other activity which precludes being available to transact business;

- Inability, or choosing not to attend certain financial proceedings, complete forms, etc.;

- Giving someone access to your finances to care for your children during your temporary absence; and

- Giving someone written authority to care for your children in your absence.

Conventional powers of attorney can be used for many needs and situations. Sometimes all that is involved is a single transaction which takes place during a set time. At the other end, a conventional power of attorney may be used to to authorize an attorney in fact to handle all financial affairs for an open-ended period of time.

A good way to demonstrate the range of transactions and type of authority that can be handled by a conventional power of attorney is by looking at several examples.

---

[1] If a power of attorney document doesn't clearly specify that it is a " durable" power of attorney—intended to last even if the principal becomes incapacitated—by definition it is a conventional power of attorney.

Example 1
Conventional power of attorney limited in time and scope

Alan is purchasing a condominium unit. Escrow has been opened at a title company, but the closing is delayed for several weeks beyond the anticipated date. Because of the delay, the closing is now scheduled for the middle of the week of Alan's long planned trip to Greece. So Alan prepares a conventional power of attorney, authorizing his friend Jennifer to sign any documents necessary to complete the closing and to withdraw any amounts of money (from an identified bank account) necessary to pay expenses and costs incurred because of the closing. Alan also specifies that Jennifer's authority expires on a set day, the date he is to come back from Greece. Finally, he specifies that Jennifer has only the authority delegated in the power of attorney document and may not engage in other transactions on his behalf.

Alan discusses his plans with both his bank and the title company before he leaves, to make sure they'll accept the power of attorney and the authority of his attorney in fact. Both organizations assure him they'll accept a valid conventional power of attorney. He has copies of his power of attorney placed in the bank's records and his file at the title company. The original power of attorney document is left with Jennifer, the attorney in fact.

Note: If you want someone to handle your financial affairs, and are also concerned with the possibility that you may become incapacitated during the time involved, it's advisable to use a durable power of attorney. (See Chapters 3, 4 and 5 for forms and instructions on how to do this.) In the durable power of attorney, include a termination clause such as: "To last until ___[whatever date you specify]___ unless I have become incapacitated before said date, in which case this durable power of attorney shall last until I have regained the capacity to manage my own financial affairs, or until my death."

Example 2
Conventional power of attorney open-ended in time, and limited in scope

Alice is owner of a summer cottage. Her friend Mary lives in the next cottage as her permanent home. Alice and Mary agree that because Mary is on the spot she'll take care of renting Mary's cottage, collecting rent and paying all house bills and costs. Alice prepares a conventional power of attorney giving Mary authority to represent Alice for "any transaction concerning my cottage located at 20 Jumping Trout Lake, including the payment of all taxes, collecting of rents, paying for repairs and any other costs." Alice specifies that this power of attorney shall continue indefinitely. She also provides that Mary has no authority to sell the house nor to represent her in any transaction which doesn't concern the house. Alice and Mary also prepare a contract between themselves to define what rights Mary has to be paid for her services, etc.

Example 3
Broad general delegation of authority to handle all finances, unlimited by time

Steven, a business investor who owns a substantial amount of property, decides he'll go to Asia to spend at least a year in a religious community reflecting on the meaning of life. However, Steven isn't currently so enlightened (or unenlightened, depending on your point of view) that he wishes to give away or neglect his property. So Steven authorizes his friend Peter to be his attorney in fact, with authority to handle all his financial transactions, pay his bills, etc. Steven puts no time limit on this power of attorney, since he isn't sure when he'll return. Steven has copies of the power of attorney placed in his bank records and with his tax accountant, his stock broker, and other people or organizations involved in his finances. When he returns from his quest, he will formally revoke the power of attorney and let everyone know.

Note: Many financial institutions have their own power of attorney forms. Before preparing a conventional power of attorney, be sure to check with the institutions which will be involved. If they have their own form, you may wish to use it for that institution. The IRS has its own power of attorney forms which you must use to authorize anyone to represent you in a proceeding before the IRS or to receive any tax information on your behalf from the IRS.

C. Conventional Power of Attorney and Children

One common use of a conventional power of attorney is to arrange for financial care of children when parents are going out of town. Children (those under age 18 or another age, depending on state law) cannot legally control large sums of money. Even if they could, it's obviously not a desirable idea. If you have children and are leaving home without them for a while, preparing a suitable power of attorney is often needed to insure the children are properly cared for in your absence.

Example 1

Doug and Missy, a married couple with two teen-age children, are planning a six-month business and pleasure trip in Europe. Neither of their children wants to go. Doug and Missy have arranged that Aunt Margaret will supervise the children during their trip. The children both attend private schools, with tuition due while their parents are traveling. Doug and Missy create a power of attorney valid for six months authorizing Aunt Margaret to pay all their bills and reasonable expenses of the children, including tuition, from certain identified bank accounts. Doug and Missy transfer enough money to those accounts to cover what they estimate those expenses will be. If the expenses run much higher, Aunt Margaret is to contact Doug and Missy for more funds. Finally, Doug and Missy contact their bank to inform them of what they've arranged, and to place a copy of the power of attorney in the bank's files.

Example 2

Colette, a single parent with a nine-year-old daughter, must go thousands of miles and several states away to care for her sick father. She doesn't want to disrupt her daughter's schooling, so she arranges for her best friend, Nancy, to care for her daughter, Alice. Colette creates a power of attorney authorizing Nancy to pay Colette's bills and all day-to-day expenses of Alice from Colette's savings account. Since Colette doesn't know how long she'll be gone, she doesn't put any ending date on the power of attorney. She sends a copy of the power of attorney to her bank. When she returns, she will revoke the power of attorney and inform the bank.

Common Sense Note: Legal guardianships giving custody and the authority to care for children cannot be authorized by a power of attorney. Still, in an emergency a power of attorney giving a responsible adult authority over the child might be honored by authorities. For example, a hospital might be more willing to accept the authority of a friend if they have signed authority from the children's parents. The same thing is true if the child has a brush with legal or school authorities. If you give a friend or relative authority over the finances necessary to care for your minor child, it may be a good idea to add a clause giving them authority over the child as well, even though legally this doesn't really give them the authority of a guardian.

Example

Colette puts the following clause in her power of attorney: "My attorney in fact, Nancy Beebstein, shall have authority to pay all living expenses of my daughter, Alice, from any of my funds at The Central Bank or any of my other assets. In addition, my attorney in fact shall have authority to make decisions for or on behalf of my daughter when I am unable or unavailable to do so, in the event of emergency or other necessity."

D. Drafting a Conventional Power of Attorney

Many of the general common sense concerns discussed in earlier chapters regarding drafting durable powers of attorney apply with equal force to conventional powers of attorney. Those concerns aren't repeated here, but a few pointers and reminders are in order.

- The choice of your attorney in fact is vitally important. The attorney in fact must be someone you trust, both in a business and ethical sense. (See Chapter 3, Section G and Chapter 6, Section D(3).)

- Conventional powers of attorney are flexible documents, and can be customized as much or as little as you determine is necessary or desirable.

- Don't state in the power of attorney document that it's revocable. That is inherently true, but stating it may discourage acceptability.

- A conventional power of attorney document should be notarized.

- A conventional power of attorney must be recorded with the county recorder of deeds if the attorney in fact will (or might) handle real estate transactions for the principal. It can often be a good idea to record a conventional power of attorney even if real estate isn't involved. Recording makes the document seem more official, and thus promotes acceptability.

- Banks and other financial institutions are reluctant to accept conventional powers of attorney that are fairly old, even though the document states that it is open-ended. For this reason, it is wise to re-do a conventional power of attorney every year or so if you wish it to stay in effect. Old copies should be destroyed and the people and institutions with old copies should be notified.

E. Sample Conventional Power of Attorney Forms

The following forms can be used or adapted to create a conventional power of attorney. As you'll see, the basic forms are open-ended. It's up to you to define the limits and nature of the authority granted to your attorney in fact. You'll find tear-out conventional power of attorney forms in the Appendix as Forms 18, 19 and 20.

1. Basic Conventional Power of Attorney

The first form isn't completed, but an explanation of the information you need is filled in.

Form 18

Recording requested by and when recorded mail to

__[principal's name]_____

__[principal's address]_____

_____

Power of Attorney

I, _____ , of
name of principal

_____ , _____ ,
city   county

_____ appoint _____ , of
state   name

_____ , _____ ,
city   county

_____ as my attorney in fact to act in my place for the purposes of
state

[specify particular powers granted]

except that my attorney in fact shall not have the power of

[specify powers reserved]

I further grant to my attorney in fact full authority to act in any manner both proper and

necessary to the exercise of the foregoing powers, including _____
specify

_____ ,

and ratify every act that _____ may lawfully perform in exercising those powers.
he/she

[modify following paragraph if power of attorney is not limited to a set time period]

This power of attorney is granted for a period of _____ and

shall become effective on _____ , 19___ and shall terminate on

_____ , 19___.

Executed this _____ day of _____ , 19___, at

_____, _____.
                 city   state

_____
                         signature

Notarization

State of _____)
) ss
County of _____)

On this _____ day of _____, in the year 19___,

before me, a Notary Public, State of _____, duly commissioned and

sworn, personally appeared _____,
                                                 name

personally known to me (or proved to me on the basis of satisfactory evidence) to be the person

whose name is subscribed to this instrument, and acknowledged that _____
                                                     he/she

executed it.

_____

Notary Public

[Notary Seal]   State of _____

My commission expires: _____, 19___

2. Sample Completed Conventional Power of Attorney

Facts: Raymond, a businessman, is leaving for a four-week pleasure and work trip to Panama. While he's gone, the following may occur:

- A loan he's been negotiating with a bank may receive final approval;

- The sale of an apartment he owns may close; and

- An antique Studebaker he has up for sale might find a buyer at his asking price of $32,000.

Raymond doesn't want any delays if any of these events occur. So he creates a power of attorney that authorizes his business assistant, Justin, to represent him in these transactions. Here the three transactions are combined in one document. Raymond could also choose to create three separate powers of attorney—this would be a particularly good idea if one of the institutions involved, such as the bank, required the power of attorney to be on their own form or if it appeared to Raymond that by authorizing so many different types of transactions in the same document he risked confusing a reader.

Finally, Raymond has this power of attorney recorded at the local recorder of deeds because it involves real estate.

Form 18

Recording requested by and when recorded mail to

Raymond Carr

41 East Avenue

Oakland CA 94607

Power of Attorney

I, _____ RAYMOND CARR _____ , of

name of principal

Oakland _____ , Alameda County _____ ,

city   county

California _____ appoint _____ JUSTIN SMITH _____ , of

state   name

100 West Street, Oakland _____ , Alameda County _____ ,

city   county

California _____ as my attorney in fact to act in my place for the purposes of

state

1. Concerning all loan transactions between myself and Commercial Bank.

2. Concerning the sale of the apartment house I own at 216 40th St., Oakland, California. The escrow for this sale is being handled by Acme Title Co., Oakland, California.

3. Concerning the sale of my antique Studebaker, license plate number MY CAR, for not less than $32,000 cash.

I further grant to my attorney in fact full authority to act in any manner both proper and

necessary to the exercise of the foregoing powers, including _____

specify

_____ ,

and ratify every act that _____ he _____ may lawfully perform in exercising those powers.

he/she

This power of attorney is granted for a period of _____ three weeks _____ and

shall become effective on _____ December 1 _____ , 19 92 and shall terminate on

December 22 _____ , 19 92.

Executed this __29th__ day of __November_____, 19_92_, at

__Oakland_____, __California_____.
              _{city}   _{state}

_____
RAYMOND CARR

Notarization

State of __California_____)
) ss

County of __Alameda_____)

On this ____29th_____ day of __November_____, in the year 19_92_,

before me, a Notary Public, State of ____California_____, duly commissioned and

sworn, personally appeared ____RAYMOND CARR_____,
                                            _{name}

personally known to me (or proved to me on the basis of satisfactory evidence) to be the person

whose name is subscribed to this instrument, and acknowledged that _____he_____
                                                    _{he/she}

executed it.

_____
        Notary Public   ROSE SHARP

[Notary Seal]   State of ____California_____

        My commission expires: _____, 19___

3. Sample Completed Conventional Power of Attorney for a Couple

A couple may jointly want to authorize someone else to handle both their financial affairs for a while. Here is a power of attorney form for a married couple, Melinda and Tom Brown, authorizing their adult daughter, Cindy, to handle the sale of certain stocks they own while Melinda and Tom spend three weeks backpacking. A joint power of attorney for a married couple is contained in the Appendix as Form 19.

Form 19

Recording requested by and when recorded mail to

_____   _____

_____

_____

Joint Power of Attorney

We, _____TOM BROWN_____ and
                                name of husband

_____MELINDA BROWN_____
                              name of wife

husband and wife, residing at ___10 Farm St._____,

City of __Zadoo, County of Ames___, State of ___Iowa_____, do hereby

jointly and severally appoint __our daughter, CINDY BROWN_____ as
                                             name

our attorney in fact, for us in our name, place, and stead to

handle all transactions, purchases and sales in our brokerage

account, #77-0154, Ace Brokers, Zadoo City, Iowa

~~except that our attorney in fact shall not have the power to~~

We further give and grant to our said attorney in fact full power and authority to do and

perform every act necessary and proper in the exercise of any of the powers granted hereunder as

fully as we might or could do if personally present, with full power of substitution and revocation,

hereby ratifying and confirming all that our said attorney in fact shall lawfully do or cause to be

done by virtue hereof.

This power of attorney is granted for a term of _____**three weeks**_____
specify period
and shall be effective on ____July 1_____, 19_91_ and shall remain in full

force and effect until ____July 22_____, 19_91_.

Dated: ____June 28_____, 19_91_

_____
signature
TOM BROWN
_____
typed name

_____
signature
MELINDA BROWN
_____
typed name

Notarization

State of ____Iowa_____)
) ss
County of ____Ames_____)

On this ___28th_____ day of _____June_____, in the year 19_91_,

before me, a Notary Public, State of ____Iowa_____, duly commissioned and

sworn, personally appeared ___TOM BROWN_____
name
and ___MELINDA BROWN_____, personally known
name
to me (or proved to me on the basis of satisfactory evidence) to be the people whose names are

subscribed to this instrument, and acknowledged that they executed it.

_____
signature

Notary Public for

the State of __Iowa_____

[Notary Seal]

My commission expires: _____, 19___

4. Sample Completed Detailed and Broad Conventional Power of Attorney

In some situations, a person may want to delegate very broad powers to the attorney in fact. This might be the case where the attorney in fact will be handling many complex financial matters and transactions. Obviously this is a different approach from that set forth in the previous two sections where the attorney in fact's power was limited to specific functions. Simultaneously, this broad authority may need to be detailed, because people or institutions that the attorney in fact will deal with may be reluctant to accept less specific wording. This can be particularly true of some employees of certain conservative bureaucracies, like banks, who are comforted by documents full of legalese. If you believe your needs are best suited by a traditional-looking legal document, use or adopt the following form, found in the Appendix as Form 20.

Form 20

Recording requested by and when recorded mail to

Byron Jones
_____

19 Williams Street
_____

New York NY
_____

General Power of Attorney

I. KNOW ALL MEN BY THESE PRESENTS, that I,

BYRON JONES
_____, residing at
                        name

19 Williams Street
_____, City
                  street address

of _New York_____, County of ___New York_____, State of

New York
_____, do hereby nominate, constitute, and appoint

MICHAEL WASHINGTON
_____, of
                        name

10 Wall Street
_____, City
                  street address

of _New York_____, County of ___New York_____, State of

New York
_____, as my true and lawful attorney in fact, for me and in my

name, place, and stead, and for my use and benefit.

II. My attorney in fact shall have all lawfully permissible authority to act for or represent me,

including, but not limited to, the authority:

A. To ask, demand, sue for, recover, collect, and receive all such sums of money, debts, dues,

accounts, legacies, bequests, interest, dividends, annuities, and demands whatsoever as are now or

shall hereafter become due, owing, payable, or belonging to me and have, use, and take all lawful

ways and means in my name or otherwise for the recovery thereof, by attachments, arrests,

distress, or otherwise, and to compromise and agree for the same and acquittances or other

sufficient discharges for the same;

B. To make, seal, and deliver, to bargain, contract, agree for, purchase, receive, and take

lands, tenements, hereditaments, and accept the possession of all lands, and all deeds and other assurances, in the law therefor, and to lease, let, demise, bargain, sell, remise, release, convey, mortgage, and hypothecate lands, tenements, and hereditaments upon such terms and conditions and under such covenants as _____he_____ shall think fit;

he/she

To bargain and agree for, buy, sell, mortgage, hypothecate, and in any and every way and manner deal in and with goods, wares, and merchandise, choses in action, and other property in possession or in action, and to make, do, and transact all and every kind of business of whatsoever nature and kind;

C. To improve, repair, maintain, manage, insure, rent, lease, sell, release, convey, subject to liens, mortgage, and hypothecate, and in any way or manner deal with all or any part of any real property whatsoever, or any interest therein, which I now own or may hereafter acquire, for me and in my name, and under such terms and conditions, and under such covenants as my attorney in fact shall deem proper;

D. To exercise, do, or perform any act, right, power, duty, or obligation whatsoever that I now have or may acquire the legal right, power, or capacity to exercise, do, or perform in connection with, arising out of, or relating to any person, item, thing, transaction, business property, real or personal, tangible or intangible, or matter whatsoever;

E. To sign, endorse, execute, acknowledge, deliver, receive, and possess such applications, contracts, agreements, options, covenants, deeds, conveyances, trust deeds, security agreements, bills of sale, leases, mortgages, assignments, insurance policies, bills of lading, warehouse receipts, documents of title, bills, bonds, debentures, checks, drafts, bills of exchange, notes, stock certificates, proxies, warrants, commercial paper, receipts, withdrawal receipts and deposit instruments relating to accounts or deposits in, or certificates of deposit of, banks, savings and loan or other institutions or associations, proofs of loss, evidence of debts, releases, and satisfaction of mortgages, judgments, liens, security agreements, and other debts and obligations, and such other instruments in writing or whatever kind and nature as may be necessary or proper in the exercise of the rights and powers herein granted.

III. Further, my attorney in fact has full power and authority to do and perform all and every act and thing whatsoever requisite, necessary, and proper to be done in the exercise of any of the rights and powers herein granted, as fully to all intents and purposes as I might or could do if personally present, with full power of substitution or revocation, hereby ratifying and confirming all that my attorney in fact shall lawfully do or cause to be done by virtue of this power of attorney and the rights and powers herein granted.

IV. This instrument is to be construed and interpreted as a general power of attorney. The enumeration of specific items, acts, rights or powers herein does not limit or restrict, and is not to be construed or interpreted as limiting or restricting the general powers herein granted to my attorney in fact.

V. All power and authority hereinabove granted shall in any event terminate on the _____20th_____ day of _____December_____, 19_92_.

IN WITNESS WHEREOF, I have hereunto signed my name this ___10th_____ day of January_____, 19_92_.

_____
Principal

BYRON JONES_____
typed name

Notarization

State of _____ New York _____

County of _____ New York _____

On this _____ 10th _____ day of _____ January _____ in the year
_____ 1992 _____, before me, a Notary Public, State of _____ New York _____, duly
commissioned and sworn, personally appeared _____ BYRON JONES _____,
personally known to me (or proved to me on the basis of satisfactory evidence) to be the person
whose name is subscribed to the within instrument, and acknowledged to me that he/she executed the same.

IN WITNESS WHEREOF, I have hereunto set my hand and affixed my official seal in the
State of _____ New York _____, County of _____ New York _____ on the date set forth
above in this certificate.

_____
Notary Public

[Notary Seal]   State of _____ New York _____

My commission expires _____

CHAPTER 10

REVOCATION OF A POWER OF ATTORNEY

A. Introduction

Any power of attorney, whether durable or conventional, can almost always be revoked at any time, as long as the principal is competent. The few rare exceptions to this rule are discussed in Section B of this chapter. The revocation of a power of attorney should always be in writing.

The revocation notice should be delivered, of course, to the (now former) attorney in fact. Revocation can create serious problems if it isn't accepted by the attorney in fact, which could occur if he claims you're now incapacitated. Obvious problems can also occur if you believe your attorney in fact has been dishonest. If you face one of these problems, consult a lawyer. (See Chapter 11.)

To make a revocation effective, it's essential, as a practical matter, that all persons or institutions who might deal, or have dealt with, the attorney in fact under the durable power of attorney be informed that the power of attorney is no longer effective, and the attorney in fact is no longer authorized to act for the principal. The reason for this is that people or institutions might still enter into transactions with the (former) attorney in fact because they don't know that the durable power of attorney has been revoked. Third parties who do this in good faith are legally protected. In other words, once you create a durable power of attorney, the legal burden is on you to be sure everyone knows you have revoked it. If you don't, you may well be held legally liable for the acts of your attorney in fact, even though you have revoked any and all of his authority.

Warning on Amending Powers of Attorney: There is no accepted form which can be used to amend a power of attorney. If you want to change or amend an existing power of attorney, either durable or conventional, the safe course is to revoke the existing document and prepare a new one.

B. Limitations

There are some limits regarding the ability of the principal to revoke a power of attorney. As you'll see, most don't apply to typical situations. I mention them primarily to be thorough.

1. If Notice of Revocation Not Given to Third Person

If not informed of the revocation, a third person or institution, such as a bank or insurance company, can rely in good faith on the apparent authority of an attorney in fact even if the principal has revoked it.

Example

Michael revokes a conventional power of attorney naming Jim as his attorney in fact to handle his bank accounts. Michael's bank isn't informed of the revocation. Jim, fraudulently acting as Michael's attorney in fact, removes money from the accounts and spends it. The bank isn't responsible to Michael for his loss. The moral to this fable is simple. When revoking a power of attorney, be sure all people or organizations who deal, or might deal, with the attorney in fact receive written notice that the power of attorney has been revoked.

2. If Power of Attorney Is Unavailable

Technically, a power of attorney isn't revoked if the document embodying it is lost or destroyed. But as a practical matter, loss or destruction of the document renders the power of attorney virtually useless. Few people are likely to accept as valid a document they can't see and are told has been lost. If you decide a power of attorney document has been lost, it's wise to formally revoke it and destroy any copies, as well as create a new one. By doing this, you minimize chances that the old power of attorney might some-day appear and confuse matters.

3. If Revocation by Incompetent Person

An incompetent or incapacitated principal cannot revoke a durable power of attorney. In this area, there can be a problem if a principal attempts to revoke the durable power of attorney but the attorney in fact believes that the principal isn't mentally competent to do so.

Example

Arthur authorizes Jim to be his attorney in fact for health care decisions. Arthur is involved in a serious automobile accident, suffers grave brain damage, and is hospitalized. Jim acts as Arthur's attorney in fact and makes medical decisions he believes are in Arthur's best interests. Arthur suddenly disputes those decisions and Jim's authority to act for him. However, the doctors tell Jim that Arthur is seriously deranged and shouldn't be allowed to make his own decisions. What can Jim do? Technically, he could try to insist that his authority hasn't been altered, because Arthur isn't competent to revoke the durable power of attorney. That might be necessary for an immediate emergency, for instance if an operation had to be decided on at once. More likely, there would have to be a court proceeding, where a judge would determine if Arthur truly was competent to revoke the durable power of attorney.

Here's another revocation situation which is somewhat more likely.

Example

Leroy creates a springing durable power of attorney, naming his friend Tony as attorney in fact for Leroy's financial affairs. Several years later, Leroy is hospitalized with severe physical and mental problems, and Tony begins to handle Leroy's financial affairs. In the hospital, Leroy meets Jane, whom Tony thinks is a designing woman out to steal Leroy's money. Leroy decides he wants to appoint Jane to be his attorney in fact, and declares in writing that he has revoked Tony's authority to serve as attorney in fact. Tony refuses to accept the revocation, asserting that Leroy isn't competent to do so. Jane and Leroy file a lawsuit to resolve this issue.

C. Legal Formalities

The actual method for revoking any power of attorney is by use of a "Notice of Revocation" document. It's called that since the purpose of revocation is to notify the attorney in fact, and those she may have been dealing with, that the principal has revoked the durable power of attorney.

Revocation of any power of attorney, whether durable or conventional, is a serious act. It's obviously important that revocation be legally effective. To insure that, observe all the following formalities:

- *Signing and Witnessing.* Any Notice of Revocation must be signed and dated by the principal. It needn't be witnessed, but witnessing may be a prudent idea, especially if questions might be raised regarding the competence of the principal.

- *Notarization.* The Notice of Revocation must be notarized. If you use witnesses, it's best to have your witnesses' signatures notarized as well as your own.

- *Recording.* Any revocation of a durable power of attorney can be recorded at your local recorder of deeds office, even if the original durable power of attorney was not. If the original form was recorded, the revocation must be recorded. Recording the revocation notice is an additional means of protection for the principal, one method of demonstrating that people shouldn't have continued to rely on the (former) attorney in fact's authority.

- *Delivery to Attorney in Fact and Others.* The former attorney in fact and all institutions and people who have dealt or might deal with the former attorney in fact must receive copies of the Notice of Revocation, as discussed in Sections A and B(1) above.

D. Sample Basic Revocation Form

This sample is a standard form used to revoke any power of attorney. A blank copy is contained in the Appendix as Form 21.

Facts: The principal, Jim Rose, revokes a durable power of attorney for health care, which names his brother, Ed Rose, as his attorney in fact. No reason for the revocation need be stated. In fact, the reason is because Ed has retired, is ill, and has moved to Florida. Jim plans to create a new durable power of attorney with his son, Tom, as his new attorney in fact. Even though the original power of attorney was "springing" and never went into effect, Jim wants the protection of a formal revocation notice.

Form 21

Recording requested by and when recorded mail to

Jim Rose
_____

37 West 261 Street
_____

New York NY
_____

Notice of Revocation of Power of Attorney

I, _____Jim Rose_____,
                            name

of ___37 West 261 Street_____,
                            street address

City of ___New York_____, County of ___New York_____,

State of _____New York_____, hereby give notice that I have revoked, and do

hereby revoke, the power of attorney dated ___August 5_____, 19 89 given to

ED ROSE_____, empowering said
                    name of attorney in fact

ED ROSE_____ to act as my true
                    name of attorney in fact

and lawful attorney in fact, and I declare that all power and authority granted under said power of

attorney is hereby revoked and withdrawn.

Dated: ___January 2_____, 19 91

                                    _____
                                    Principal
                                    JIM ROSE
                                    _____
                                            typed name

Witnesses

_____ of _____2188 Clear Lake Drive,_____

New York, NY _____

_____ of _____300 16th Avenue,_____

New York, NY _____

Notarization

State of __New York_____

County of New York _____

On this ___2nd_____ day of _____January_____ in the year 19_91, before

me a Notary Public, State of _____New York_____, duly commissioned and

sworn, personally appeared _JIM ROSE_____,

name

personally known to me (or proved to me on the basis of satisfactory evidence) to be the person

whose name is subscribed to in the within instrument as principal, and acknowledged to me that

___he_____ executed the same.

he/she

IN WITNESS WHEREOF, I have hereunto set my hand and affixed my official seal in the

State of _____New York_____, County of New York_____ on the date

set forth above in this certificate.

_____

Notary Public

[Notary Seal]   State of __New York_____

My commission expires: _____, 19___

E. Sample Completed Revocation Form for Recorded Power of Attorney

The standard form used to revoke any power of attorney which has been recorded is contained in the Appendix as Form 22. Following is a completed sample.

Facts: Josie Jones revokes a conventional power of attorney authorizing her friend Jane Smith to represent her regarding the sale of Josie's house. Josie had planned a trip to the Far East, but became ill and had to postpone it. She can now handle the sale herself.

Form 22

Recording requested by and when recorded mail to

Josie Jones

1 Berkeley Way

Berkeley, California

Notice of Revocation of Recorded Power of Attorney

I, JOSIE JONES ,

name

of 1 Berkeley Way ,

street address

City of Berkeley , County of Alameda ,

State of California , executed a power of attorney dated

July 10 , 19 90 appointing JANE SMITH ,

name of attorney in fact

of 2 Berkeley Way ,

street address

City of Berkeley , County of Alameda ,

State of California , my true and lawful attorney in fact with

full power to act for me and in my name as therein specified, and such power of attorney was duly

recorded on July 10 in Book 98 , at Page 104 , of the

date of recordation

Official Records, County of Alameda , State of

California .

I hereby revoke said power of attorney given to said JANE SMITH ,

name of attorney in fact

and all power and authority contained therein.

Dated: August 20 , 19 90

_____
Principal
JOSIE JONES
_____
typed name

Witnesses

_____ of ____221 Shattuck Avenue_____

Berkeley CA
_____

_____ of ____9113 Shafter Avenue_____

Oakland CA
_____

Notarization

State of ___California_____

County of _Alameda_____

On this ____20th_____ day of _____August_____ in the year 19_90_, before

me a Notary Public, State of ____California_____, duly commissioned and

sworn, personally appeared __JOSIE JONES_____,
                                              name

personally known to me (or proved to me on the basis of satisfactory evidence) to be the person

whose name is subscribed to in the within instrument as principal, and acknowledged to me that

____she_____ executed the same.
        he/she

IN WITNESS WHEREOF, I have hereunto set my hand and affixed my official seal in the

State of _____California_____, County of _____Alameda_____ on the

date set forth above in this certificate.

_____
Notary Public

[Notary Seal]   State of ___California_____

                                 My commission expires: _____, 19___

CHAPTER 11

LAWYERS AND LEGAL RESEARCH

For a variety of reasons, you may determine that you need more legal information than is presented in this book. In the last analysis, you're the only one who can make the decision as to what's required to prepare the power of attorney you desire.

Doing more research or visiting a lawyer can be particularly important if you live in a state where there may be legal concerns or limits regarding a financial durable power of attorney (see Chapter 3, Section B(1), Chart 3) or for health care (see Chapter 6, Section B(1), Chart 4). Or, you might want to check out your state's laws carefully, so you're sure no technicality has been overlooked. Beyond these needs, there are several other possible reasons why you might want further, more specific information. Perhaps you want precise information regarding the duties your state imposes on attorneys in fact (i.e., trust, fair dealing, etc.). Maybe you want to learn about matters related to your durable power of attorney, such as the preparation of a will or a trust.

Realistically, if you need further legal information, you have three options:

- Hire a lawyer to find out all the answers you want;

- Learn to do your own legal research; or

- Combine these approaches.

Let's explore these options.

A. Using Lawyers[1]

If you decide you want a lawyer to review your draft power of attorney, first be clear with yourself about what you expect the lawyer to do. For most intelligent consumers, consulting with a lawyer should not mean that you tell him, "I want a power of attorney, so please prepare one for me."

---

[1] Ambrose Bierce defines a lawyer as "one skilled in circumvention of the law."

At a minimum, you should take the time to understand your needs, and prepare your own draft power of attorney. Most readers of this book will probably want an attorney to do little more than check their draft over, answer specific questions and insure that the finished product complies with all their state's legal requirements. If you do the initial drafting work yourself, a lawyer's fees should be reasonable.

What type of lawyer do you want? Probably a lawyer with some experience with estate planning, or, better yet, actually preparing powers of attorney. Particularly if you have questions or uncertainty about an aspect of your state's laws, you want someone with experience in the field. As I've explained, it's a relatively new one, and many general practice attorneys aren't very familiar with it. If you do see an estate planning lawyer, be sure to tell her what you want, and discuss and agree on her fee before you hire her. Except for complicated cases (unusual in this area), a lawyer should be able to review your document in no more than an hour or so. Since lawyers' fees are generally charged on an hours-worked basis, you're not getting into an open-ended, big-fee situation.

1. Finding a Lawyer

All this sounds good, you may think, but how do I find a lawyer? The trick isn't just finding (or being found by) any lawyer, but retaining one who is trustworthy, competent, and charges fairly. A few words of advice may be helpful.

It's important that you feel personal rapport with your lawyer. At the same time, you want a lawyer who treats you as an equal. In this regard, you obviously don't want to let the lawyer cast you in the role of a passive "client" (interestingly, the Latin root of the word client translates as "to obey," "to hear"). If he tries to do this, it's probably wise to hire someone else.

Personal contacts are the traditional, and probably the best, means for locating a good lawyer. If you've got a close friend who found an estate planning lawyer he liked, chances are you'll like her too. If you can't get a recommendation from a friend, here are some suggestions for finding a lawyer you'll be pleased with:

- Check with people you know who own their own businesses. Almost anyone running a small business has had to use a lawyer at some time. Chances are they've found one they like. Even if that lawyer doesn't do estate planning, she'll probably know one who does.

- Check with people you know in any political or social organization you're involved with. They may know of a lawyer whose attitudes are similar to yours.

- Call referral panels set up by local bar associations, but be cautious—there's often a charge for referral. While lawyers are supposed to be screened as to their specialty to get on these panels, screening is usually perfunctory. Normally the main qualification to get listed on the panel is that the lawyer needs business, so never assume a bar association referral is a seal of approval. Question the lawyer and make your own judgment, just as you would if you got a referral any other way.

- Check the classified ads under "Attorneys," especially for estate planning attorneys. Young attorneys just starting out often advertise low rates to build up a practice. Also, there are quite a few attorneys around who are no longer interested in handling court-contested matters, but provide consultations at low rates. This could be just what you need.

When you find a lawyer, talk to her personally so you can get an idea of how friendly and sympathetic she is to your concerns. Explain that you've drafted your own power of attorney, and you want the attorney to check it over for you. Ask some specific questions. If the lawyer answers them clearly and

concisely, explaining, not talking down to you, fine. On the other hand, if a lawyer acts wise but says little, except to ask that the problem be placed in her hands (with the appropriate fee, of course), watch out. You're either dealing with someone who isn't knowledgeable about powers of attorney and won't admit it (fairly common) or someone who finds it impossible to let go of the "me expert, you peasant" view of life (even more common).

2. Paying a Lawyer

While fancy offices, three-piece suits and solemn faces are no guarantee (or even any indication) that a lawyer is one you'll like, this traditional style will typically insure that you'll be charged a high fee. If you select a lawyer with a suite on top of a downtown office building, remember you'll be charged substantially for that high overhead, impressive view and repressed demeanor. Also remember that your consultation is likely to seem quite minor compared to those corporate clients who pay $200 to $500 per hour. At Nolo, our experience tells us that high fees and quality service don't necessarily go hand in hand. Indeed, the attorneys we think most highly of tend to charge fairly moderate fees.

Again, when you do locate a lawyer, settle your fee arrangement before you agree to a meeting. Generally, we feel that fees in the range of $75 to $150 per hour are fair depending on the area of the country and what you want the lawyer to do. Simply checking and making minor corrections to a power of attorney shouldn't take more than an hour or two. If a lawyer says that powers of attorney are complex and costly matters, call someone else.

B. Doing Your Own Legal Research

Doing your own research is a definite alternative to hiring a lawyer to review your power of attorney. For those who are willing to learn how, there can be real benefits. Not only will you save some money, you'll gain a sense of mastery over an area of law, generating a confidence that will benefit you should you deal with other legal matters.

Fortunately, researching powers of attorney, whether conventional or durable, is an area well suited to doing your own research. Primarily, you need only check the statutes of your state to see what requirements they impose on powers of attorney, particularly durable powers of attorney.

How can you locate and understand your state's statutes? First, go to a law library (often located in your county courthouse), or a public library with a good law collection. Law libraries are normally supported by your tax dollars, or the fees paid to file legal papers, and are open to the public. In my experience, law librarians are usually helpful and courteous to nonlawyers who wish to learn to do their own legal research. Ask them how you can locate the state's statutes (these are called "codes," "laws," or "statutes," depending on the state). Usually you want an "annotated version," which contains both your state's statutes and excerpts from any relevant judicial decisions and cross references to related articles and commentaries.

Once you've found your state's statutes, check the general index for provisions dealing with "Powers of Attorney" or "Durable Powers of Attorney." Generally, you'll find what you want in the volume of statutes dealing with your state's basic civil laws. These will be called a name such as "Civil Code." These codes are numbered sequentially, and once you get the correct number in the index, it's easy to find the statute you need. If you have trouble, the law librarian will usually be happy to help.

Once you've looked at the basic law you'll probably want to check any recent court decisions mentioned in the "Annotation" section of the code immediately following the law itself. (Check the back of the statute book to see if there's a "pocket part" inserted inside the back cover which will contain statutory changes and court decisions since the hardback book was printed.)

Also very helpful can be form books, how-to-do-it books written primarily for lawyers. There will likely be a "form book" which contains sample durable power of attorney forms valid in your state. You may ask the law librarian for help with this. Once you find the forms which are in use in your state, check them against any sample form you wish to use from this book.

To do further legal research about power of attorney law, you'll need a basic understanding which includes more depth on how statutes and code books work and how you can read and comprehend them. The best book explaining how to do your own legal work is *Legal Research: How to Find and Understand the Law* by Stephen Elias (Nolo Press). If you ever plan to enter a law library, you'll want to have it tucked under your arm.

APPENDIX

Warning: If you re-type any of these forms, all type which is printed in bold face on the tear-out forms must be typewritten in capital letters.

This appendix contains the following forms in the order listed. Do not complete a tear-out form until you have read this book.

Form 1

Recording requested by and when recorded mail to

_____

_____

_____

Financial Durable Power of Attorney

WARNING TO PERSON EXECUTING THIS DOCUMENT

THIS IS AN IMPORTANT LEGAL DOCUMENT. IT CREATES A DURABLE POWER OF ATTORNEY. BEFORE EXECUTING THIS DOCUMENT, YOU SHOULD KNOW THESE IMPORTANT FACTS:

1. THIS DOCUMENT MAY PROVIDE THE PERSON YOU DESIGNATE AS YOUR ATTORNEY IN FACT WITH BROAD POWERS TO MANAGE, DISPOSE, SELL, AND CONVEY YOUR REAL AND PERSONAL PROPERTY AND TO BORROW MONEY USING YOUR PROPERTY AS SECURITY FOR THE LOAN.

2. THESE POWERS WILL EXIST FOR AN INDEFINITE PERIOD OF TIME UNLESS YOU LIMIT THEIR DURATION IN THIS DOCUMENT. THESE POWERS WILL CONTINUE TO EXIST NOTWITHSTANDING YOUR SUBSEQUENT DISABILITY OR INCAPACITY.

3. YOU HAVE THE RIGHT TO REVOKE OR TERMINATE THIS DURABLE POWER OF ATTORNEY.

IF THERE IS ANYTHING ABOUT THIS FORM THAT YOU DO NOT UNDERSTAND, YOU SHOULD ASK A LAWYER TO EXPLAIN IT TO YOU.

Durable Power of Attorney

1. Creation of Durable Power of Attorney

By signing this document, I, _____,
name

intend to create a durable power of attorney. This durable power of attorney shall not be affected

by my subsequent disability or incapacity, and shall remain effective until my death, or until

revoked by me in writing.

2. Effective Date

This durable power of attorney shall become effective as of the date of my signing it.

3. Designation of Attorney in Fact

I, ______________________________, hereby appoint
name

______________________________ of
name

______________________________ as my
address

attorney in fact, to act for me and in my name and for my use and benefit. Should

____
name

for any reasons fail to serve or cease to serve as my attorney in fact, I appoint

______________________________ of
name

____
address

to be my attorney in fact.

4. Authority of Attorney in Fact

(A) Except as specified in Paragraph 4(B), I grant my attorney in fact full power and authority over all my property, real and personal, and authorize ______________ (him/her) to do and perform all and every act which I as an owner of said property could do or perform and I hereby ratify and confirm all that my attorney in fact shall do or cause to be done under this durable power of attorney.

(B) My attorney in fact has no authority to give any of my property to, or use any of my property for the benefit of ______________________ (himself/herself).

5. Reliance by Third Parties

The powers conferred on my attorney in fact by this durable power of attorney may be exercisable by my attorney in fact alone, and my attorney in fact's signature or act under the authority granted in this durable power of attorney may be accepted by any third person or organization as fully authorized by me and with the same force and effect as if I were personally present, competent and acting on my own behalf.

No person or organization who relies on this durable power of attorney or any representation

my attorney in fact makes regarding _____ authority, including, but not limited to:

(i)   the fact that this durable power of attorney has not been revoked;

(ii) that I, _____ was competent

      to execute this power of attorney;

(iii) the authority of my attorney in fact under this durable power of attorney;

shall incur any liability to me, my estate, heirs, successors or assigns because of such reliance on

this durable power of attorney or on any such representation by my attorney in fact.

Executed this _____ day of _____, 19____, at

_____.

_____

Principal

Witnesses

_____ of _____

_____

_____ of _____

_____

Notarization

State of _____

County of _____

On this _____ day of _____ in the year 19___,

before me a Notary Public, State of _____, duly commissioned

and sworn, personally appeared _____,

personally known to me (or proved to me on the basis of satisfactory evidence) to be the person

whose name is subscribed to in this instrument, and acknowledged to me that _____
he/she

executed the same.

IN WITNESS WHEREOF, I have hereunto set my hand and affixed my official seal in the

State of _____, County of _____

on the date set forth above in this certificate.

_____

Notary Public

[Notary Seal]   State of _____

My commission expires _____

Form 2

Recording requested by and when recorded mail to

_____

_____

_____

Springing Financial Durable Power of Attorney

WARNING TO PERSON EXECUTING THIS DOCUMENT

THIS IS AN IMPORTANT LEGAL DOCUMENT. IT CREATES A DURABLE POWER OF ATTORNEY. BEFORE EXECUTING THIS DOCUMENT, YOU SHOULD KNOW THESE IMPORTANT FACTS:

1. THIS DOCUMENT MAY PROVIDE THE PERSON YOU DESIGNATE AS YOUR ATTORNEY IN FACT WITH BROAD POWERS TO MANAGE, DISPOSE, SELL, AND CONVEY YOUR REAL AND PERSONAL PROPERTY AND TO BORROW MONEY USING YOUR PROPERTY AS SECURITY FOR THE LOAN.

2. THESE POWERS WILL EXIST FOR AN INDEFINITE PERIOD OF TIME UNLESS YOU LIMIT THEIR DURATION IN THIS DOCUMENT. THESE POWERS WILL CONTINUE TO EXIST NOTWITHSTANDING YOUR SUBSEQUENT DISABILITY OR INCAPACITY.

3. YOU HAVE THE RIGHT TO REVOKE OR TERMINATE THIS DURABLE POWER OF ATTORNEY.

IF THERE IS ANYTHING ABOUT THIS FORM THAT YOU DO NOT UNDERSTAND, YOU SHOULD ASK A LAWYER TO EXPLAIN IT TO YOU.

Durable Power of Attorney

1. Creation of Durable Power of Attorney

By signing this document, I, _____,
name

intend to create a durable power of attorney. This durable power of attorney shall not be affected

by my subsequent disability or incapacity, and shall remain effective until my death, or until

revoked by me in writing.

2. Effective Date

This durable power of attorney shall become effective only in the event that I become

incapacitated or disabled so that I am not able to manage my financial affairs in which case it

shall become effective as of the date of the written statement by a physician, as provided in

Paragraph 3. If the durable power of attorney becomes effective, it shall remain effective during any period when I am incapacitated or disabled until my death, or until revoked by me.

3. Determination of Incapacity

The determination of whether I have become incapacitated or disabled so that I am not able to manage my financial affairs shall be made in writing by a licensed physician; if possible, the physician shall be _____ of

_____.
address

In the event that a licensed physician has made a written determination that I have become incapacitated or disabled and am not able to manage my own financial affairs, that written statement shall be attached to the original of this durable power of attorney.

4. Designation of Attorney in Fact

If I become incapacitated or disabled so that I am not able to manage my financial affairs, I,

_____, hereby appoint
name

_____ of
name

_____
address

as my attorney in fact, to act for me and in my name and for my use and benefit. Should

_____ for any reasons fail to serve or cease
name

to serve as my attorney in fact, I appoint _____ of
name

_____
address

to be my attorney in fact.

5. Authority of Attorney in Fact

(A) Except as specified in Paragraph 5(B), I grant my attorney in fact full power and authority over all my property, real and personal, and authorize _____ to do and perform
him/her

all and every act which I as an owner of said property could do or perform and I hereby ratify and confirm all that my attorney in fact shall do or cause to be done under this durable power of attorney.

(B) My attorney in fact has no authority to give any of my property to, or use any of my

property for the benefit of _____.
himself/herself

6. Reliance by Third Parties

The powers conferred on my attorney in fact by this durable power of attorney may be

exercisable by my attorney in fact alone, and my attorney in fact's signature or act under the

authority granted in this durable power of attorney may be accepted by any third person or

organization as fully authorized by me and with the same force and effect as if I were personally

present, competent and acting on my own behalf.

No person or organization who relies on this durable power of attorney or any representation

my attorney in fact makes regarding _____ authority, including, but not limited to:
his/her

(i)   the fact that this durable power of attorney has not been revoked;

(ii) that I, _____ was competent
name
      to execute this power of attorney;

(iii) the authority of my attorney in fact under this durable power of attorney;

shall incur any liability to me, my estate, heirs, successors or assigns because of such reliance on

this durable power of attorney or on any such representation by my attorney in fact.

Executed this _____ day of _____, 19___, at

_____.

_____

Principal

Witnesses

_____ of _____

_____

_____ of _____

_____

Notarization

State of _____

County of _____

On this _____ day of _____ in the year 19___,

before me a Notary Public, State of _____, duly commissioned

and sworn, personally appeared _____,

personally known to me (or proved to me on the basis of satisfactory evidence) to be the person

whose name is subscribed to in this instrument, and acknowledged to me that _____

_{he/she}

executed the same.

IN WITNESS WHEREOF, I have hereunto set my hand and affixed my official seal in the

State of _____, County of _____

on the date set forth above in this certificate.

_____

Notary Public

[Notary Seal]   State of _____

My commission expires _____

Form 3

California Statutory Short Form Durable Power of Attorney

WARNING! UNLESS YOU LIMIT THE POWER IN THIS DOCUMENT, THIS DOCUMENT GIVES YOUR AGENT THE POWER TO ACT FOR YOU IN ANY WAY YOU COULD ACT FOR YOURSELF. FOR EXAMPLE, YOUR AGENT CAN:

- BUY, SELL, AND MANAGE REAL AND PERSONAL PROPERTY FOR YOU. THIS MEANS THAT YOUR AGENT CAN SELL YOUR HOME, YOUR SECURITIES AND YOUR OTHER PROPERTY.
- DEPOSIT AND WITHDRAW MONEY FROM YOUR CHECKING AND SAVINGS ACCOUNTS.
- BORROW MONEY USING YOUR PROPERTY AS SECURITY FOR THE LOAN.
- PUT THINGS IN AND TAKE THINGS OUT OF YOUR SAFETY DEPOSIT BOX.
- OPERATE YOUR BUSINESS FOR YOU.
- PREPARE AND FILE TAX RETURNS FOR YOU AND ACT FOR YOU IN TAX MATTERS.
- ESTABLISH TRUSTS FOR YOU AND TAKE OTHER ACTIONS FOR YOU IN CONNECTION WITH PROBATE AND ESTATE PLANNING MATTERS.
- PROVIDE FOR THE SUPPORT AND WELFARE OF YOUR SPOUSE, CHILDREN, AND DEPENDENTS.
- CONTINUE PAYMENTS TO THE CHURCH AND OTHER ORGANIZATIONS OF WHICH YOU ARE A MEMBER AND MAKE GIFTS TO YOUR SPOUSE, DESCENDANTS, AND CHARITIES.

THIS DOCUMENT DOES NOT AUTHORIZE YOUR AGENT TO MAKE MEDICAL AND OTHER HEALTH CARE DECISIONS FOR YOU. YOU CAN DESIGNATE AN AGENT TO MAKE HEALTH CARE DECISIONS FOR YOU ONLY BY A SEPARATE DOCUMENT.

IT MAY BE IN YOUR BEST INTEREST TO CONSULT WITH A CALIFORNIA LAWYER BECAUSE THE POWERS GRANTED BY THIS DOCUMENT ARE BROAD AND SWEEPING. THEY ARE DEFINED IN SECTIONS 2460 TO 2473, INCLUSIVE, OF THE CALIFORNIA CIVIL CODE.

THE POWERS GRANTED BY THIS DOCUMENT WILL EXIST FOR AN INDEFINITE PERIOD OF TIME UNLESS YOU LIMIT THEIR DURATION IN THIS DOCUMENT. THESE POWERS WILL CONTINUE TO EXIST NOTWITHSTANDING YOUR SUBSEQUENT DISABILITY OR INCAPACITY UNLESS YOU INDICATE OTHERWISE IN THIS DOCUMENT.

YOU CAN ELIMINATE POWERS OF YOUR AGENT BY CROSSING OUT ANY ONE OR MORE OF THE POWERS LISTED IN PARAGRAPH 3 OF THIS FORM. YOU CAN WRITE OTHER LIMITATIONS AND SPECIAL PROVISIONS IN PARAGRAPH 4 OF THIS FORM. HOWEVER, IF YOU DO NOT WANT TO GRANT YOUR AGENT THE POWER TO ACT FOR YOU IN ANY WAY YOU COULD ACT FOR YOURSELF, IT MAY BE IN YOUR BEST INTEREST TO CONSULT WITH A LAWYER INSTEAD OF USING THIS FORM.

THIS DOCUMENT MUST BE SIGNED BY TWO WITNESSES AND BE NOTARIZED TO BE VALID.

YOU HAVE THE RIGHT TO REVOKE OR TERMINATE THIS POWER OF ATTORNEY.

YOU ARE NOT REQUIRED TO USE THIS FORM; YOU MAY USE A DIFFERENT POWER OF ATTORNEY IF THAT IS DESIRED BY THE PARTIES CONCERNED.

IF THERE IS ANYTHING ABOUT THIS FORM THAT YOU DO NOT UNDERSTAND, YOU SHOULD ASK A LAWYER TO EXPLAIN IT TO YOU.

1. Designation of Agent

I, _____

_____ [Insert your name and address] do hereby appoint

_____

[Insert name and address of your agent or each agent if you want to designate more than one] as

my-attorney in fact (agent) to act for me and in my name as authorized in this document.

2. Creation of Durable Power of Attorney

By this document I intend to create a general power of attorney under Sections 2450 to 2473,

inclusive, of the California Civil Code. Subject to any limitations in this document, this power of

attorney is a durable power of attorney and shall not be affected by my subsequent incapacity.

[If you want this power of attorney to terminate automatically when you lack capacity, you

must so state in paragraph 4 ("Special Provisions and Limitations") below.]

3. Statement of Authority Granted

Subject to any limitations in this document, I hereby grant to my agent(s) full power and

authority to act for me and in my name, in any way which I myself could act, if I were personally

present and able to act, with respect to the following matters as each of them is defined in

Chapter 3 (commencing with Section 2450) of Title 9 of Part 4 of Division 3 of the California

Civil Code to the extent that I am permitted by law to act through an agent.

    (1)   Real estate transactions.
    (2)   Tangible personal property transactions.
    (3)   Bond, share, and commodity transactions.
    (4)   Financial institution transactions.
    (5)   Business operating transactions.
    (6)   Insurance transactions.
    (7)   Retirement plan transactions.
    (8)   Estate transactions.
    (9)   Claims and litigation.
    (10)   Tax matters.
    (11)   Personal relationships and affairs.
    (12)   Benefits from military service.
    (13)   Records, reports, and statements.
    (14)   Full and unqualified authority to my agent(s) to delegate any or all of the foregoing powers to any person or persons whom my agent(s) shall select.
    (15)   All other matters.

[Strike out any one or more of the items above to which you do not desire to give your agent authority. Such elimination of any one or more of items (1) to (14), inclusive, automatically constitutes an elimination of item (15). TO STRIKE OUT AN ITEM, YOU MUST DRAW A LINE THROUGH THE TEXT OF THAT ITEM.]

4. Special Provisions and Limitations

In exercising the authority under this power of attorney, my agent(s) is subject to the following special provisions and limitations:

_____

_____

_____

_____

[Special provisions and limitations may be included in the statutory short form power of attorney only if they conform to the requirements of Section 2455 of the California Civil Code.]

5. Exercise of Power of Attorney Where More than One Agent Designated

If I have designated more than one agent, the agents are to act

_____.

[If you designate more than one agent and wish each agent alone to be able to exercise this power, insert in this blank the word "severally." Failure to make an insertion or the insertion of the word "jointly" will require that the agents act jointly.]

6. Duration

[The powers granted by this document will exist for an indefinite period of time unless you limit their duration below.]

This power of attorney expires on _____.

[Fill in this space ONLY if you want the authority of your agent to terminate before your death.]

7. Nomination of a Conservator of Estate

[A conservator of the estate may be appointed for you if a court decides that one should be appointed. The conservator is responsible for the management of your financial affairs and your property. You are not required to nominate a conservator but you may do so. The court will appoint the person you nominate unless that would be contrary to your best interests. You may, but are not required to, nominate as your conservator the same person you named in paragraph 1 as your agent. You may nominate a person as your conservator by completing the space below.]

If conservator of the estate is to be appointed for me, I nominate the following person to serve as conservator of the estate _____.

Date and Signature of Principal

[YOU MUST DATE AND SIGN THIS POWER OF ATTORNEY]

I sign my name to this Statutory Short Form Power of Attorney on _____,
date

19_____ at _____, _____.
city state

_____
signature

[THIS POWER OF ATTORNEY WILL NOT BE VALID UNLESS IT IS BOTH (1) SIGNED BY TWO ADULT WITNESSES WHO ARE PRESENT WHEN YOU SIGN OR ACKNOWLEDGE YOUR SIGNATURE; AND (2) ACKNOWLEDGED BEFORE A NOTARY PUBLIC IN CALIFORNIA.]

Statement of Witnesses

[**READ CAREFULLY BEFORE SIGNING.** You can sign as a witness only if you personally know the principal or the identity of the principal is proved to you by convincing evidence.]

[To have convincing evidence of the identity of the principal, you must be presented with and reasonably rely on any one or more of the following:

(1) An identification card or driver's license issued by the California Department of Motor Vehicles that is current or has been issued within five years.

(2) A passport issued by the Department of State of the United States that is current or has been issued within five years.

(3) Any of the following documents if the document is current or has been issued within five years and contains a photograph and description of the person named on it, is signed by the person, and bears a serial or other identifying number:

(a) A passport issued by a foreign government that has been stamped by the United States Immigration and Naturalization Service.

(b) A driver's license issued by a state other than California or by a Canadian or Mexican public agency authorized to issue driver's licenses.

(c) An identification card issued by a state other than California.

(d) An identification card issued by any branch of the armed forces of the United States.]

(Other kinds of proof of identity are not allowed.)

I declare under penalty of perjury under the laws of California that the person who signed or acknowledged this document is personally known to me (or proved to me on the basis of convincing evidence) to be the principal, that the principal signed or acknowledged this power of attorney in my presence, and that the principal appears to be of sound mind and under no duress, fraud, or undue influence.

Signature:_____ Residence Address:_____

Print Name:_____ _____

Date:_____ _____

Signature:_____ Residence Address:_____

Print Name:_____ _____

Date:_____ _____

Notarization

State of _____)
) ss.

County of _____)

On this _____ day of _____, in the year 19___, before me,

_____
name of notary public

personally appeared _____,
name of principal

personally known to me (or proved to me on the basis of satisfactory evidence) to be the person

whose name is subscribed to this instrument, and acknowledged that he or she executed it.

[Notary Seal]   _____
                                              signature of notary public

Form 4

New York General Power of Attorney

WARNING: MUST BE NOTARIZED

NOTICE: THE POWERS GRANTED BY THIS DOCUMENT ARE BROAD AND SWEEPING. THEY ARE DEFINED IN NEW YORK GENERAL OBLIGATIONS LAW, ARTICLE 5, TITLE 15, SECTIONS 5-1502A THROUGH 5-1503, WHICH EXPRESSLY PERMITS THE USE OF ANY OTHER OR DIFFERENT FORM OF POWER OF ATTORNEY DESIRED BY THE PARTIES CONCERNED.

Know All Men By These Presents, which are intended to constitute a General Power of

Attorney pursuant to Article 5, Title 15 of the New York General Obligations Law:

That I _____
insert name and address of the principal

do hereby appoint _____
insert name and address of the agent, or each agent, if more than one is designated

_____ my attorney(s)-in-fact to act

_____.

(a) If more than one agent is designated and the principal wishes each agent alone to be able

to exercise the power conferred, insert in this blank the word "severally." Failure to make any

insertion or the insertion of the word "jointly" will require the agents to act jointly.

In my name, place and stead in any way which I myself could do, if I were personally present,

with respect to the following matters as each of them is defined in Title 15 of Article 5 of the

New York General Obligations Law to the extent that I am permitted by law to act through an

agent:

[Strike out and initial in the opposite box any one or more of the subdivisions as to which

the principal does NOT desire to give the agent authority. Such elimination of any one or more

of subdivisions (A) to (L), inclusive, shall automatically constitute an elimination also of subdivi-

sion (M).]

To strike out any subdivision the principal must draw a line through the text of that subdivi-

sion AND write his initials in the box opposite.

(A)	real estate transactions;	[ ]
(B)	chattel and goods transactions;	[ ]
(C)	bond, share and commodity transactions;	[ ]

(D) banking transactions;   [   ]

(E) business operating transactions;   [   ]

(F) insurance transactions;   [   ]

(G) estate transactions;   [   ]

(H) claims and litigation;   [   ]

(I) personal relationships and affairs;   [   ]

(J) benefits from military service;   [   ]

(K) records, reports and statements;   [   ]

(L) full and unqualified authority to my
     attorney(s)-in-fact to delegate any or
     all of the foregoing powers to any
     person or persons whom my
     attorney(s)-in-fact shall select;   [   ]

(M) all other matters   [   ]

[Special provisions and limitations may be included in the statutory short form power of

attorney only if they conform to the requirements of the section 5-1503 of the New York General

Obligations Law.]

This power of attorney shall not be affected by the subsequent disability or incompetence of

the principal.

In Witness Whereof, I have hereunto signed my name and affixed my seal this _____ day

of _____ , 19___.

                                        _____
                                                signature of principal

STATE OF NEW YORK   )
) ss.
COUNTY OF   )

On _____,19___ before me came

_____, known to me to be,

or proved on the basis of satisfactory evidence to be, the individual who executed the foregoing

durable power of attorney, and ____ acknowledged to me that ____ executed the same.

[Notary Seal]   _____

Form 5

Durable Power of Attorney for Health Care

1. Creation of Durable Power of Attorney

To my family, relatives, friends and my physicians, health care providers, community care facilities and any other person who may have an interest or duty in my medical care or treatment:

I, _____, being of sound mind,
　　　　　　　　　　　　　　　　name

willfully and voluntarily intend to create by this document a durable power of attorney for my health care by appointing the person designated as my attorney in fact to make health care decisions for me. This power of attorney shall not be affected by my subsequent incapacity.

2. Designation of Attorney in Fact

The person designated to be my attorney in fact for health care is

_____ of
　　　　　　　　　　　　　　　　name

_____ . If
　　　　　　　　　　　　　　　　address

_____ for any
　　　　　　　　　　　　　　　　name

reason shall fail to serve or ceases to serve as my attorney in fact for health care,

_____ of
　　　　　　　　　　　　　　　　name

_____ shall be
　　　　　　　　　　　　　　　　address

my attorney in fact for health care.

3. Effective on Signing

This durable power of attorney shall become effective as of the date I sign it [or specify some other specific date].

4. Authority of My Attorney in Fact

My attorney in fact shall have all lawful authority permissible to make health care decisions for me, including the authority to consent, or withdraw consent or refuse consent to any care, treatment, service or procedure to maintain, diagnose or treat my physical or mental condition, EXCEPT

5. Inspection and Disclosure of Information Relating to My Physical or Mental Health

Subject to any limitations in this document, my attorney in fact has the power and authority to do all of the following:

(a) Request, review, and receive any information, verbal or written, regarding my physical or mental health, including, but not limited to, medical and hospital records.

(b) Execute on my behalf any releases or other documents that may be required in order to obtain this information.

(c) Consent to the disclosure of this information.

6. Signing Documents, Waivers, and Releases

Where necessary to implement the health care decisions that my attorney in fact is authorized by this document to make, my attorney in fact has the power and authority to execute on my behalf all of the following:

(a) Documents titled or purporting to be a "Refusal to Permit Treatment" and "Leaving Hospital Against Medical Advice."

(b) Any necessary waiver or release from liability required by a hospital or physician.

7. Duration

I intend that this Durable Power of Attorney remain effective until my death, or until revoked by me in writing.

Executed this _____ day of _____,

19____ at _____.

_____
Principal

Witnesses

I declare that the principal is personally known to me, that the principal signed or acknow-ledged this durable power of attorney in my presence, and that the principal appears to be of sound mind and under no duress, fraud, or undue influence.

I further declare that I am not related to the principal by blood, marriage, or adoption, and to the best of my knowledge, I am not entitled to any part of the estate of the principal upon the death of the principal under a Will now existing or by operation of law.

_____ of _____

_____

_____ of _____

_____

Notarization

State of _____

County of _____

On this _____ day of _____ in the year 19___, before me a Notary Public, State of _____, duly commissioned and sworn, personally appeared _____, personally known to me (or proved to me on the basis of satisfactory evidence) to be the person whose name is subscribed to in this instrument, and acknowledged to me that _____ he/she executed the same.

IN WITNESS WHEREOF, I have hereunto set my hand and affixed my official seal in the State of _____, County of _____ on the date set forth above in this certificate.

_____

Notary Public

[Notary Seal]   State of _____

My commission expires _____

Form 6

Springing Durable Power of Attorney for Health Care

1. Creation of Durable Power of Attorney

To my family, relatives, friends and my physicians, health care providers, community care facilities and any other person who may have an interest or duty in my medical care or treatment:

I, _____, being of sound

name

mind, willfully and voluntarily intend to create by this document a durable power of attorney for my health care by appointing the person designated as my attorney in fact to make health care decisions for me in the event I become incapacitated and am unable to make health care decisions for myself. This power of attorney shall not be affected by my subsequent incapacity.

2. Designation of Attorney in Fact

The person designated to be my attorney in fact for health care in the event I become

incapacitated is _____ of

name

_____. If

address

_____

name

for any reason shall fail to serve or ceases to serve as my attorney in fact for health care,

_____ of

name

_____ shall be

address

my attorney in fact for health care.

3. Effective on Incapacity

This durable power of attorney shall become effective in the event I become incapacitated and am unable to make health care decisions for myself, in which case it shall become effective as of the date of the written statement by a physician, as provided in Paragraph 4.

4. Determination of Incapacity

(a) The determination that I have become incapacitated and am unable to make health care decisions shall be made in writing by a licensed physician. If possible, the determination shall be

made by _____,
name of physician

_____.
address

(b) In the event that a licensed physician has made a written determination that I have become incapacitated and am not able to make health care decisions for myself, that written statement shall be attached to the original document of this durable power of attorney.

5. Authority of My Attorney in Fact

My attorney in fact shall have all lawful authority permissible to make health care decisions for me, including the authority to consent, or withdraw consent or refuse consent to any care, treatment, service or procedure to maintain, diagnose or treat my physical or mental condition, EXCEPT

6. Inspection and Disclosure of Information Relating to My Physical or Mental Health

Subject to any limitations in this document, my attorney in fact has the power and authority to do all of the following:

(a) Request, review, and receive any information, verbal or written, regarding my physical or mental health, including, but not limited to, medical and hospital records.

(b) Execute on my behalf any releases or other documents that may be required in order to obtain this information.

(c) Consent to the disclosure of this information.

7. Signing Documents, Waivers, and Releases

Where necessary to implement the health care decisions that my attorney in fact is authorized by this document to make, my attorney in fact has the power and authority to execute on my behalf all of the following:

(a) Documents titled or purporting to be a "Refusal to Permit Treatment" and "Leaving Hospital Against Medical Advice."

(b) Any necessary waiver or release from liability required by a hospital or physician.

8. Duration

I intend that this Durable Power of Attorney remain effective until my death, or until revoked by me in writing.

Executed this _____ day of _____,

19____ at _____.

_____
Principal

Witnesses

I declare that the principal is personally known to me, that the principal signed or acknowledged this durable power of attorney in my presence, that the principal appears to be of sound mind and under no duress, fraud, or undue influence.

I further declare that I am not related to the principal by blood, marriage, or adoption, and to the best of my knowledge, I am not entitled to any part of the estate of that principal upon the death of the principal under a Will now existing or by operation of law.

_____ of _____

_____

_____ of _____

_____

Notarization

State of _____

County of _____

On this _____ day of _____ in the year 19___,

before me a Notary Public, State of _____, duly commissioned

and sworn, personally appeared _____,

personally known to me (or proved to me on the basis of satisfactory evidence) to be the person

whose name is subscribed to in this instrument, and acknowledged to me that _____
                                                                              he/she

executed the same.

IN WITNESS WHEREOF, I have hereunto set my hand and affixed my official seal in the

State of _____, County of _____ on

the date set forth above in this certificate.

_____

Notary Public

[Notary Seal]   State of _____

My commission expires _____

Idaho: A Durable Power of Attorney For Health Care

1. **Designation of Health Care Agent.** I, _____

insert your name and address

_____

do hereby designate and appoint _____

_____

[Insert name, address, and telephone number of one individual only as your agent to make health care decisions for you. None of the following may be designated as your agent: (1) your treating health care provider, (2) a nonrelative employee of your treating health care provider, (3) an operator of a community care facility, (4) a nonrelative employee of an operator of a community care facility.]

as my attorney in fact (agent) to make health care decisions for me as authorized in this document. For the purposes of this document, "health care decision" means consent, refusal of consent, or withdrawal of consent to any care, treatment, service, or procedure to maintain, diagnose, or treat an individual's physical condition.

2. **Creation of Durable Power of Attorney For Health Care.** By this document I intend to create a durable power of attorney for health care. This power of attorney shall not be affected by my subsequent incapacity.

3. **General Statement of Authority Granted.** Subject to any limitations in this document, I hereby grant to my agent full power and authority to make health care decisions for me to the same extent that I could make such decisions for myself if I had the capacity to do so. In exercising this authority, my agent shall make health care decisions that are consistent with my desires as stated in this document or otherwise made known to my agent, including, but not limited to, my desires concerning obtaining or refusing or withdrawing life-prolonging care, treatment, services, and procedures.

[If you want to limit the authority of your agent to make health care decisions for you, you can state the limitations in paragraph 4 ("Statement of Desires, Special Provisions, and Limitations") below. You can indicate your desires by including a statement of your desires in the same paragraph.]

4. Statement of Desires, Special Provisions, and Limitations.

[Your agent must make health care decisions that are consistent with your known desires. You can, but are not required to, state your desires in the space provided below. You should consider whether you want to include a statement of your desires concerning life-prolonging care, treatment, services, and procedures. You can also include a statement of your desires concerning other matters relating to your health care. You can also make your desires known to your agent by discussing your desires with your agent or by some other means. If there are any types of treatment that you do not want to be used, you should state them in the space below. If you want to limit in any other way the authority given your agent by this document, you should state the limits in the space below. If you do not state any limits, your agent will have broad powers to make health care decisions for you, except to the extent that there are limits provided by law.]

In exercising the authority under this durable power of attorney for health care, my agent shall act consistently with my desires as stated below and is subject to the special provisions and limitations stated in the living will. Additional statement of desires, special provisions, and limitations:

_____

_____

_____

_____

_____

[You may attach additional pages if you need more space to complete your statement. If you attach additional pages, you must date and sign each of the additional pages at the same time you date and sign this document.]

5. Inspection and Disclosure of Information Relating To My Physical Or Mental Health. Subject to any limitations in this document, my agent has the power and authority to do all of the following:

(a) Request, review, and receive any information, verbal or written, regarding my physical or mental health, including, but not limited to, medical and hospital records.

(b) Execute on my behalf any releases or other documents that may be required in order to obtain this information.

(c) Consent to the disclosure of this information.

(d) Consent to the donation of any of my organs for medical purposes.

[If you want to limit the authority of your agent to receive and disclose information relating to your health, you must state the limitations in paragraph 4 ("Statement of Desires, Special Provisions, and Limitations") above.]

6. Signing Documents, Waivers, and Releases. Where necessary to implement the health care decisions that my agent is authorized by this document to make, my agent has the power and authority to execute on my behalf all of the following:

(a) Documents titled or purporting to be a "Refusal to Permit Treatment" and "Leaving Hospital Against Medical Advice."

(b) Any necessary waiver or release from liability required by a hospital or physician.

7. Designation of Alternate Agents.

[You are not required to designate any alternate agents but you may do so. Any alternate agent you designate will be able to make the same health care decisions as the agent you designated in paragraph 1, above, in the event that agent is unable or ineligible to act as your agent. If the agent you designated is your spouse, he or she becomes ineligible to act as your agent if your marriage is dissolved.]

If the person designated as my agent in paragraph 1 is not available or becomes ineligible to act as my agent to make a health care decision for me or loses the mental capacity to make health care decisions for me, or if I revoke that person's appointment or authority to act as my agent to make health care decisions for me, then I designate and appoint the following persons to serve as my agent to make health care decisions for me as authorized in this document, such persons to serve in the order listed below:

A. First Alternate Agent _____

insert name, address, and telephone number of first alternate agent

_____

B. Second Alternate Agent _____

insert name, address, and telephone number of second alternate agent

_____

8. Prior Designations Revoked. I revoke any prior durable power of attorney for health care.

Date and Signature of Principal

(YOU MUST DATE AND SIGN THIS POWER OF ATTORNEY)

I sign my name to this Statutory Form Durable Power of Attorney for Health Care on

_____, at _____,
date   city

_____.
state

            _____

                             you sign here

(THIS POWER OF ATTORNEY WILL NOT BE VALID UNLESS IT IS SIGNED BY TWO QUALIFIED WITNESSES WHO ARE PRESENT WHEN YOU SIGN OR ACKNOWLEDGE YOUR SIGNATURE. IF YOU HAVE ATTACHED ANY ADDITIONAL PAGES TO THIS FORM, YOU MUST DATE AND SIGN EACH OF THE ADDITIONAL PAGES AT THE SAME TIME YOU DATE AND SIGN THIS POWER OF ATTORNEY.)

Statement of Witnesses

[This document must be witnessed by two qualified adult witnesses. None of the following may be used as a witness: (1) a person you designate as your agent or alternate agent, (2) a health care provider, (3) an employee of a health care provider, (4) the operator of a community care facility, (5) an employee of an operator of a community care facility. At least one of the witnesses must make the additional declaration set out following the place where the witnesses sign.]

I declare under penalty of perjury under the laws of Idaho that the person who signed or acknowledged this document is personally known to me (or proved to me on the basis of convincing evidence) to be the principal, that the principal signed or acknowledged this durable power of attorney in my presence, that the principal appears to be of sound mind and under no duress, fraud, or undue influence, that I am not the person appointed as attorney in fact by this document, and that I am not a health care provider, an employee of a health care provider, the operator of a community care facility, nor an employee of an operator of a community care facility.

Signature: _____

Print Name: _____

Date: _____ Residence Address: _____

_____

Signature: _____

Print Name: _____

Date: _____ Residence Address: _____

_____

(AT LEAST ONE OF THE ABOVE WITNESSES MUST ALSO SIGN.)

I further declare under penalty of perjury that I am not related to the principal by blood, marriage, or adoption, and, to the best of my knowledge, I am not entitled to any part of the estate of the principal upon the death of the principal under a will now existing or by operation of law.

Signature: _____

Signature: _____

Notary

(Signer of instrument may either have it witnessed as above or have his/her signature notarized as below, to legalize this instrument.)

State of Idaho

County of _____ ss.

On this ____ day of _____, 19___ before me personally appeared

_____, to me known
full name of signer of instrument

(or proved to me on the basis of satisfactory evidence) to be the person whose name is subscribed to this instrument, and acknowledged that he/she executed it. I declare under penalty of perjury that the person whose name is subscribed to this instrument appears to be of sound mind and under no duress, fraud, or undue influence.

[Notary Seal]   _____
                                                       signature of notary

Form 8

Nevada Durable Power of Attorney For Health Care Decisions

WARNING TO PERSON EXECUTING THIS DOCUMENT

THIS IS AN IMPORTANT LEGAL DOCUMENT. IT CREATES A DURABLE POWER OF ATTORNEY FOR HEALTH CARE. BEFORE EXECUTING THIS DOCUMENT, YOU SHOULD KNOW THESE IMPORTANT FACTS:

(1) THIS DOCUMENT GIVES THE PERSON YOU DESIGNATE AS YOUR ATTORNEY-IN-FACT THE POWER TO MAKE HEALTH CARE DECISIONS FOR YOU. THIS POWER IS SUBJECT TO ANY LIMITATIONS OR STATEMENT OF YOUR DESIRES THAT YOU INCLUDE IN THIS DOCUMENT. THE POWER TO MAKE HEALTH CARE DECISIONS FOR YOU MAY INCLUDE CONSENT, REFUSAL OF CONSENT, OR WITHDRAWAL OF CONSENT TO ANY CARE, TREATMENT, SERVICE, OR PROCEDURE TO MAINTAIN, DIAGNOSE, OR TREAT A PHYSICAL OR MENTAL CONDITION. YOU MAY STATE IN THIS DOCUMENT ANY TYPES OF TREATMENT OR PLACEMENTS THAT YOU DO NOT DESIRE.

(2) THE PERSON YOU DESIGNATE IN THIS DOCUMENT HAS A DUTY TO ACT CONSISTENT WITH YOUR DESIRES AS STATED IN THIS DOCUMENT OR OTHERWISE MADE KNOWN OR, IF YOUR DESIRES ARE UNKNOWN, TO ACT IN YOUR BEST INTERESTS.

(3) EXCEPT AS YOU OTHERWISE SPECIFY IN THIS DOCUMENT, THE POWER OF THE PERSON YOU DESIGNATE TO MAKE HEALTH CARE DECISIONS FOR YOU MAY INCLUDE THE POWER TO CONSENT TO YOUR DOCTOR NOT GIVING TREATMENT OR STOPPING TREATMENT WHICH WOULD KEEP YOU ALIVE.

(4) UNLESS YOU SPECIFY A SHORTER PERIOD IN THIS DOCUMENT, THIS POWER WILL EXIST INDEFINITELY FROM THE DATE YOU EXECUTE THIS DOCUMENT AND, IF YOU ARE UNABLE TO MAKE HEALTH CARE DECISIONS FOR YOURSELF, THIS POWER WILL CONTINUE TO EXIST UNTIL THE TIME WHEN YOU BECOME ABLE TO MAKE HEALTH CARE DECISIONS FOR YOURSELF.

(5) NOTWITHSTANDING THIS DOCUMENT, YOU HAVE THE RIGHT TO MAKE MEDICAL AND OTHER HEALTH CARE DECISIONS FOR YOURSELF SO LONG AS YOU CAN GIVE INFORMED CONSENT WITH RESPECT TO THE PARTICULAR DECISION. IN ADDITION, NO TREATMENT MAY BE GIVEN TO YOU OVER YOUR OBJECTION, AND HEALTH CARE NECESSARY TO KEEP YOU ALIVE MAY NOT BE STOPPED IF YOU OBJECT.

(6) YOU HAVE THE RIGHT TO REVOKE THE APPOINTMENT OF THE PERSON DESIGNATED IN THIS DOCUMENT TO MAKE HEALTH CARE DECISIONS FOR YOU BY NOTIFYING THAT PERSON OF THE REVOCATION ORALLY OR IN WRITING.

(7) YOU HAVE THE RIGHT TO REVOKE THE AUTHORITY GRANTED TO THE PERSON DESIGNATED IN THIS DOCUMENT TO MAKE HEALTH CARE DECISIONS FOR YOU BY NOTIFYING THE TREATING PHYSICIAN, HOSPITAL, OR OTHER PROVIDER OF HEALTH CARE ORALLY OR IN WRITING.

(8) THE PERSON DESIGNATED IN THIS DOCUMENT TO MAKE HEALTH CARE DECISIONS FOR YOU HAS THE RIGHT TO EXAMINE YOUR MEDICAL RECORDS AND TO CONSENT TO THEIR DISCLOSURE UNLESS YOU LIMIT THIS RIGHT IN THIS DOCUMENT.

(9) THIS DOCUMENT REVOKES ANY PRIOR DURABLE POWER OF ATTORNEY FOR HEALTH CARE.

(10) IF THERE IS ANYTHING IN THIS DOCUMENT THAT YOU DO NOT UNDERSTAND, YOU SHOULD ASK A LAWYER TO EXPLAIN IT TO YOU.

1. Designation of Health Care Agent. I, _____ (insert your

name) do hereby designate and appoint:

Name: _____

Address:_____ Phone:_____

as my attorney-in-fact to make health care decisions for me as authorized in this document.

(Insert the name and address of the person you wish to designate as your attorney-in-fact to

make health care decisions for you. None of the following may be designated as your attorney-in-

fact: (1) your treating provider of health care, (2) an employee of your treating provider of health

care, (3) an operator of a health care facility, (4) an employee of an operator of a health care

facility.)

2. Creation of Durable Power of Attorney for Health Care. By this document I intend to

create a durable power of attorney by appointing the person designated above to make health care

decisions for me. This power of attorney shall not be affected by my subsequent incapacity.

3. General Statement of Authority Granted. In the event that I am incapable of giving

informed consent with respect to health care decisions, I hereby grant to the attorney-in-fact

named above full power and authority to make health care decisions for me before or after my

death, including: consent, refusal of consent, or withdrawal of consent to any care, treatment,

service, or procedure to maintain, diagnose, or treat a physical or mental condition, subject only

to the limitations and special provisions, if any, set forth in paragraph 4 or 6.

4. Special Provisions and Limitations. (Your attorney-in-fact is not permitted to consent to

any of the following: commitment to or placement in a mental health treatment facility, convul-

sive treatment, psychosurgery, sterilization, or abortion. If there are any other types of treatment

or placement that you do not want your attorney-in-fact's authority to give consent for or other

restrictions you wish to place on his or her attorney-in-fact's authority, you should list them in

the space below. If you do not write any limitations, your attorney-in-fact will have the broad

powers to make health care decisions on your behalf which are set forth in paragraph 3, except to

the extent that there are limits provided by law.)

In exercising the authority under this durable power of attorney for health care, the authority of my attorney-in-fact is subject to the following special provisions and limitations:

_____

_____

_____

_____

5. Duration. I understand that this power of attorney will exist indefinitely from the date I execute this document unless I establish a shorter time. If I am unable to make health care decisions for myself when this power of attorney expires, the authority I have granted my attorney-in-fact will continue to exist until the time when I become able to make health care decisions for myself.

(IF APPLICABLE)

I wish to have this power of attorney end on the following date: _____.

6. Statement of Desires. (With respect to decisions to withhold or withdraw life-sustaining treatment, your attorney-in-fact must make health care decisions that are consistent with your known desires. You can, but are not required to, indicate your desires below. If your desires are unknown, your attorney-in-fact has the duty to act in your best interests; and, under some circumstances, a judicial proceeding may be necessary so that a court can determine the health care decision that is in your best interests. If you wish to indicate your desires, you may INITIAL the statement or statements that reflect your desires and/or write your own statements in the space below.)

(If the statement reflects your desires, initial the box next to the statement.)

1. I desire that my life be prolonged to the greatest extent possible, without regard to my condition, the chances I have for recovery or long-term survival, or the cost of the procedures.

2. If I am in a coma which my doctors have reasonably concluded is irreversible, I desire that life-sustaining or prolonging treatments not be used. (You also should utilize provisions of NRS 449.610 et seq., the Nevada Withholding or Withdrawal of Life-Sustaining Procedures Act "Directive to Physicians," if you initial this subparagraph.)

3. If I have an incurable or terminal condition or illness and no reasonable hope of long-term recovery or survival, I desire that life-sustaining or prolonging treatments not be used. (You also should utilize provision of NRS 449.610 et seq. if you initial this subparagraph.)

4. I do not desire treatment to be provided and/or continued if the burdens of the treatment outweigh the expected benefits. My attorney-in-fact is to consider the relief of suffering, the preservation or restoration of functioning, and the quality as well as the extent of the possible extension of my life.

(If you wish to change your answer, you may do so by drawing an "X" through the answer you do not want, and circling the answer you prefer.)

Other or Additional Statements of Desires:

_____

_____

_____

_____

7. Designation of Alternate Attorney-in-Fact. (You are not required to designate any alternative attorney-in-fact but you may do so. Any alternative attorney-in-fact you designate will be able to make the same health care decisions as the attorney-in-fact designated in paragraph 1, page 2, in the event he or she is unable or unwilling to act as your attorney-in-fact. Also, if the attorney-in-fact designated in paragraph 1 is your spouse, his or her designation as your attorney-in-fact is automatically revoked by law if your marriage is dissolved.)

If the person designated in paragraph 1 as my attorney-in-fact is unable to make health care decisions for me, then I designate the following persons to serve as my attorney-in-fact to make health care decisions for me as authorized in this document, such persons to serve in the order listed below:

A. First Alternative Attorney-in-fact

Name:_____

Address: _____

_____ Phone_____

B. Second Alternative Attorney-in-fact

Name:_____

Address: _____

_____ Phone_____

8. Prior Designations Revoked. I revoke any prior durable power of attorney for health care

(YOU MUST DATE AND SIGN THIS POWER OF ATTORNEY)

I sign my name to this Durable Power of Attorney for Health Care on

_____ at _____
        date   city   state

_____
                                   signature

(THIS POWER OF ATTORNEY WILL NOT BE VALID FOR MAKING HEALTH CARE DECISIONS UNLESS IT IS EITHER (1) SIGNED BY AT LEAST TWO QUALIFIED WITNESSES WHO ARE PERSONALLY KNOWN TO YOU AND WHO ARE PRESENT WHEN YOU SIGN OR ACKNOWLEDGE YOUR SIGNATURE OR (2) ACKNOWLEDGED BEFORE A NOTARY PUBLIC.)

Certificate of Acknowledgement of Notary Public

(You may use acknowledgement before a notary public instead of the statement of witnesses.)

State of Nevada _____)

County of _____) ss.

On this ____ day of _____, in the year _____, before me,

_____, personally appeared
                          name of notary public

_____, personally known to me (or proved to
                     name of principal

me on the basis of satisfactory evidence) to be the person whose name is subscribed to this

instrument, and acknowledged that he or she executed it. I declare under penalty of perjury that

the person whose name is ascribed to this instrument appears to be of sound mind and under no

duress, fraud, or undue influence.

[Notarial Seal]   _____
                                         signature of notary public

Statement of Witnesses

(You should carefully read and follow this witnessing procedure. This document will not be valid unless you comply with the witnessing procedure. If you elect to use witnesses instead of having this document notarized, you must use two qualified adult witnesses. None of the following may be used as a witness: (1) a person you designate as your attorney-in-fact, (2) a provider of health care, (3) an employee of a provider of health care, (4) the operator of a health care facility, (5) an employee of an operator of a health care facility. At least one of the witnesses must make the additional declaration set out following the place where the witnesses sign.)

I declare under penalty of perjury that the principal is personally known to me, that the principal signed or acknowledged this durable power of attorney in my presence, that the principal appears to be of sound mind and under no duress, fraud, or undue influence, that I am not the person appointed as attorney in fact by this document, and that I am not a provider of health care, an employee of a provider of health care, the operator of a community care facility, nor an employee of an operator of a health care facility.

Signature: _____ Date:_____

Print Name: _____

Address: _____

Signature: _____ Date:_____

Print Name: _____

Address: _____

(AT LEAST ONE OF THE ABOVE WITNESSES MUST ALSO SIGN THE FOLLOWING DECLARATION.)

I declare under penalty of perjury that I am not related to the principal by blood, marriage, or adoption, and to the best of my knowledge I am not entitled to any part of the estate of the principal upon the death of the principal under a will now existing or by operation of law.

Signature: _____ Date:_____

Print Name: _____

Address: _____

Copies: You should retain an executed copy of this document and give one to your attorney-in-fact. The power of attorney should be available so a copy may be given to your providers of health care.

Form 9

Rhode Island Statutory Form Durable Power of Attorney for Health Care

WARNING TO PERSON EXECUTING THIS DOCUMENT

THIS IS AN IMPORTANT LEGAL DOCUMENT WHICH IS AUTHORIZED BY THE GENERAL LAWS OF THIS STATE. BEFORE EXECUTING THIS DOCUMENT, YOU SHOULD KNOW THESE IMPORTANT FACTS:

YOU MUST BE AT LEAST EIGHTEEN (18) YEARS OF AGE AND A RESIDENT OF THE STATE OF RHODE ISLAND FOR THIS DOCUMENT TO BE LEGALLY VALID AND BINDING.

THIS DOCUMENT GIVES THE PERSON YOU DESIGNATE AS YOUR AGENT (THE ATTORNEY IN FACT) THE POWER TO MAKE HEALTH CARE DECISIONS FOR YOU. YOUR AGENT MUST ACT CONSISTENTLY WITH YOUR DESIRES AS STATED IN THIS DOCUMENT OR OTHERWISE MADE KNOWN.

EXCEPT AS YOU OTHERWISE SPECIFY IN THIS DOCUMENT, THIS DOCUMENT GIVES YOUR AGENT THE POWER TO CONSENT TO YOUR DOCTOR NOT GIVING TREATMENT OR STOPPING TREATMENT NECESSARY TO KEEP YOU ALIVE.

NOTWITHSTANDING THIS DOCUMENT, YOU HAVE THE RIGHT TO MAKE MEDICAL AND OTHER HEALTH CARE DECISIONS FOR YOURSELF SO LONG AS YOU CAN GIVE INFORMED CONSENT WITH RESPECT TO THE PARTICULAR DECISION. IN ADDITION, NO TREATMENT MAY BE GIVEN TO YOU OVER YOUR OBJECTION AT THE TIME, AND HEALTH CARE NECESSARY TO KEEP YOU ALIVE MAY NOT BE STOPPED OR WITHHELD IF YOU OBJECT AT THE TIME.

THIS DOCUMENT GIVES YOUR AGENT AUTHORITY TO CONSENT, TO REFUSE TO CONSENT, OR TO WITHDRAW CONSENT TO ANY CARE, TREATMENT, SERVICE, OR PROCEDURE TO MAINTAIN, DIAGNOSE, OR TREAT A PHYSICAL OR MENTAL CONDITION. THIS POWER IS SUBJECT TO ANY STATEMENT OF YOUR DESIRES AND ANY LIMITATION THAT YOU INCLUDE IN THIS DOCUMENT. YOU MAY STATE IN THIS DOCUMENT ANY TYPES OF TREATMENT THAT YOU DO NOT DESIRE. IN ADDITION, A COURT CAN TAKE AWAY THE POWER OF YOUR AGENT TO MAKE HEALTH CARE DECISIONS FOR YOU IF YOUR AGENT (1) AUTHORIZES ANYTHING THAT IS ILLEGAL, (2) ACTS CONTRARY TO YOUR KNOWN DESIRES, OR (3) WHERE YOUR DESIRES ARE NOT KNOWN, DOES ANYTHING THAT IS CLEARLY CONTRARY TO YOUR BEST INTERESTS.

UNLESS YOU SPECIFY A SPECIFIC PERIOD, THIS POWER WILL EXIST UNTIL YOU REVOKE IT.

YOU HAVE THE RIGHT TO REVOKE THE AUTHORITY OF YOUR AGENT BY NOTIFYING YOUR AGENT OR YOUR TREATING DOCTOR, HOSPITAL, OR OTHER HEALTH CARE PROVIDER ORALLY OR IN WRITING OF THE REVOCATION.

YOUR AGENT HAS THE RIGHT TO EXAMINE YOUR MEDICAL RECORDS AND TO CONSENT TO THEIR DISCLOSURE UNLESS YOU LIMIT THIS RIGHT IN THIS DOCUMENT.

THIS DOCUMENT REVOKES ANY PRIOR DURABLE POWER OF ATTORNEY FOR HEALTH CARE.

YOU SHOULD CAREFULLY READ AND FOLLOW THE WITNESSING PROCEDURE DESCRIBED AT THE END OF THIS FORM. THIS DOCUMENT WILL NOT BE VALID UNLESS YOU COMPLY WITH THE WITNESSING PROCEDURE.

IF THERE IS ANYTHING IN THIS DOCUMENT THAT YOU DO NOT UNDERSTAND, YOU SHOULD ASK A LAWYER TO EXPLAIN IT TO YOU.

YOUR AGENT MAY NEED THIS DOCUMENT IMMEDIATELY IN CASE OF AN EMERGENCY THAT REQUIRES A DECISION CONCERNING YOUR HEALTH CARE. EITHER KEEP THIS DOCUMENT WHERE IT IS IMMEDIATELY AVAILABLE TO YOUR AGENT AND ALTERNATE AGENTS OR GIVE EACH OF THEM AN EXECUTED COPY OF THIS DOCUMENT. YOU MAY ALSO WANT TO GIVE YOUR DOCTOR AN EXECUTED COPY OF THIS DOCUMENT.

1. **Designation of Health Care Agent.** I, _____

insert your name and address

_____

do hereby designate and appoint:_____

_____

[Insert name, address, and telephone number of one individual only as your agent to make health care decisions for you. None of the following may be designated as your agent: (1) your treating health care provider, (2) a nonrelative employee of your treating health care provider, (3) an operator of a community care facility, or (4) a nonrelative employee of an operator of a community care facility.]

as my attorney in fact (agent) to make health care decisions for me as authorized in this document. For the purposes of this document, "health care decision" means consent, refusal or consent, or withdrawal of consent to any care, treatment, service, or procedure to maintain, diagnose, or treat an individual's physical or mental condition.

2. **Creation of Durable Power of Attorney For Health Care.** By this document I intend to create a durable power of attorney for health care.

3. **General Statement of Authority Granted.** Subject to any limitations in this document, I hereby grant to my agent full power and authority to make health care decisions for me to the same extent that I could make such decisions for myself if I had the capacity to do so. In exercising this authority, my agent shall make health care decisions that are consistent with my desires as stated in this document or otherwise made known to my agent, including, but not limited to, my desires concerning obtaining or refusing or withdrawing life-prolonging care, treatment, services, and procedures.

[If you want to limit the authority of your agent to make health care decisions for you, you can state the limitation in paragraph 4 ("Statement of Desires, Special Provisions, and Limitations") below. You can indicate your desires by including a statement of your desires in the same paragraph.]

4. Statement of Desires, Special Provisions, and Limitations. (Your agent must make health care decisions that are consistent with your known desires. You can, but are not required to, state your desires in the space provided below. You should consider whether you want to include a statement of your desires concerning life-prolonging care, treatment, services, and procedures. You can also include a statement of your desires concerning other matters relating to your health care. You can also make your desires known to your agent by discussing your desires with your agent or by some other means. If there are any types of treatment that you do not want to be used, you should state them in the space below. If you want to limit in any other way the authority given your agent by this document, you should state the limits in the space below. If you do not state any limits, your agent will have broad powers to make health care decisions for you, except to the extent that there are limits provided by law.)

In exercising the authority under this durable power of attorney for health care, my agent shall act consistently with my desire as stated below and is subject to the special provisions and limitations stated below:

(a) Statement of desire concerning life-prolonging care, treatment, service, and procedures:

_____

_____

_____

_____

_____

_____

_____

(b) Additional statement of desires, special provisions, and limitations regarding health care decisions:

_____

_____

_____

_____

_____

_____

_____

_____

[You may attach additional pages if you need more space to complete your statement. If you attach additional pages, you must date and sign **each** of the additional pages at the same time you date and sign this document.] If you wish to make a gift of any bodily organ you may do so pursuant to the Uniform Anatomical Gift Act.

5. Inspection and Disclosure of Information Relating To My Physical Or Mental Health. Subject to any limitation in this document, my agent has the power and authority to do all of the following:

(a) Request, review, and receive any information, verbal or written, regarding my physical or mental health, including, but not limited to, medical and hospital records.

(b) Execute on my behalf any releases or other documents that may be required in order to obtain this information.

(c) Consent to the disclosure of this information.

[If you want to limit the authority of your agent to receive and disclose information relating to your health, you must state the limitations in paragraph 4 ("Statement of Desires, Special Provisions, and Limitations") above.]

6. Signing Documents, Waivers, and Releases. Where necessary to implement the health care decisions that my agent is authorized by this document to make, my agent has the power and authority to execute on my behalf all of the following:

(a) Documents titled or purporting to be a "Refusal to Permit Treatment" and "Leaving Hospital Against Medical Advice."

(b) Any necessary waiver or release from liability required by a hospital or physician.

7. Duration. (Unless you specify a shorter period in the space below, this power of attorney will exist until it is revoked.)

This durable power of attorney for health care expires on

_____.

fill in this space only if you want the authority of your agent to end on a specific date

8. Designation of Alternate Agents. [You are not required to designate any alternate agent, but you may do so. Any alternate agent you designate will be able to make the same health care decisions as the agent you designated in paragraph 1, above, in the event that agent is unable or ineligible to act as your agent. If the agent you designated is your spouse, he or she becomes ineligible to act as your agent if your marriage is dissolved.]

If the person designated as my agent in paragraph 1 is not available or becomes ineligible to act as my agent to make a health care decision for me or loses the mental capacity to make health care decisions for me, or if I revoke that person's appointment or authority to act as my agent to make health care decisions for me, then I designate and appoint the following persons to serve as my agent to make health care decisions for me as authorized in this document, such persons to serve in the order listed below:

A. First Alternate Agent _____
insert name, address, and telephone number of first alternate agent

_____

B. Second Alternate Agent _____
insert name, address, and telephone number of second alternate agent

_____

9. Prior Designations Revoked. I revoke any prior durable power of attorney for health care.

Date and Signature of Principal
(YOU MUST DATE AND SIGN THIS POWER OF ATTORNEY)

I sign my name to this Statutory Form Durable Power of Attorney for Health Care on

_____ at _____
date   city

_____.
state

_____
you sign here

[THIS POWER OF ATTORNEY WILL NOT BE VALID UNLESS IT IS SIGNED BY TWO (2) QUALIFIED WITNESSES WHO ARE PRESENT WHEN YOU SIGN OR ACKNOWLEDGE YOUR SIGNATURE. IF YOU HAVE ATTACHED ANY ADDITIONAL PAGES TO THIS FORM, YOU MUST DATE AND SIGN EACH OF THE ADDITIONAL PAGES AT THE SAME TIME YOU DATE AND SIGN THIS POWER OF ATTORNEY.]

Statement of Witnesses

(This document must be witnessed by two (2) qualified adult witnesses. None of the following may be used as a witness: (1) a person you designate as your agent or alternate agent, (2) a health care provider, (3) an employee of a health care provider, (4) the operator of a community care facility, (5) an employee of an operator of a community care facility. At least one of the witnesses must make the additional declaration set out following the place where the witnesses sign.)

I declare under penalty of perjury that the person who signed or acknowledged this document is personally known to me to be the principal, that the principal signed or acknowledged this durable power of attorney in my presence, that the principal appears to be of sound mind and under no duress, fraud, or undue influence, that I am not the person appointed as attorney in fact by this document, and that I am not a health care provider, an employee of a health care provider, the operator of a community care facility, nor an employee of an operator of a community care facility.

Signature: _____   Residence Address: _____

Print Name: _____   _____

Date: _____   _____

Signature: _____   Residence Address: _____

Print Name: _____   _____

Date: _____   _____

(AT LEAST ONE OF THE ABOVE WITNESSES MUST ALSO SIGN THE FOLLOWING DECLARATION.)

I further declare under penalty of perjury that I am not related to the principal by blood, marriage, or adoption, and, to the best of my knowledge, I am not entitled to any part of the estate of the principal upon the death of the principal under a will now existing or by operation of law.

Signature: _____   Signature: _____

Print Name: _____   Print Name: _____

Vermont Durable Power of Attorney for Health Care

INFORMATION CONCERNING THE DURABLE POWER OF ATTORNEY FOR HEALTH CARE

THIS IS AN IMPORTANT LEGAL DOCUMENT. BEFORE SIGNING THIS DOCUMENT, YOU SHOULD KNOW THESE IMPORTANT FACTS:

EXCEPT TO THE EXTENT YOU STATE OTHERWISE, THIS DOCUMENT GIVES THE PERSON YOU NAME AS YOUR AGENT THE AUTHORITY TO MAKE ANY AND ALL HEALTH CARE DECISIONS FOR YOU WHEN YOU ARE NO LONGER CAPABLE OF MAKING THEM YOURSELF. "HEALTH CARE" MEANS ANY TREATMENT, SERVICE OR PROCEDURE TO MAINTAIN, DIAGNOSE OR TREAT YOUR PHYSICAL OR MENTAL CONDITION. YOUR AGENT THEREFORE CAN HAVE THE POWER TO MAKE A BROAD RANGE OF HEALTH CARE DECISIONS FOR YOU. YOUR AGENT MAY CONSENT, REFUSE TO CONSENT, OR WITHDRAW CONSENT TO MEDICAL TREATMENT AND MAY MAKE DECISIONS ABOUT WITHDRAWING OR WITHHOLDING LIFE-SUSTAINING TREATMENT.

YOU MAY STATE IN THIS DOCUMENT ANY TREATMENT YOU DO NOT DESIRE OR TREATMENT YOU WANT TO BE SURE YOU RECEIVE. YOUR AGENT'S AUTHORITY WILL BEGIN WHEN YOUR DOCTOR CERTIFIES THAT YOU LACK THE CAPACITY TO MAKE HEALTH CARE DECISIONS. YOU MAY ATTACH ADDITIONAL PAGES IF YOU NEED MORE SPACE TO COMPLETE YOUR STATEMENT.

YOUR AGENT WILL BE OBLIGATED TO FOLLOW YOUR INSTRUCTIONS WHEN MAKING DECISIONS ON YOUR BEHALF. UNLESS YOU STATE OTHERWISE, YOUR AGENT WILL HAVE THE SAME AUTHORITY TO MAKE DECISIONS ABOUT YOUR HEALTH CARE AS YOU WOULD HAVE HAD.

IT IS IMPORTANT THAT YOU DISCUSS THIS DOCUMENT WITH YOUR PHYSICIAN OR OTHER HEALTH CARE PROVIDERS BEFORE YOU SIGN IT TO MAKE SURE THAT YOU UNDERSTAND THE NATURE AND RANGE OF DECISIONS WHICH MAY BE MADE ON YOUR BEHALF. IF YOU DO NOT HAVE A PHYSICIAN, YOU SHOULD TALK WITH SOMEONE ELSE WHO IS KNOWLEDGEABLE ABOUT THESE ISSUES AND CAN ANSWER YOUR QUESTIONS. YOU DO NOT NEED A LAWYER'S ASSISTANCE TO COMPLETE THIS DOCUMENT, BUT IF THERE IS ANYTHING IN THIS DOCUMENT THAT YOU DO NOT UNDERSTAND, YOU SHOULD ASK A LAWYER TO EXPLAIN IT TO YOU.

THE PERSON YOU APPOINT AS AGENT SHOULD BE SOMEONE YOU KNOW AND TRUST AND MUST BE AT LEAST 18 YEARS OLD. IF YOU APPOINT YOUR HEALTH OR RESIDENTIAL CARE PROVIDER (E.G., YOUR PHYSICIAN, OR AN EMPLOYEE OF A HOME HEALTH AGENCY, HOSPITAL, NURSING HOME, OR RESIDENTIAL CARE HOME, OTHER THAN A RELATIVE), THAT PERSON WILL HAVE TO CHOOSE BETWEEN ACTING AS YOUR AGENT OR AS YOUR HEALTH OR RESIDENTIAL CARE PROVIDER; THE LAW DOES NOT PERMIT A PERSON

TO DO BOTH AT THE SAME TIME.

YOU SHOULD INFORM THE PERSON YOU APPOINT THAT YOU WANT HIM OR HER TO BE YOUR HEALTH CARE AGENT. YOU SHOULD DISCUSS THIS DOCUMENT WITH YOUR AGENT AND YOUR PHYSICIAN AND GIVE EACH A SIGNED COPY. YOU SHOULD INDICATE ON THE DOCUMENT ITSELF THE PEOPLE AND INSTITUTIONS WHO WILL HAVE SIGNED COPIES. YOUR AGENT WILL NOT BE LIABLE FOR HEALTH CARE DECISIONS MADE IN GOOD FAITH ON YOUR BEHALF.

EVEN AFTER YOU HAVE SIGNED THIS DOCUMENT, YOU HAVE THE RIGHT TO MAKE HEALTH CARE DECISIONS FOR YOURSELF AS LONG AS YOU ARE ABLE TO DO SO, AND TREATMENT CANNOT BE GIVEN TO YOU OR STOPPED OVER YOUR OBJECTION. YOU HAVE THE RIGHT TO REVOKE THE AUTHORITY GRANTED TO YOUR AGENT BY INFORMING HIM OR HER OR YOUR HEALTH CARE PROVIDER ORALLY OR IN WRITING.

THIS DOCUMENT MAY NOT BE CHANGED OR MODIFIED. IF YOU WANT TO MAKE CHANGES IN THE DOCUMENT, YOU MUST MAKE AN ENTIRELY NEW ONE.

YOU MAY WISH TO DESIGNATE AN ALTERNATE AGENT IN THE EVENT THAT YOUR AGENT IS UNWILLING, UNABLE OR INELIGIBLE TO ACT AS YOUR AGENT. ANY ALTERNATE AGENT YOU DESIGNATE WILL HAVE THE SAME AUTHORITY TO MAKE HEALTH CARE DECISIONS FOR YOU.

THIS POWER OF ATTORNEY WILL NOT BE VALID UNLESS IT IS SIGNED IN THE PRESENCE OF TWO (2) OR MORE QUALIFIED WITNESSES WHO MUST BOTH BE PRESENT WHEN YOU SIGN OR ACKNOWLEDGE YOUR SIGNATURE. THE FOLLOWING PERSONS MAY NOT ACT AS WITNESSES:
- THE PERSON YOU HAVE DESIGNATED AS YOUR AGENT;
- YOUR HEALTH OR RESIDENTIAL CARE PROVIDER OR ONE OF THEIR EMPLOYEES;
- YOUR SPOUSE;
- YOUR LAWFUL HEIRS OR BENEFICIARIES NAMED IN YOUR WILL OR A DEED;
- CREDITORS OR PERSONS WHO HAVE A CLAIM AGAINST YOU.

THE DURABLE POWER OF ATTORNEY SHALL BE IN SUBSTANTIALLY THE FOLLOWING FORM:

Durable Power of Attorney for Health Care

I, _____, hereby appoint

_____ of _____

_____ as my agent to make any and all health

care decisions for me, except to the extent I state otherwise in this document. This durable power

of attorney for health care shall take effect in the event I become unable to make my own health

care decisions.

(a) Statement of desires, special provisions, and limitations regarding health care decisions.

Here you may include any specific desires or limitations you deem appropriate, such as when or what life-sustaining measures should be withheld; directions whether to continue or discontinue artificial nutrition and hydration; or instructions to refuse any specific types of treatment that are inconsistent with your religious beliefs or unacceptable to you for any other reason.

_____

_____

_____

_____

_____

attach additional pages as necessary

(b) The subject of life-sustaining treatment is of particular importance.

For your convenience in dealing with that subject, some general statements concerning the withholding or removal of life-sustaining treatment are set forth below.

If you agree with one of these statements, you may include the statement in the blank space above:

If I suffer a condition from which there is no reasonable prospect of regaining my ability to think and act for myself, I want only care directed to my comfort and dignity, and authorize my agent to decline all treatment (including artificial nutrition and hydration) the primary purpose of which is to prolong my life.

If I suffer a condition from which there is no reasonable prospect of regaining the ability to think and act for myself, I want care directed to my comfort and dignity, and also want artificial nutrition and hydration if needed, but authorize my agent to decline all other treatment the primary purpose of which is to prolong my life.

I want my life sustained by any reasonable medical measures, regardless of my condition.

In the event the person I appoint above is unable, unwilling or unavailable to act as my

heath care agent, I hereby appoint _____ of

_____ as alternate agent.

I hereby acknowledge that I have been provided with a disclosure statement explaining the

effect of this document. I have read and understand the information contained in the disclosure

statement.

The original of this document will be kept at _____

and the following persons and institutions will have signed copies.

_____

_____

_____

In witness whereof, I have hereunto signed my name this _____ day of

_____, 19_____.

_____
signature

I declare that the principal appears to be of sound mind and free from duress at the time the

durable power of attorney for health care is signed and that the principal has affirmed that he or

she is aware of the nature of the document and is signing it freely and voluntarily.

Witness:_____   Address:_____

Witness:_____   Address:_____

**STATEMENT OF OMBUDSMAN, HOSPITAL REPRESENTATIVE OR OTHER
AUTHORIZED PERSON (TO BE SIGNED ONLY IF THE PRINCIPAL IS IN OR IS
BEING ADMITTED TO A HOSPITAL, NURSING HOME OR RESIDENTIAL CARE
HOME):**

I declare that I have personally explained the nature and effect of this durable power of

attorney to the principal and that the principal understands the same.

Date:_____

Name:_____

Address:_____

Form 11

District of Columbia Power of Attorney for Health Care

INFORMATION ABOUT THIS DOCUMENT

THIS IS AN IMPORTANT LEGAL DOCUMENT. BEFORE SIGNING THIS DOCUMENT, IT IS VITAL FOR YOU TO KNOW AND UNDERSTAND THESE FACTS:

THIS DOCUMENT GIVES THE PERSON YOU NAME AS YOUR ATTORNEY IN FACT THE POWER TO MAKE HEALTH-CARE DECISIONS FOR YOU IF YOU CANNOT MAKE THE DECISIONS FOR YOURSELF.

AFTER YOU HAVE SIGNED THIS DOCUMENT, YOU HAVE THE RIGHT TO MAKE HEALTH-CARE DECISIONS FOR YOURSELF IF YOU ARE MENTALLY COMPETENT TO DO SO. IN ADDITION, AFTER YOU HAVE SIGNED THIS DOCUMENT, NO TREATMENT MAY BE GIVEN TO YOU OR STOPPED OVER YOUR OBJECTION IF YOU ARE MENTALLY COMPETENT TO MAKE THAT DECISION.

YOU MAY STATE IN THIS DOCUMENT ANY TYPE OF TREATMENT THAT YOU DO NOT DESIRE AND ANY THAT YOU WANT TO MAKE SURE YOU RECEIVE.

YOU HAVE THE RIGHT TO TAKE AWAY THE AUTHORITY OF YOUR ATTORNEY IN FACT, UNLESS YOU HAVE BEEN ADJUDICATED INCOMPETENT, BY NOTIFYING YOUR ATTORNEY IN FACT OR HEALTH-CARE PROVIDER EITHER ORALLY OR IN WRITING. SHOULD YOU REVOKE THE AUTHORITY OF YOUR ATTORNEY IN FACT, IT IS ADVISABLE TO REVOKE IN WRITING AND TO PLACE COPIES OF THE REVOCATION WHEREVER THIS DOCUMENT IS LOCATED.

IF THERE IS ANYTHING IN THIS DOCUMENT THAT YOU DO NOT UNDERSTAND, YOU SHOULD ASK A SOCIAL WORKER, LAWYER OR OTHER PERSON TO EXPLAIN IT TO YOU.

YOU SHOULD KEEP A COPY OF THIS DOCUMENT AFTER YOU HAVE SIGNED IT. GIVE A COPY TO THE PERSON YOU NAME AS YOUR ATTORNEY IN FACT. IF YOU ARE IN A HEALTH-CARE FACILITY, A COPY OF THIS DOCUMENT SHOULD BE INCLUDED IN YOUR MEDICAL RECORD.

I, _____, hereby appoint

_____   _____
name   home address

_____   _____
home telephone number

_____   _____
work telephone number

as my attorney in fact to make health-care decisions for me if I become unable to make my own

health-care decisions. This gives my attorney in fact the power to grant, refuse, or withdraw

consent on my behalf for any health-care service, treatment or procedure. My attorney in fact also has the authority to talk to health-care personnel, get information and sign forms necessary to carry out these decisions.

If the person named as my attorney in fact is not available or is unable to act as my attorney in fact, I appoint the following person to serve in the order listed below:

1. _____   _____
    name   home address

_____   _____
home telephone number

_____   _____
work telephone number

2. _____   _____
    name   home address

_____   _____
home telephone number

_____   _____
work telephone number

With this document, I intend to create a power of attorney for health care, which shall take effect if I become incapable of making my own health care decisions and shall continue during that incapacity.

My attorney in fact shall make health-care decisions as I direct below or as I make known to my attorney in fact in some other way.

(a) Statement of Directives Concerning Life-Prolonging Care, Treatment, Services and Procedures:

_____

_____

_____

_____

_____

(b) Special Provisions and Limitations:

_____

_____

_____

_____

_____

BY MY SIGNATURE, I INDICATE THAT I UNDERSTAND THE PURPOSE AND EFFECT OF THIS DOCUMENT.

I sign my name to this form on _____

date

at: _____.

address

_____

signature

Witnesses

I declare that the person who signed or acknowledged this document is personally known to me, that the person signed or acknowledged this durable power of attorney for health care in my presence, and that the person appears to be of sound mind and under no duress, fraud, or undue influence. I am not the person appointed as the attorney in fact by this document, nor am I a health-care provider of the principal or an employee of the health-care provider of the principal.

First Witness | Second Witness

Signature: _____   Signature: _____

Home Address:_____   Home Address:_____

_____   _____

Print Name: _____   Print Name: _____

Date: _____   Date: _____

(AT LEAST 1 OF THE WITNESSES LISTED ABOVE SHALL ALSO SIGN THE FOLLOWING DECLARATION.)

I further declare that I am not related to the principal by blood, marriage or adoption, and, to the best of my knowledge, I am not entitled to any part of the estate of the principal under a currently-existing will or by operation of law.

Signature: _____   Signature: _____

Form 12

Illinois Statutory Short Form Power of Attorney for Health Care

(NOTICE: THE PURPOSE OF THIS POWER OF ATTORNEY IS TO GIVE THE PERSON YOU DESIGNATE (YOUR "AGENT") BROAD POWERS TO MAKE HEALTH CARE DECISIONS FOR YOU, INCLUDING POWER TO REQUIRE, CONSENT TO OR WITHDRAW ANY TYPE OF PERSONAL CARE OR MEDICAL TREATMENT FOR ANY PHYSICAL OR MENTAL CONDITION AND TO ADMIT YOU TO OR DISCHARGE YOU FROM ANY HOSPITAL, HOME OR OTHER INSTITUTION. THIS FORM DOES NOT IMPOSE A DUTY ON YOUR AGENT TO EXERCISE GRANTED POWERS; BUT WHEN A POWER IS EXERCISED, YOUR AGENT WILL HAVE TO USE DUE CARE TO ACT FOR YOUR BENEFIT AND IN ACCORDANCE WITH THIS FORM. A COURT CAN TAKE AWAY THE POWERS OF YOUR AGENT IF IT FINDS THE AGENT IS NOT ACTING PROPERLY. YOU MAY NAME SUCCESSOR AGENTS UNDER THIS FORM BUT NOT CO-AGENTS, AND NO HEALTH CARE PROVIDER MAY BE NAMED. UNLESS YOU EXPRESSLY LIMIT THE DURATION OF THIS POWER IN THE MANNER PROVIDED BELOW, UNTIL YOU REVOKE THIS POWER OR A COURT ACTING ON YOUR BEHALF TERMINATES IT, YOUR AGENT MAY EXERCISE THE POWERS GIVEN HERE THROUGHOUT YOUR LIFETIME, EVEN AFTER YOU BECOME DISABLED. THE POWERS YOU GIVE YOUR AGENT, YOUR RIGHT TO REVOKE THOSE POWERS AND THE PENALTIES FOR VIOLATING THE LAW ARE EXPLAINED MORE FULLY IN SECTIONS 4-5, 4-6, 4-9 AND 4-10(b) OF THE ILLINOIS "POWERS OF ATTORNEY FOR HEALTH CARE LAW" OF WHICH THIS FORM IS A PART (SEE THE BACK OF THIS FORM). THAT LAW EXPRESSLY PERMITS THE USE OF ANY DIFFERENT FORM OF POWER OF ATTORNEY YOU MAY DESIRE. IF THERE IS ANYTHING ABOUT THIS FORM THAT YOU DO NOT UNDERSTAND, YOU SHOULD ASK A LAWYER TO EXPLAIN IT TO YOU.)

POWER OF ATTORNEY MADE THIS . . . . DAY OF . . . .
month & year

1. I, _____
insert name and address of principal

_____

hereby appoint: _____
insert name and address of agent

_____

as my attorney-in-fact (my "agent") to act for me and in my name (in any way I could act in

person) to make any and all decisions for me concerning my personal care, medical treatment,

hospitalization and health care and to require, withhold or withdraw any type of medical treat-

ment or procedure, even though my death may ensue. My agent shall have the same access to my

medical records that I have, including the right to disclose the contents to others. My agent shall also have full power to make a disposition of any part or all of my body for medical purposes, authorize an autopsy and direct the disposition of my remains.

(THE ABOVE GRANT OF POWER IS INTENDED TO BE AS BROAD AS POSSIBLE SO THAT YOUR AGENT WILL HAVE AUTHORITY TO MAKE ANY DECISION YOU COULD MAKE TO OBTAIN OR TERMINATE ANY TYPE OF HEALTH CARE, INCLUDING WITHDRAWAL OF FOOD AND WATER AND OTHER LIFE-SUSTAINING MEASURES, IF YOUR AGENT BELIEVES SUCH ACTION WOULD BE CONSISTENT WITH YOUR INTENT AND DESIRES. IF YOU WISH TO LIMIT THE SCOPE OF YOUR AGENT'S POWERS OR PRESCRIBE SPECIAL RULES OR LIMIT THE POWER TO MAKE AN ANATOMICAL GIFT, AUTHORIZE AUTOPSY OR DISPOSE OF REMAINS, YOU MAY DO SO IN THE FOLLOWING PARAGRAPHS.)

2. The powers granted above shall not include the following powers or shall be subject to the following rules or limitations (here you may include any specific limitations you deem appropriate, such as: your own definition of when life-sustaining measures should be withheld; a direction to continue food and fluids or life-sustaining treatment in all events; or instructions to refuse any specific types of treatment that are inconsistent with your religious beliefs or unacceptable to you for any other reason, such as blood transfusion, electro-convulsive therapy, amputation, psychosurgery, voluntary admission to a mental institution, etc):

_____

_____

_____

_____

(THE SUBJECT OF LIFE-SUSTAINING TREATMENT IS OF PARTICULAR IMPORTANCE. FOR YOUR CONVENIENCE IN DEALING WITH THAT SUBJECT, SOME GENERAL STATEMENTS CONCERNING THE WITHHOLDING OR REMOVAL OF LIFE-SUSTAINING TREATMENT ARE SET FORTH BELOW. IF YOU AGREE WITH ONE OF THESE STATEMENTS, YOU MAY INITIAL THAT STATEMENT; BUT DO NOT INITIAL MORE THAN ONE):

I do not want my life to be prolonged, nor do I want life-sustaining treatment to be provided or continued if my agent believes the burdens of the treatment outweigh the expected benefits. I want my agent to consider the relief of suffering, the expense involved and the quality as well as the possible extension of my life in making decisions concerning life-sustaining treatment.

Initialed _____

I want my life to be prolonged and I want life-sustaining treatment to be provided or continued unless I am in a coma which my attending physician believes to be irreversible, in accordance with reasonable medical standards at the time of reference. If and when I have suffered irreversible coma, I want life-sustaining treatment to be withheld or discontinued.

Initialed _____

I want my life to be prolonged to the greatest extent possible without regard to my condition, the chances I have for recovery or the cost of the procedures.

Initialed _____

(THIS POWER OF ATTORNEY MAY BE AMENDED OR REVOKED BY YOU AT ANY TIME AND IN ANY MANNER WHILE YOU HAVE THE CAPACITY TO DO SO. ABSENT AMENDMENT OR REVOCATION, THE AUTHORITY GRANTED IN THIS POWER OF ATTORNEY WILL BECOME EFFECTIVE AT THE TIME THIS POWER IS SIGNED AND WILL CONTINUE UNTIL YOUR DEATH, AND BEYOND IF ANATOMICAL GIFT, AUTOPSY OR DISPOSITION OF REMAINS IS AUTHORIZED, UNLESS A LIMITATION ON THE BEGINNING DATE OR DURATION IS MADE BY INITIALING AND COMPLETING EITHER OR BOTH OF THE FOLLOWING:)

3. (   ) This power of attorney shall become effective on _____
insert a future date or event during your lifetime,

_____
such as court determination of your disability, when you want this power to first take effect

4. (   ) This power of attorney shall terminate on _____
insert a future date or event, such as court determination of

_____
your disability, when you want this power to terminate prior to your death

(IF YOU WISH TO NAME SUCCESSOR AGENTS, INSERT THE NAMES AND ADDRESSES OF SUCH SUCCESSORS IN THE FOLLOWING PARAGRAPH.)

5. If any agent named by me shall die, become legally disabled, resign, refuse to act or be unavailable, I name the following (each to act alone and successively, in the order named) as

successors to such agent: _____

_____

_____

(IF YOU WISH TO NAME A GUARDIAN OF YOUR PERSON IN THE EVENT A COURT DECIDES THAT ONE SHOULD BE APPOINTED, YOU MAY, BUT ARE NOT REQUIRED TO, DO SO BY INSERTING THE NAME OF SUCH GUARDIAN IN THE FOLLOWING PARAGRAPH. THE COURT WILL APPOINT THE PERSON NOMINATED BY YOU IF THE COURT FINDS THAT SUCH APPOINTMENT WILL SERVE YOUR BEST INTERESTS AND WELFARE. YOU MAY, BUT ARE NOT REQUIRED TO, NOMINATE AS YOUR GUARDIAN THE SAME PERSON NAMED IN THIS FORM AS YOUR AGENT.)

6. If a guardian of my person is to be appointed, I nominate the following to serve as such

guardian: _____
insert name and address of nominated guardian of the person

_____

7. I am fully informed as to all the contents of this form and understand the full import of this

grant of powers to my agent.

Signed _____
principal

The principal has had an opportunity to read the above form and has signed the form or

acknowledged his or her signature or mark on the form in my presence.

_____ Residing at _____
witness

(YOU MAY, BUT ARE NOT REQUIRED TO, REQUEST YOUR AGENT AND SUCCESSOR AGENTS TO PROVIDE SPECIMEN SIGNATURES BELOW. IF YOU INCLUDE SPECIMEN SIGNATURES IN THIS POWER OF ATTORNEY, YOU MUST COMPLETE THE CERTIFICATION OPPOSITE THE SIGNATURES OF THE AGENTS.)

Specimen signatures of agent (and successors)   I certify that the signature of my agent (and successors) are correct.

_____   _____
agent   principal

_____   _____
successor agent   principal

_____   _____
successor agent   principal

Form 13

Statutory Form Durable Power of Attorney for Health Care
(California Civil Code Section 2500)

WARNING TO PERSON EXECUTING THIS DOCUMENT

THIS IS AN IMPORTANT LEGAL DOCUMENT WHICH IS AUTHORIZED BY THE KEENE HEALTH CARE AGENT ACT. BEFORE EXECUTING THIS DOCUMENT, YOU SHOULD KNOW THESE IMPORTANT FACTS:

THIS DOCUMENT GIVES THE PERSON YOU DESIGNATE AS YOUR AGENT (THE ATTORNEY IN FACT) THE POWER TO MAKE HEALTH CARE DECISIONS FOR YOU. YOUR AGENT MUST ACT CONSISTENTLY WITH YOUR DESIRES AS STATED IN THIS DOCUMENT OR OTHERWISE MADE KNOWN.

EXCEPT AS YOU OTHERWISE SPECIFY IN THIS DOCUMENT, THIS DOCUMENT GIVES YOUR AGENT THE POWER TO CONSENT TO YOUR DOCTOR NOT GIVING TREATMENT OR STOPPING TREATMENT NECESSARY TO KEEP YOU ALIVE.

NOTWITHSTANDING THIS DOCUMENT, YOU HAVE THE RIGHT TO MAKE MEDICAL AND OTHER HEALTH CARE DECISIONS FOR YOURSELF SO LONG AS YOU CAN GIVE INFORMED CONSENT WITH RESPECT TO THE PARTICULAR DECISION. IN ADDITION, NO TREATMENT MAY BE GIVEN TO YOU OVER YOUR OBJECTION AT THE TIME, AND HEALTH CARE NECESSARY TO KEEP YOU ALIVE MAY NOT BE STOPPED OR WITHHELD IF YOU OBJECT AT THE TIME.

THIS DOCUMENT GIVES YOUR AGENT AUTHORITY TO CONSENT, TO REFUSE TO CONSENT, OR TO WITHDRAW CONSENT TO ANY CARE, TREATMENT, SERVICE, OR PROCEDURE TO MAINTAIN, DIAGNOSE, OR TREAT A PHYSICAL OR MENTAL CONDITION. THIS POWER IS SUBJECT TO ANY STATEMENT OF YOUR DESIRES AND ANY LIMITATIONS THAT YOU INCLUDE IN THIS DOCUMENT. YOU MAY STATE IN THIS DOCUMENT ANY TYPES OF TREATMENT THAT YOU DO NOT DESIRE. IN ADDITION, A COURT CAN TAKE AWAY THE POWER OF YOUR AGENT TO MAKE HEALTH CARE DECISIONS FOR YOU IF YOUR AGENT (1) AUTHORIZES ANYTHING THAT IS ILLEGAL, (2) ACTS CONTRARY TO YOUR KNOWN DESIRES, OR (3) WHERE YOUR DESIRES ARE NOT KNOWN, DOES ANYTHING THAT IS CLEARLY CONTRARY TO YOUR BEST INTERESTS.

UNLESS YOU SPECIFY A SHORTER PERIOD IN THIS DOCUMENT, THIS POWER WILL EXIST FOR SEVEN YEARS FROM THE DATE YOU EXECUTE THIS DOCUMENT AND, IF YOU ARE UNABLE TO MAKE HEALTH CARE DECISIONS FOR YOURSELF AT THE TIME WHEN THIS SEVEN-YEAR PERIOD ENDS, THE POWER WILL CONTINUE TO EXIST UNTIL THE TIME WHEN YOU BECOME ABLE TO MAKE HEALTH CARE DECISIONS FOR YOURSELF.

YOU HAVE THE RIGHT TO REVOKE THE AUTHORITY OF YOUR AGENT BY NOTIFYING YOUR AGENT OR YOUR TREATING DOCTOR, HOSPITAL, OR OTHER HEALTH CARE PROVIDER ORALLY OR IN WRITING OF THE REVOCATION.

YOUR AGENT HAS THE RIGHT TO EXAMINE YOUR MEDICAL RECORDS AND TO CONSENT TO THEIR DISCLOSURE UNLESS YOU LIMIT THIS RIGHT IN THIS DOCUMENT.

UNLESS YOU OTHERWISE SPECIFY IN THIS DOCUMENT, THIS DOCUMENT GIVES YOUR AGENT THE POWER AFTER YOU DIE TO (1) AUTHORIZE AN AUTOPSY, (2) DONATE YOUR BODY OR PARTS THEREOF FOR TRANSPLANT OR THERAPEUTIC OR EDUCATIONAL OR SCIENTIFIC PURPOSES, AND (3) DIRECT THE DISPOSITION OF YOUR REMAINS.

THIS DOCUMENT REVOKES ANY PRIOR DURABLE POWER OF ATTORNEY FOR HEALTH CARE.

YOU SHOULD CAREFULLY READ AND FOLLOW THE WITNESSING PROCEDURE DESCRIBED AT THE END OF THIS FORM. THIS DOCUMENT WILL NOT BE VALID UNLESS YOU COMPLY WITH THE WITNESSING PROCEDURE.

IF THERE IS ANYTHING IN THIS DOCUMENT THAT YOU DO NOT UNDERSTAND, YOU SHOULD ASK A LAWYER TO EXPLAIN IT TO YOU.

YOUR AGENT MAY NEED THIS DOCUMENT IMMEDIATELY IN CASE OF AN EMERGENCY THAT REQUIRES A DECISION CONCERNING YOUR HEALTH CARE. EITHER KEEP THIS DOCUMENT WHERE IT IS IMMEDIATELY AVAILABLE TO YOUR AGENT AND ALTERNATE AGENTS OR GIVE EACH OF THEM AN EXECUTED COPY OF THIS DOCUMENT. YOU MAY ALSO WANT TO GIVE YOUR DOCTOR AN EXECUTED COPY OF THIS DOCUMENT.

DO NOT USE THIS FORM IF YOU ARE A CONSERVATEE UNDER THE LANTERMAN-PETRIS-SHORT ACT AND YOU WANT TO APPOINT YOUR CONSERVATOR AS YOUR AGENT. YOU CAN DO THAT ONLY IF THE APPOINTMENT DOCUMENT INCLUDES A CERTIFICATE OF YOUR ATTORNEY.

1. Designation of Health Care Agent. I, _____

insert your name and address

_____

do hereby designate and appoint _____

_____.

[Insert name, address, and telephone number of one individual only as your agent to make health care decisions for you. None of the following may be designated as your agent: (1) your treating health care provider, (2) a nonrelative employee of your treating health care provider, (3) an operator of a community care facility, (4) a nonrelative employee of an operator of a community care facility, (5) an operator of a residential care facility for the elderly, or (6) a nonrelative employee of an operator of a residential care facility for the elderly.]

as my attorney in fact (agent) to make health care decisions for me as authorized in this document. For the purposes of this document, "health care decision" means consent, refusal of consent, or withdrawal of consent to any care, treatment, service, or procedure to maintain, diagnose, or treat an individual's physical or mental condition.

2. Creation of Durable Power of Attorney For Health Care. By this document I intend to create a durable power of attorney for health care under Sections 2430 to 2443, inclusive, of the

California Civil Code. This power of attorney is authorized by the Keene Health Care Agent Act and shall be construed in accordance with the provisions of Sections 2500 to 2506, inclusive, of the California Civil Code. This power of attorney shall not be affected by my subsequent incapacity.

3. General Statement of Authority Granted. Subject to any limitations in this document, I hereby grant to my agent full power and authority to make health care decisions for me to the same extent that I could make such decisions for myself if I had the capacity to do so. In exercising this authority, my agent shall make health care decisions that are consistent with my desires as stated in this document or otherwise made known to my agent, including, but not limited to, my desires concerning obtaining or refusing or withdrawing life-prolonging care, treatment, services, and procedures.

[If you want to limit the authority of your agent to make health care decisions for you, you can state the limitation in paragraph 4 ("Statement of Desires, Special Provisions, and Limitations") below. You can indicate your desires by including a statement of your desires in the same paragraph.]

4. Statement of Desires, Special Provisions, and Limitations. (Your agent must make health care decisions that are consistent with your known desires. You can, but are not required to, state your desires in the space provided below. You should consider whether you want to include a statement of your desires concerning life-prolonging care, treatment, services, and procedures. You can also include a statement of your desires concerning other matters relating to your health care. You can also make your desires known to your agent by discussing your desires with your agent or by some other means. If there are any types of treatment that you do not want to be used, you should state them in the space below. If you want to limit in any other way the authority given your agent by this document, you should state the limits in the space below. If you do not state any limits, your agent will have broad powers to make health care decisions for you, except to the extent that there are limits provided by law.)

In exercising the authority under this durable power of attorney for health care, my agent shall act consistently with my desires as stated below and is subject to the special provisions and limitations stated below:

(a) Statement of desire concerning life-prolonging care, treatment, service, and procedures:

_____

_____

_____

_____

_____

_____

_____

_____

(b) Additional statement of desires, special provisions, and limitations:

_____

_____

_____

_____

_____

_____

_____

[You may attach additional pages if you need more space to complete your statement. If you attach additional pages, you must date and sign each of the additional pages at the same time you date and sign this document.]

5. Inspection and Disclosure of Information Relating To My Physical Or Mental Health. Subject to any limitation in this document, my agent has the power and authority to do all of the following:

(a) Request, review, and receive any information, verbal or written, regarding my physical or mental health, including, but not limited to, medical and hospital records.

(b) Execute on my behalf any releases or other documents that may be required in order to obtain this information.

(c) Consent to the disclosure of this information.

[If you want to limit the authority of your agent to receive and disclose information relating to your health, you must state the limitations in paragraph 4 ("Statement of Desires, Special Provisions, and Limitations") above.]

6. Signing Documents, Waivers, and Releases. Where necessary to implement the health care decisions that my agent is authorized by this document to make, my agent has the power and authority to execute on my behalf all of the following:

(a) Documents titled or purporting to be a "Refusal to Permit Treatment" and "Leaving Hospital Against Medical Advice."

(b) Any necessary waiver or release from liability required by a hospital or physician.

7. Autopsy; Anatomical Gifts; Disposition of Remains. Subject to any limitations in this document, my agent has the power and authority to do all of the following:

(a) Authorize an autopsy under Section 7113 of the Health and Safety Code.

(b) Make a disposition of a part or parts of my body under the Uniform Anatomical Gift Act (Chapter 3.5 (commencing with Section 7150) of Part 1 of Division 7 of the Health and Safety Code).

(c) Direct the disposition of my remains under Section 7100 of the Health and Safety Code.

[If you want to limit the authority of your agent to consent to an autopsy, make an anatomical gift, or direct the disposition of your remains, you must state the limitations in paragraph 4 ("Statement of Desires, Special Provisions, and Limitations") above.]

8. Duration. (Unless you specify a shorter period in the space below, this power of attorney will exist for seven years from the date you execute this document and, if you are unable to make health care decisions for yourself at the time when this seven-year period ends, the power will continue to exist until the time when you become able to make health care decisions for yourself.)

This durable power of attorney for health care expires on

_____.

fill in this space only if you want the authority of your agent to end earlier than the seven-year period described above

9. Designation of Alternate Agents. (You are not required to designate any alternate agent but you may do so. Any alternate agent you designate will be able to make the same health care decisions as the agent you designated in paragraph 1, above, in the event that agent is unable or ineligible to act as your agent. If the agent you designated is your spouse, he or she becomes ineligible to act as your agent if your marriage is dissolved.)

If the person designated as my agent in paragraph 1 is not available or becomes ineligible to act as my agent to make a health care decision for me or loses the mental capacity to make health care decisions for me, or if I revoke that person's appointment or authority to act as my agent to make health care decisions for me, then I designate and appoint the following persons to serve as my agent to make health care decisions for me as authorized in this document, such persons to serve in the order listed below:

A. First Alternate Agent _____

insert name, address, and telephone number of first alternate agent

_____

B. Second Alternate Agent _____
insert name, address, and telephone number of second alternate agent

_____

10. Nomination of Conservator of Person. (A conservator of the person may be appointed for you if a court decides that one should be appointed. The conservator is responsible for your physical care, which under some circumstances includes making health care decisions for you. You are not required to nominate a conservator but you may do so. The court will appoint the person you nominate unless that would be contrary to your best interests. You may, but are not required to, nominate as your conservator the same person you named in paragraph 1 as your health care agent. You can nominate an individual as your conservator by completing the space below.)

If a conservator of the person is to be appointed for me, I nominate the following individual to serve as conservator of the person _____
insert name and address of person nominated as conservator of the person

_____.

11. Prior Designations Revoked. I revoke any prior durable power of attorney for health care.

Date and Signature of Principal

(YOU MUST DATE AND SIGN THIS POWER OF ATTORNEY)

I sign my name to this Statutory Form Durable Power of Attorney for Health Care

on_____ at _____,
          date   city

_____.
        state

_____
              you sign here

(THIS POWER OF ATTORNEY WILL NOT BE VALID UNLESS IT IS SIGNED BY TWO QUALIFIED WITNESSES WHO ARE PRESENT WHEN YOU SIGN OR ACKNOWLEDGE YOUR SIGNATURE. IF YOU HAVE ATTACHED ANY ADDITIONAL PAGES TO THIS FORM, YOU MUST DATE AND SIGN EACH OF THE ADDITIONAL PAGES AT THE SAME TIME YOU DATE AND SIGN THIS POWER OF ATTORNEY.)

Statement of Witnesses

(This document must be witnessed by two qualified adult witnesses. None of the following may be used as a witness: (1) a person you designate as your agent or alternate agent, (2) a health care provider, (3) an employee of a health care provider, (4) the operator of a community care facility, (5) an employee of an operator of a community care facility, (6) the operator of a residential care facility for the elderly, or (7) an employee of an operator of a residential care facility for the elderly. At least one of the witnesses must make the additional declaration set out following the place where the witnesses sign.)

(READ CAREFULLY BEFORE SIGNING. You can sign as a witness only if you personally know the principal or the identity of the principal is proved to you by convincing evidence.)

(To have convincing evidence of the identity of the principal, you must be presented with and reasonably rely on any one or more of the following:

(1) An identification card or driver's license issued by the California Department of Motor Vehicles that is current or has been issued within five years.

(2) A passport issued by the Department of State of the United States that is current or has been issued within five years.

(3) Any of the following documents if the document is current or has been issued within five years and contains a photograph and description of the person named on it, is signed by the person, and bears a serial or other identifying number:

(a) A passport issued by a foreign government that has been stamped by the United States Immigration and Naturalization Service.

(b) A driver's license issued by a state other than California or by a Canadian or Mexican public agency authorized to issue driver's licenses.

(c) An identification card issued by a state other than California.

(d) An identification card issued by any branch of the armed forces of the United States.)

(Other kinds of proof of identity are not allowed.)

I declare under penalty of perjury under the laws of California that the person who signed or acknowledged this document is personally known to me (or proved to me on the basis of convincing evidence) to be the principal, that the principal signed or acknowledged this durable power of attorney in my presence, that the principal appears to be of sound mind and under no duress, fraud, or undue influence, that I am not the person appointed as attorney in fact by this document, and that I am not a health care provider, an employee of a health care provider, the operator of a community care facility, an employee of an operator of a community care facility, the operator of a residential care facility for the elderly, nor an employee of an operator of a residential care facility for the elderly.

Signature: _____ Residence Address: _____

Print Name: _____ _____

Date: _____ _____

Signature: _____ Residence Address: _____

Print Name: _____ _____

Date: _____ _____

(AT LEAST ONE OF THE ABOVE WITNESSES MUST ALSO SIGN THE FOLLOWING DECLARATION.)

I further declare under penalty of perjury under the laws of California that I am not related to the principal by blood, marriage, or adoption, and, to the best of my knowledge, I am not entitled to any part of the estate of the principal upon the death of the principal under a will now existing or by operation of law.

Signature: _____

Signature: _____

Statement of Patient Advocate or Ombudsman

(If you are a patient in a skilled nursing facility, one of the witnesses must be a patient advocate or ombudsman. The following statement is required only if you are a patient in a skilled nursing facility—a health care facility that provides the following basic services: skilled nursing care and supportive care to patients whose primary need is for availability of skilled nursing care on an extended basis. The patient advocate or ombudsman must sign both parts of the "Statement of Witnesses" above **and** must also sign the following statement.)

I further declare under penalty of perjury under the laws of California that I am a patient advocate or ombudsman as designated by the State Department of Aging and that I am serving as a witness as required by subdivision (f) of Section 2432 of the Civil Code.

Signature: _____

California Springing Durable Power of Attorney (Health Care)

WARNING TO PERSON EXECUTING THIS DOCUMENT

THIS IS AN IMPORTANT LEGAL DOCUMENT. IT CREATES A DURABLE POWER OF ATTORNEY FOR HEALTH CARE. BEFORE EXECUTING THIS DOCUMENT, YOU SHOULD KNOW THESE IMPORTANT FACTS.

THIS DOCUMENT GIVES THE PERSON YOU DESIGNATE AS YOUR AGENT (THE ATTORNEY IN FACT) THE POWER TO MAKE HEALTH CARE DECISIONS FOR YOU. YOUR AGENT MUST ACT CONSISTENTLY WITH YOUR DESIRES AS STATED IN THIS DOCUMENT OR OTHERWISE MADE KNOWN.

EXCEPT AS YOU OTHERWISE SPECIFY IN THIS DOCUMENT, THIS DOCUMENT GIVES YOUR AGENT THE POWER TO CONSENT TO YOUR DOCTOR NOT GIVING TREATMENT OR STOPPING TREATMENT NECESSARY TO KEEP YOU ALIVE.

NOTWITHSTANDING THIS DOCUMENT, YOU HAVE THE RIGHT TO MAKE MEDICAL AND OTHER HEALTH CARE DECISIONS FOR YOURSELF SO LONG AS YOU CAN GIVE INFORMED CONSENT WITH RESPECT TO THE PARTICULAR DECISION. IN ADDITION, NO TREATMENT MAY BE GIVEN TO YOU OVER YOUR OBJECTION, AND HEALTH CARE NECESSARY TO KEEP YOU ALIVE MAY NOT BE STOPPED OR WITHHELD IF YOU OBJECT AT THE TIME.

THIS DOCUMENT GIVES YOUR AGENT AUTHORITY TO CONSENT, TO REFUSE TO CONSENT, OR TO WITHDRAW CONSENT TO ANY CARE, TREATMENT, SERVICE, OR PROCEDURE TO MAINTAIN, DIAGNOSE, OR TREAT A PHYSICAL OR MENTAL CONDITION. THIS POWER IS SUBJECT TO ANY STATEMENT OF YOUR DESIRES AND ANY LIMITATIONS THAT YOU INCLUDE IN THIS DOCUMENT. YOU MAY STATE IN THIS DOCUMENT ANY TYPES OF TREATMENT THAT YOU DO NOT DESIRE. IN ADDITION, A COURT CAN TAKE AWAY THE POWER OF YOUR AGENT TO MAKE HEALTH CARE DECISIONS FOR YOU IF YOUR AGENT (1) AUTHORIZES ANYTHING THAT IS ILLEGAL, (2) ACTS CONTRARY TO YOUR KNOWN DESIRES, OR (3) WHERE YOUR DESIRES ARE NOT KNOWN, DOES ANYTHING THAT IS CLEARLY CONTRARY TO YOUR BEST INTERESTS.

UNLESS YOU SPECIFY A SHORTER PERIOD IN THIS DOCUMENT, THIS POWER WILL EXIST FOR SEVEN YEARS FROM THE DATE YOU EXECUTE THIS DOCUMENT AND, IF YOU ARE UNABLE TO MAKE HEALTH CARE DECISIONS FOR YOURSELF AT THE TIME WHEN THIS SEVEN-YEAR PERIOD ENDS, THIS POWER WILL CONTINUE TO EXIST UNTIL THE TIME WHEN YOU BECOME ABLE TO MAKE HEALTH CARE DECISIONS FOR YOURSELF.

YOU HAVE THE RIGHT TO REVOKE THE AUTHORITY OF YOUR AGENT BY NOTIFYING YOUR AGENT OR YOUR TREATING DOCTOR, HOSPITAL, OR OTHER HEALTH CARE PROVIDER ORALLY OR IN WRITING OF THE REVOCATION.

YOUR AGENT HAS THE RIGHT TO EXAMINE YOUR MEDICAL RECORDS AND TO CONSENT TO THEIR DISCLOSURE UNLESS YOU LIMIT THIS RIGHT IN THIS DOCUMENT.

UNLESS YOU OTHERWISE SPECIFY IN THIS DOCUMENT, THIS DOCUMENT GIVES YOUR AGENT THE POWER AFTER YOU DIE TO (1) AUTHORIZE AN AUTOPSY, (2) DONATE YOUR BODY OR PARTS THEREOF FOR TRANSPLANT OR THERAPEUTIC OR EDUCATIONAL OR SCIENTIFIC PURPOSES, AND (3) DIRECT THE DISPOSITION OF YOUR REMAINS.

IF THERE IS ANYTHING IN THIS DOCUMENT THAT YOU DO NOT UNDERSTAND, YOU SHOULD ASK A LAWYER TO EXPLAIN IT TO YOU.

THIS POWER OF ATTORNEY WILL NOT BE VALID FOR MAKING HEALTH CARE DECISIONS UNLESS IT IS EITHER (1) SIGNED BY TWO QUALIFIED ADULT WITNESSES WHO PERSONALLY KNOW YOU AND WHO ARE PRESENT WHEN YOU SIGN OR ACKNOWLEDGE YOUR SIGNATURE OR (2) ACKNOWLEDGED BEFORE A NOTARY PUBLIC IN CALIFORNIA.

Durable Power of Attorney for Health Care

1. Creation of Durable Power of Attorney

To my family, relatives, friends and my physicians, health care providers, community care facilities and any other person who may have an interest or duty in my medical care or treatment:

I, _____, being of sound
name

mind, willfully and voluntarily intend to create by this document a durable power of attorney for my health care by appointing the person designated as my attorney in fact to make health care decisions for me in the event I become incapacitated and am unable to make health care decisions for myself. This power of attorney shall not be affected by my subsequent incapacity.

2. Designation of Attorney in Fact

The person designated to be my attorney in fact for health care in the event I become incapacitated is _____ of
name

_____. If
address

_____ for any
name

reason shall fail to serve or ceases to serve as my attorney in fact for health care,

_____ of
name

_____ shall be
address

my attorney in fact for health care.

3. Effective on Incapacity

This durable power of attorney shall become effective in the event I become incapacitated and am unable to make health care decisions for myself, in which case it shall become effective as of the date of the written statement by a physician, as provided in Paragraph 4.

4. Determination of Incapacity

The determination that I have become incapacitated and am unable to make health care decisions shall be made in writing by a licensed physician. If possible, the determination shall be made by _____,

name of physician

_____.

address

5. Authority of My Attorney in Fact

My attorney in fact shall have all lawful authority permissible to make health care decisions for me, including the authority to consent, or withdraw consent or refuse consent to any care, treatment, service or procedure to maintain, diagnose or treat my physical or mental condition, EXCEPT

6. Inspection and Disclosure of Information Relating to My Physical or Mental Health

Subject to any limitations in this document, my attorney in fact has the power and authority to do all of the following:

(a) Request, review, and receive any information, verbal or written, regarding my physical or mental health, including, but not limited to, medical and hospital records.

(b) Execute on my behalf any releases or other documents that may be required in order to obtain this information.

(c) Consent to the disclosure of this information.

7. Signing Documents, Waivers, and Releases

Where necessary to implement the health care decisions that my attorney in fact is authorized by this document to make, my attorney in fact has the power and authority to execute on my behalf all of the following:

(a) Documents titled or purporting to be a "Refusal to Permit Treatment" and "Leaving Hospital Against Medical Advice."

(b) Any necessary waiver or release from liability required by a hospital or physician.

8. Duration

I intend that this Durable Power of Attorney remain effective until my death, or until revoked by me in writing.

Executed this _____ day of _____,

19___ at _____.

_____
Principal

Statement of Witnesses

(This document must be witnessed by two qualified adult witnesses. None of the following may be used as a witness: (1) a person you designate as your agent or alternate agent, (2) a health care provider, (3) an employee of a health care provider, (4) the operator of a community care facility, (5) an employee of an operator of a community care facility, (6) the operator of a residential care facility for the elderly, (7) an employee of an operator of a residential care facility for the elderly. At least one of the witnesses must make the additional declaration set out following the place where the witnesses sign.)

(READ CAREFULLY BEFORE SIGNING. You can sign as a witness only if you personally know the principal or the identity of the principal is proved to you by convincing evidence.)

(To have convincing evidence of the identity of the principal, you must be presented with and reasonably rely on any one or more of the following:

(1) An identification card or driver's license issued by the California Department of Motor Vehicles that is current or has been issued within five years.

(2) A passport issued by the Department of State of the United States that is current or has been issued within five years.

(3) Any of the following documents if the document is current or has been issued within five

years and contains a photograph and description of the person named on it, is signed by the person, and bears a serial or other identifying number:

(a) A passport issued by a foreign government that has been stamped by the United States Immigration and Naturalization Service.

(b) A driver's license issued by a state other than California or by a Canadian or Mexican public agency authorized to issue driver's licenses.

(c) An identification card issued by a state other than California.

(d) An identification card issued by any branch of the armed forces of the United States.)

(Other kinds of proof of identity are not allowed.)

I declare under penalty of perjury under the laws of California that the person who signed or acknowledged this document is personally known to me (or proved to me on the basis of convincing evidence) to be the principal, that the principal signed or acknowledged this Durable Power of Attorney in my presence, that the principal appears to be of sound mind and under no duress, fraud, or undue influence, that I am not the person appointed as attorney-in-fact by this document, and that I am not a health care provider, an employee of a health care provider, the operator of a community care facility, nor an employee of an operator of a community care facility, an operator of a residential care facility for the elderly, nor an employee of an operator of a residential care facility for the elderly.

Signature: _____ Print Name: _____

Residence Address: _____

Date: _____

Signature: _____ Print Name: _____

Residence Address: _____

Date: _____

(AT LEAST ONE OF THE ABOVE WITNESSES MUST ALSO SIGN THE FOLLOWING DECLARATION.)

I further declare under penalty of perjury under the laws of California that I am not related to the principal by blood, marriage, or adoption, and, to the best of my knowledge, I am not entitled to any part of the estate of the principal upon the death of the principal under a will now existing or by operation of law.

Signature: _____

Signature: _____

Statement of Patient Advocate or Ombudsman

(If you are a patient in a skilled nursing facility, one of the witnesses must be a patient advocate or ombudsman. The following statement is required only if you are a patient in a skilled nursing facility—a health care facility that provides the following basic services: skilled nursing care and supportive care to patients whose primary need is for availability of skilled nursing care on an extended basis. The patient advocate or ombudsman must sign both parts of the "Statement of Witnesses" above AND must also sign the following statement.)

I further declare under penalty of perjury under the laws of California that I am a patient advocate or ombudsman as designated by the State Department of Aging and that I am serving as a witness as required by subdivision (f) of Section 2432 of the Civil Code.

Signature:_____

Notarization

State of California   )
) ss

County of _____   )

On this _____ day of _____, in the year 19___,

before me, a Notary Public, State of California, duly commissioned and sworn, personally appeared _____, personally known

name of principal

to me (or proved to me on the basis of satisfactory evidence) to be the person whose name is subscribed to this instrument, and acknowledged that _____ executed it. I declare under

he/she

penalty of perjury that the person whose name is subscribed to this instrument appears to be of sound mind and under no duress, fraud, or undue influence.

_____

signature of notary public

[Notary Seal]   Notary Public for the State of California

My commission expires:_____, 19_____

Form 15

California Durable Power of Attorney (Health Care)

WARNING TO PERSON EXECUTING THIS DOCUMENT

THIS IS AN IMPORTANT LEGAL DOCUMENT. IT CREATES A DURABLE POWER OF ATTORNEY FOR HEALTH CARE. BEFORE EXECUTING THIS DOCUMENT, YOU SHOULD KNOW THESE IMPORTANT FACTS.

THIS DOCUMENT GIVES THE PERSON YOU DESIGNATE AS YOUR AGENT (THE ATTORNEY IN FACT) THE POWER TO MAKE HEALTH CARE DECISIONS FOR YOU. YOUR AGENT MUST ACT CONSISTENTLY WITH YOUR DESIRES AS STATED IN THIS DOCUMENT OR OTHERWISE MADE KNOWN.

EXCEPT AS YOU OTHERWISE SPECIFY IN THIS DOCUMENT, THIS DOCUMENT GIVES YOUR AGENT THE POWER TO CONSENT TO YOUR DOCTOR NOT GIVING TREATMENT OR STOPPING TREATMENT NECESSARY TO KEEP YOU ALIVE.

NOTWITHSTANDING THIS DOCUMENT, YOU HAVE THE RIGHT TO MAKE MEDICAL AND OTHER HEALTH CARE DECISIONS FOR YOURSELF SO LONG AS YOU CAN GIVE INFORMED CONSENT WITH RESPECT TO THE PARTICULAR DECISION. IN ADDITION, NO TREATMENT MAY BE GIVEN TO YOU OVER YOUR OBJECTION, AND HEALTH CARE NECESSARY TO KEEP YOU ALIVE MAY NOT BE STOPPED OR WITHHELD IF YOU OBJECT AT THE TIME.

THIS DOCUMENT GIVES YOUR AGENT AUTHORITY TO CONSENT, TO REFUSE TO CONSENT, OR TO WITHDRAW CONSENT TO ANY CARE, TREATMENT, SERVICE, OR PROCEDURE TO MAINTAIN, DIAGNOSE, OR TREAT A PHYSICAL OR MENTAL CONDITION. THIS POWER IS SUBJECT TO ANY STATEMENT OF YOUR DESIRES AND ANY LIMITATIONS THAT YOU INCLUDE IN THIS DOCUMENT. YOU MAY STATE IN THIS DOCUMENT ANY TYPES OF TREATMENT THAT YOU DO NOT DESIRE. IN ADDITION, A COURT CAN TAKE AWAY THE POWER OF YOUR AGENT TO MAKE HEALTH CARE DECISIONS FOR YOU IF YOUR AGENT (1) AUTHORIZES ANYTHING THAT IS ILLEGAL, (2) ACTS CONTRARY TO YOUR KNOWN DESIRES, OR (3) WHERE YOUR DESIRES ARE NOT KNOWN, DOES ANYTHING THAT IS CLEARLY CONTRARY TO YOUR BEST INTERESTS.

UNLESS YOU SPECIFY A SHORTER PERIOD IN THIS DOCUMENT, THIS POWER WILL EXIST FOR SEVEN YEARS FROM THE DATE YOU EXECUTE THIS DOCUMENT AND, IF YOU ARE UNABLE TO MAKE HEALTH CARE DECISIONS FOR YOURSELF AT THE TIME WHEN THIS SEVEN-YEAR PERIOD ENDS, THIS POWER WILL CONTINUE TO EXIST UNTIL THE TIME WHEN YOU BECOME ABLE TO MAKE HEALTH CARE DECISIONS FOR YOURSELF.

YOU HAVE THE RIGHT TO REVOKE THE AUTHORITY OF YOUR AGENT BY NOTIFYING YOUR AGENT OR YOUR TREATING DOCTOR, HOSPITAL, OR OTHER HEALTH CARE PROVIDER ORALLY OR IN WRITING OF THE REVOCATION.

YOUR AGENT HAS THE RIGHT TO EXAMINE YOUR MEDICAL RECORDS AND TO CONSENT TO THEIR DISCLOSURE UNLESS YOU LIMIT THIS RIGHT IN THIS DOCUMENT.

UNLESS YOU OTHERWISE SPECIFY IN THIS DOCUMENT, THIS DOCUMENT GIVES YOUR AGENT THE POWER AFTER YOU DIE TO (1) AUTHORIZE AN AUTOPSY, (2) DONATE YOUR BODY OR PARTS THEREOF FOR TRANSPLANT OR THERAPEUTIC OR EDUCATIONAL OR SCIENTIFIC PURPOSES, AND (3) DIRECT THE DISPOSITION OF YOUR REMAINS.

IF THERE IS ANYTHING IN THIS DOCUMENT THAT YOU DO NOT UNDERSTAND, YOU SHOULD ASK A LAWYER TO EXPLAIN IT TO YOU.

THIS POWER OF ATTORNEY WILL NOT BE VALID FOR MAKING HEALTH CARE DECISIONS UNLESS IT IS EITHER (1) SIGNED BY TWO QUALIFIED ADULT WITNESSES WHO PERSONALLY KNOW YOU AND WHO ARE PRESENT WHEN YOU SIGN OR ACKNOWLEDGE YOUR SIGNATURE OR (2) ACKNOWLEDGED BEFORE A NOTARY PUBLIC IN CALIFORNIA.

Durable Power of Attorney for Health Care

1. Creation of Durable Power of Attorney

To my family, relatives, friends and my physicians, health care providers, community care

facilities and any other person who may have an interest or duty in my medical care or treatment:

I, _____, being of sound
name

mind, willfully and voluntarily intend to create by this document a durable power of attorney for

my health care by appointing the person designated as my attorney in fact to make health care

decisions for me in the event I become incapacitated and am unable to make health care deci-

sions for myself. This power of attorney shall not be affected by my subsequent incapacity.

2. Designation of Attorney in Fact

The person designated to be my attorney in fact for health care in the event I become

incapacitated is _____ of
name

_____. If
address

_____ for any
name

reason shall fail to serve or ceases to serve as my attorney in fact for health care,

_____ of
name

_____ shall be
address

my attorney in fact for health care.

3. Effective on Signing

This durable power of attorney shall become effective as of the date I sign it.

4. Authority of My Attorney in Fact

My attorney in fact shall have all lawful authority permissible to make health care decisions for me, including the authority to consent, or withdraw consent or refuse consent to any care, treatment, service or procedure to maintain, diagnose or treat my physical or mental condition, EXCEPT

5. Inspection and Disclosure of Information Relating to My Physical or Mental Health

Subject to any limitations in this document, my attorney in fact has the power and authority to do all of the following:

(a) Request, review, and receive any information, verbal or written, regarding my physical or mental health, including, but not limited to, medical and hospital records.

(b) Execute on my behalf any releases or other documents that may be required in order to obtain this information.

(c) Consent to the disclosure of this information.

6. Signing Documents, Waivers, and Releases

Where necessary to implement the health care decisions that my attorney in fact is authorized by this document to make, my attorney in fact has the power and authority to execute on my behalf all of the following:

(a) Documents titled or purporting to be a "Refusal to Permit Treatment" and "Leaving Hospital Against Medical Advice."

(b) Any necessary waiver or release from liability required by a hospital or physician.

7. Duration

I understand that this Durable Power of Attorney will exist for seven years from the date I execute this document, and that if I am unable to make health care decisions for myself when this

Durable Power of Attorney expires, the authority I have granted my attorney in fact will continue to exist until the time when I become able to make health care decisions for myself.

Executed this _____ day of _____,

19___ at _____.

_____
Principal

Statement of Witnesses

(This document must be witnessed by two qualified adult witnesses. None of the following may be used as a witness: (1) a person you designate as your agent or alternate agent, (2) a health care provider, (3) an employee of a health care provider, (4) the operator of a community care facility, (5) an employee of an operator of a community care facility, (6) the operator of a residential care facility for the elderly, (7) an employee of an operator of a residential care facility for the elderly. At least one of the witnesses must make the additional declaration set out following the place where the witnesses sign.)

(READ CAREFULLY BEFORE SIGNING. You can sign as a witness only if you personally know the principal or the identity of the principal is proved to you by convincing evidence.)

(To have convincing evidence of the identity of the principal, you must be presented with and reasonably rely on any one or more of the following:

(1) An identification card or driver's license issued by the California Department of Motor Vehicles that is current or has been issued within five years.

(2) A passport issued by the Department of State of the United States that is current or has been issued within five years.

(3) Any of the following documents if the document is current or has been issued within five years and contains a photograph and description of the person named on it, is signed by the person, and bears a serial or other identifying number:

(a) A passport issued by a foreign government that has been stamped by the United States Immigration and Naturalization Service.

(b) A driver's license issued by a state other than California or by a Canadian or Mexican public agency authorized to issue driver's licenses.

(c) An identification card issued by a state other than California.

(d) An identification card issued by any branch of the armed forces of the United States.)

(Other kinds of proof of identity are not allowed.)

I declare under penalty of perjury under the laws of California that the person who signed or acknowledged this document is personally known to me (or proved to me on the basis of convincing evidence) to be the principal, that the principal signed or acknowledged this Durable Power of Attorney in my presence, that the principal appears to be of sound mind and under no duress, fraud, or undue influence, that I am not the person appointed as attorney-in-fact by this document, and that I am not a health care provider, an employee of a health care provider, the operator of a community care facility, nor an employee of an operator of a community care facility, an operator of a residential care facility for the elderly, nor an employee of an operator of a residential care facility for the elderly.

Signature: _____ Print Name: _____

Residence Address: _____

Date: _____

Signature: _____ Print Name: _____

Residence Address: _____

Date: _____

(AT LEAST ONE OF THE ABOVE WITNESSES MUST ALSO SIGN THE FOLLOWING DECLARATION.)

I further declare under penalty of perjury under the laws of California that I am not related to the principal by blood, marriage, or adoption, and, to the best of my knowledge, I am not entitled to any part of the estate of the principal upon the death of the principal under a will now existing or by operation of law.

Signature: _____

Signature: _____

Statement of Patient Advocate or Ombudsman

(If you are a patient in a skilled nursing facility, one of the witnesses must be a patient advocate or ombudsman. The following statement is required only if you are a patient in a skilled nursing facility—a health care facility that provides the following basic services: skilled nursing care and supportive care to patients whose primary need is for availability of skilled nursing care on an extended basis. The patient advocate or ombudsman must sign both parts of the "Statement of Witnesses" above AND must also sign the following statement.)

I further declare under penalty of perjury under the laws of California that I am a patient advocate or ombudsman as designated by the State Department of Aging and that I am serving as a witness as required by subdivision (f) of Section 2432 of the Civil Code.

Signature:_____

Notarization

State of California   )
) ss

County of _____)

On this _____ day of _____, in the year 19___,

before me, a Notary Public, State of California, duly commissioned and sworn, personally appeared _____, personally known
name of principal

to me (or proved to me on the basis of satisfactory evidence) to be the person whose name is subscribed to this instrument, and acknowledged that _____ executed it. I declare under
he/she
penalty of perjury that the person whose name is subscribed to this instrument appears to be of sound mind and under no duress, fraud, or undue influence.

_____
signature of notary public

[Notary Seal]   Notary Public for the State of California

My commission expires:_____, 19___

Form 16

California Living Will and Directive to My Physicians

Directive made this _____ day of _____, 19___.

I, _____, residing in the County
　　　　　　　　　　　　　　name

of _____, State of _____,

being of sound mind, willfully and voluntarily make known my desire that my life shall not be ar-

tificially prolonged under the circumstances set forth below and do hereby declare:

1. If at any time I should have an incurable injury, disease, or illness certified to be a terminal

condition by two physicians, and where the application of life-sustaining procedures would serve

only to artificially prolong the moment of my death and where my physician determines that my

death is imminent whether or not life-sustaining procedures are utilized, I direct that such

procedures be withheld or withdrawn, and that I be permitted to die naturally.

2. In the absence of my ability to give directions regarding the use of such life-sustaining

procedures, it is my intention that this directive shall be honored by my family and physician(s)

as the final expression of my legal right to refuse medical or surgical treatment and accept the

consequences from such refusal.

3. If I have been diagnosed as pregnant and that diagnosis is known to my physician, this

directive shall have no force or effect during the course of my pregnancy.

4. I have been diagnosed and notified at least 14 days ago as having a terminal condition by

_____, M.D., whose address is
　　　　　　　physician's name

_____, and whose
　　　　　　　　　　　　address

telephone number is _____. I understand that if I have not filled in the

physician's name and address, it shall be presumed that I did not have a terminal condition when

I made out this directive.

5. This directive shall have no force or effect five years from the date filled in above.

6. I understand the full import of this directive and I am emotionally and mentally competent to make this directive.

Dated: _____, 19____

_____
Principal

_____
city, county and state of residence

This declarant has been personally known to me and I believe him or her to be of sound mind.

_____

Residing at _____

_____, _____

_____

Residing at _____

_____, _____

Form 17

Determination of Incapacity

I, _____, declare: I am a
name

physician licensed to practice in the State of _____.

I have examined _____. It is my
name

professional opinion that _____ is
name

incapacitated and is therefore unable to make health care decisions for _____.
himself/herself

Dated:_____ _____

_____
signature of physician

Form 18

Recording requested by and when recorded mail to

_____

_____

_____

Power of Attorney

I, _____ , of
name of principal

_____ , _____ ,
city   county

_____ appoint _____ , of
state   name

_____ , _____ ,
city   county

_____ as my attorney in fact to act in my place for the purposes of
state

except that my attorney in fact shall not have the power of

I further grant to my attorney in fact full authority to act in any manner both proper and

necessary to the exercise of the foregoing powers, including _____
specify

_____ ,

and ratify every act that _____ may lawfully perform in exercising those powers.
he/she

This power of attorney is granted for a period of _____
specify

_____ and shall become effective on

_____ , 19___ and shall terminate on _____ , 19___.

Executed this _____ day of _____ , 19___, at

_____ , _____ .

             city   state

_____

                        signature

Notarization

State of _____)

) ss

County of _____)

On this _____ day of _____ , in the year 19___,

before me, a Notary Public, State of _____ , duly commissioned and

sworn, personally appeared _____ ,

                                                           name

personally known to me (or proved to me on the basis of satisfactory evidence) to be the person

whose name is subscribed to this instrument, and acknowledged that _____

                                                              he/she

executed it.

_____

                        Notary Public

[Notary Seal]   State of _____

                        My commission expires: _____ , 19___

Form 19

Recording requested by and when recorded mail to

_____

_____

_____

Joint Power of Attorney

We, _____ and

name of husband

_____

name of wife

husband and wife, residing at _____,

City of _____, State of _____, do hereby

jointly and severally appoint _____ _____ as

name

our attorney in fact, for us in our name, place, and stead to

except that our attorney in fact shall not have the power to

We further give and grant to our said attorney in fact full power and authority to do and

perform every act necessary and proper in the exercise of any of the powers granted hereunder as

fully as we might or could do if personally present, with full power of substitution and revocation,

hereby ratifying and confirming all that our said attorney in fact shall lawfully do or cause to be

done by virtue hereof.

This power of attorney is granted for a term of _____
                                                                                    specify period

and shall be effective on _____, 19____ and shall remain in full

force and effect until _____, 19____.

Dated: _____, 19____

                                    _____
                                                        signature

                                    _____
                                                       typed name

                                    _____
                                                        signature

                                    _____
                                                       typed name

Notarization

State of _____   )
) ss
County of _____   )

On this _____ day of _____, in the year 19___,

before me, a Notary Public, State of _____, duly commissioned and

sworn, personally appeared _____
                                                        name

and _____, personally known
                          name

to me (or proved to me on the basis of satisfactory evidence) to be the people whose names are

subscribed to this instrument, and acknowledged that they executed it.

                                    _____
                                    signature

                                    Notary Public for

[Notary Seal]   the State of _____

                                    My commission expires: _____, 19___

Form 20

Recording requested by and when recorded mail to

_____

_____

_____

General Power of Attorney

I. KNOW ALL MEN BY THESE PRESENTS, that I,

_____ _____, residing at

name

_____, City

street address

of _____, County of _____, State of

_____, do hereby nominate, constitute, and appoint

_____, of

name

_____, City

street address

of _____, County of _____, State of

_____, as my true and lawful attorney in fact, for me and in my

name, place, and stead, and for my use and benefit.

II. My attorney in fact shall have all lawfully permissible authority to act for or represent me,

including, but not limited to, the authority:

A. To ask, demand, sue for, recover, collect, and receive all such sums of money, debts, dues,

accounts, legacies, bequests, interest, dividends, annuities, and demands whatsoever as are now or

shall hereafter become due, owing, payable, or belonging to me and have, use, and take all lawful

ways and means in my name or otherwise for the recovery thereof, by attachments, arrests,

distress, or otherwise, and to compromise and agree for the same and acquittances or other

sufficient discharges for the same;

B. To make, seal, and deliver, to bargain, contract, agree for, purchase, receive, and take

lands, tenements, hereditaments, and accept the possession of all lands, and all deeds and other assurances, in the law therefor, and to lease, let, demise, bargain, sell, remise, release, convey, mortgage, and hypothecate lands, tenements, and hereditaments upon such terms and conditions and under such covenants as _____ shall think fit;

_{he/she}

To bargain and agree for, buy, sell, mortgage, hypothecate, and in any and every way and manner deal in and with goods, wares, and merchandise, choses in action, and other property in possession or in action, and to make, do, and transact all and every kind of business of whatsoever nature and kind;

C. To improve, repair, maintain, manage, insure, rent, lease, sell, release, convey, subject to liens, mortgage, and hypothecate, and in any way or manner deal with all or any part of any real property whatsoever, or any interest therein, which I now own or may hereafter acquire, for me and in my name, and under such terms and conditions, and under such covenants as my attorney in fact shall deem proper;

D. To exercise, do, or perform any act, right, power, duty, or obligation whatsoever that I now have or may acquire the legal right, power, or capacity to exercise, do, or perform in connection with, arising out of, or relating to any person, item, thing, transaction, business property, real or personal, tangible or intangible, or matter whatsoever;

E. To sign, endorse, execute, acknowledge, deliver, receive, and possess such applications, contracts, agreements, options, covenants, deeds, conveyances, trust deeds, security agreements, bills of sale, leases, mortgages, assignments, insurance policies, bills of lading, warehouse receipts, documents of title, bills, bonds, debentures, checks, drafts, bills of exchange, notes, stock certificates, proxies, warrants, commercial paper, receipts, withdrawal receipts and deposit instruments relating to accounts or deposits in, or certificates of deposit of, banks, savings and loan or other institutions or associations, proofs of loss, evidence of debts, releases, and satisfaction of mortgages, judgments, liens, security agreements, and other debts and obligations, and such other instruments in writing or whatever kind and nature as may be necessary or proper in the exercise of the rights and powers herein granted.

III. Further, my attorney in fact has full power and authority to do and perform all and every act and thing whatsoever requisite, necessary, and proper to be done in the exercise of any of the rights and powers herein granted, as fully to all intents and purposes as I might or could do if personally present, with full power of substitution or revocation, hereby ratifying and confirming all that my attorney in fact shall lawfully do or cause to be done by virtue of this power of attorney and the rights and powers herein granted.

IV. This instrument is to be construed and interpreted as a general power of attorney. The enumeration of specific items, acts, rights or powers herein does not limit or restrict, and is not to be construed or interpreted as limiting or restricting the general powers herein granted to my attorney in fact.

V. All power and authority hereinabove granted shall in any event terminate on the

_____ day of _____, 19 __.

IN WITNESS WHEREOF, I have hereunto signed my name this _____ day of

_____, 19___.

_____
Principal

_____
typed name

Notarization

State of _____

County of _____

On this _____ day of _____ in the year

_____, before me, a Notary Public, State of _____, duly

commissioned and sworn, personally appeared _____,

name

personally known to me (or proved to me on the basis of satisfactory evidence) to be the person

whose name is subscribed to the within instrument, and acknowledged to me that he/she exe-

cuted the same.

IN WITNESS WHEREOF, I have hereunto set my hand and affixed my official seal in the

State of _____, County of _____ on the

date set forth above in this certificate.

_____

Notary Public

[Notary Seal]   State of _____

My commission expires _____

Form 21

Recording requested by and when recorded mail to

_____

_____

_____

Notice of Revocation of Power of Attorney

I, _____,
                                    name

of _____ _____,
                          street address

City of _____, County of _____,

State of _____, hereby give notice that I have revoked, and do

hereby revoke, the power of attorney dated _____ _____, 19___ given to

_____, empowering said
          name of attorney in fact

_____ to act as my true
          name of attorney in fact

and lawful attorney in fact, and I declare that all power and authority granted under said power of

attorney is hereby revoked and withdrawn.

Dated: _____, 19___

                              _____
                              Principal

                              _____
                                        typed name

Witnesses

_____ of _____

_____

_____ of _____

_____

Notarization

State of _____

County of _____

On this _____ day of _____ in the year 19___, before

me a Notary Public, State of _____, duly commissioned and

sworn, personally appeared _____,
name

personally known to me (or proved to me on the basis of satisfactory evidence) to be the person

whose name is subscribed to in the within instrument as principal, and acknowledged to me that

_____ executed the same.
he/she

IN WITNESS WHEREOF, I have hereunto set my hand and affixed my official seal in the

State of _____, County of _____ on the date

set forth above in this certificate.

_____

Notary Public

[Notary Seal]   State of _____

My commission expires: _____, 19___

Form 22

Recording requested by and when recorded mail to

_____

_____

_____

Notice of Revocation of Recorded Power of Attorney

I, _____,
name

of _____,
street address

City of _____, County of _____,

State of _____, executed a power of attorney dated

_____, 19___ appointing _____ _____,
name of attorney in fact

of _____,
street address

City of _____, County of _____,

State of _____, my true and lawful attorney in fact with

full power to act for me and in my name as therein specified, and such power of attorney was duly

recorded on _____ in Book _____, at Page _____, of the
date of recordation

Official Records, County of _____, State of

_____.

I hereby revoke said power of attorney given to said _____
name of attorney in fact

_____, and all power and authority contained therein.

Dated: _____, 19___

_____
Principal

_____
typed name

Witnesses

_____ of _____

_____

_____ of _____

_____

Notarization

State of _____

County of _____

On this _____ day of _____ in the year 19___, before

me a Notary Public, State of _____, duly commissioned and

sworn, personally appeared _____,
name

personally known to me (or proved to me on the basis of satisfactory evidence) to be the person

whose name is subscribed to in the within instrument as principal, and acknowledged to me that

_____ executed the same.
he/she

IN WITNESS WHEREOF, I have hereunto set my hand and affixed my official seal in the

State of _____, County of _____ on the

date set forth above in this certificate.

_____

Notary Public

[Notary Seal]   State of _____

My commission expires: _____, 19___

D

It's no secret that our legal system offers most Americans poor access to justice. Especially when it comes to relatively straightforward legal tasks, many people knew that too often lawyers charge too much, explain too little, and provide inadequate services.

Nolo Press, founded in 1971, pioneered a different approach: helping people gain the knowledge necessary to cope with their own routine legal problems. Nolo now publishes over 60 self-help law books and software programs. Our materials are affordable, they explain—in plain English—what the law says, and they show readers how to complete many routine legal tasks (including court appearances) without a lawyer.

Bar associations thundered against Nolo's first book, *How To Do Your Own Divorce in California*, claiming it was a "danger to consumers." In the next few years the public was repeatedly warned that doing your own legal paperwork, for even the simplest legal task, was akin to doing your own brain surgery. Fortunately, consumers took a hard look at the expensive alternatives the legal profession offered, examined Nolo books, and made up their own minds. Today, close to 60% of the uncontested divorces in California are done without lawyers, most of them with the help of Nolo's divorce book, which has sold close to half a million copies.

In the late 1970s, after publishing a dozen successful California self-help law books in areas as diverse as tenants' rights and incorporating a small business, Nolo broadened its focus to the whole country. We now have national books on wills, patents, estate planning, and partnerships, to mention just a few. In 1981 Nolo began publishing a quarterly self-help law newspaper, the *Nolo News— Access to Law*. It keeps readers up-to-date on law changes that affect our books, encourages new self-help approaches, and provides consumer information.

An important part of Nolo's purpose is to spread the word that our legal system can easily be made more affordable, accessible, and fair if it is redesigned to serve consumers instead of the legal profession. To take but one example, Nolo has repeatedly urged that competent non-lawyers (independent paralegals) be permitted to provide reasonably priced legal form completion services.

More recently, Nolo expanded into self-help legal software with a number of easy-to-use programs, including *WillMaker* (with Legisoft). With over 100,000 sold, it's fair to estimate that *WillMaker* has made more wills than any law firm in history.

Currently, we're busy creating new programs, writing new books, and keeping our existing titles up to date. Nolo has grown from a home-base business with a couple of part-time employees to one that employs close to 50 people.

One thing that hasn't changed since Nolo's undeniably humble beginnings is our commitment to quality. Our books and software are as clear, accurate, up-to-date and useful as we can make them. To help with this process we enclose a tear-out feedback card in this book and urge you to take a minute to give us the benefit of your suggestions. Every suggestion is read by a Nolo author or editor.

ABOUT THE AUTHOR

DENIS CLIFFORD is a lawyer who specializes in estate planning and has been involved in the developing uses of durable powers of attorney. He is the author of several Nolo titles, including *Nolo's Simple Will Book* and *Plan Your Estate*. A graduate of Columbia Law School, where he was editor of *The Law Review*, he has practiced law in various ways, and is convinced that people can do much of the legal work they need themselves.

ABOUT THE ILLUSTRATOR

MARI STEIN is a free lance illustrator and writer. Her published work has been eclectic, covering a wide range of subjects: humor, whimsy, health education, juvenile, fables and yoga. She has illustrated a number of books for Nolo Press, including *29 Reasons Not to Go to Law School*, *Plan Your Estate*, *WillMaker* and *How to Form Your Own Corporation*, and has produced audio tapes on Hatha Yoga and meditation. She now enjoys the life of a writer/illustrator/yoga teacher/spinner and shepherdess on Enchanted Rabbit Mountain, an 175-acre ranch on the summit of the Greensprings in Ashland, Oregon.

FAMILY MATTERS

A Legal Guide for Lesbian and Gay Couples

ATTORNEYS HAYDEN CURRY & DENIS CLIFFORD
NATIONAL 5TH ED.

Laws designed to regulate and protect married couples don't apply to lesbian and gay couples. This book shows you, step-by-step, how to write a living-together contract, plan for medical emergencies (using durable powers of attorney), and plan your estates (wills and probate avoidance techniques). It also discusses legal aspects of having and raising children and relating to ex-spouses and children of former marriages. Complete with forms, sample agreements and lists of both national lesbian and gay legal organizations, and AIDS organizations.
$17.95 / LG

The Guardianship Book

BY LISA GOLDOFTAS &
ATTORNEY DAVID BROWN
CALIFORNIA 1ST ED.

Thousands of children in California are left without a guardian because their parents have died, abandoned them or are unable to care for them. *The Guardianship Book* provides step-by-step instructions and the forms needed to obtain a legal guardianship without a lawyer.
$19.95 / GB

How to Do Your Own Divorce

ATTORNEY CHARLES E. SHERMAN
(TEXAS ED. BY SHERMAN & SIMONS)
CALIFORNIA 15TH ED. & TEXAS 2ND ED.

This is the book that launched Nolo Press and advanced the self-help law movement. During the past 18 years, over 500,000 copies have been sold, saving consumers at least $50 million in legal fees (assuming 100,000 have each saved $500—certainly a conservative estimate). Contains all the forms and instructions you need to do your divorce without a lawyer.
CALIFORNIA $18.95 / CDIV
TEXAS $14.95 / TDIV

Practical Divorce Solutions

ATTORNEY CHARLES E. SHERMAN
CALIFORNIA 1ST ED.

This book is a valuable guide to the emotional aspects of divorce as well as an overview of the legal and financial decisions that must be made.
$12.95 / PDS

The Living Together Kit

ATTORNEYS TONI IHARA & RALPH WARNER
NATIONAL 6TH ED.

"Written in plain language, free of legal mumbo jumbo, and spiced with witty personal observations."

—**Associated Press**

The Living Together Kit is a detailed guide designed to help the increasing number of unmarried couples living together understand the laws that affect them. *The Living Together Kit* contains comprehensive information on estate planning, paternity agreements, living together agreements, buying real estate, and much more. Sample agreements and instructions are included.
$17.95 / LTK

How to Adopt You Stepchild in California

FRANK ZAGONE & ATTORNEY MARY RANDOLPH
CALIFORNIA 3RD ED.

For many families that include stepchildren, adoption is a sure-fire way to avoid confusion over inheritance or guardianship. This book provides sample forms and complete step-by-step instructions for completing a simple uncontested stepparent adoption in California.
$19.95 / ADOP

How to Modify and Collect Child Support in California

ATTORNEYS JOSEPH MATTHEWS, WARREN SIEGEL & MARY WILLIS
CALIFORNIA 3RD ED.

Using this book, parents can determine the level of child support they are entitled to receive, or obliged to pay, and can go to court to modify existing support to the appropriate level.
$17.95 / SUPP

California Marriage & Divorce Law

ATTORNEYS RALPH WARNER, TONI IHARA & STEPHEN ELIAS
CALIFORNIA 10TH ED.

This practical handbook is for the Californian who wants to understand marriage and divorce laws. It explains community property, pre-nuptial contracts, foreign marriages, buying a house, the steps for getting a divorce, dividing property, and much more.
$17.95 / MARR

PATENT, COPYRIGHT & TRADEMARK

Patent it Yourself

ATTORNEY DAVID PRESSMAN
NATIONAL 2ND ED.

Every step of the patent process is presented in order in this gem of a book, complete with official forms…"

—**San Francisco Chronicle**

This state-of-the-art guide is a must for all inventors interested in obtaining patents—from the patent search to the actual application. Patent attorney and former patent examiner David Pressman covers use and licensing, successful marketing, and how to deal with infringement.
$29.95 / PAT

The Inventor's Notebook

GRISSOM & ATTORNEY PRESSMAN
NATIONAL 1ST ED.

The best protection for your patent is adequate records. *The Inventor's Notebook* helps you document the process of successful independent inventing by providing forms, instructions, references to relevant areas of patent law, a bibliography of legal and non-legal aids, and more.
$19.95 / INOT

How to Copyright Software

ATTORNEY M.J. SALONE
NATIONAL 3RD ED.

"Written by practicing lawyers in the straightforward and informative Nolo style, the book covers just about everything that might be of interest to a software developer or publisher. Even those who are employed by a company on a full-time or contractual basis will find much to ponder here."

—**PC Week**

Now that you've spent hours of time and sleepless nights perfecting your software creation, learn how to protect it from plagiarism. Copyright laws give you rights against those who use your work without your permission. This book tells you how to enforce those rights, how to register your copyright for maximum protection, and discusses who owns a copyright on software developed by more than one person.
$34.95 / COPY

Legal Care for Your Software

ATTORNEYS DANIEL REMER & STEPHEN ELIAS
NATIONAL

Legal Care for Your Software is out of print. Nolo authors are in the process of writing a new 4th edition of this book.

BUSINESS

The Independent Paralegal's Handbook

ATTORNEY RALPH WARNER
NATIONAL 1ST ED.

A large percentage of routine legal work in this country is performed by typists, secretaries, researchers and other law office helpers generally labeled paralegals. For those who want to take these services out of the law office and offer them for a reasonable fee in an independent business, attorney Ralph Warner provides legal and business guidelines.

$12.95 / PARA

Getting Started as an Independent Paralegal

(TWO AUDIO TAPES)
ATTORNEY RALPH WARNER
NATIONAL 1ST ED.

Approximately three hours in all, these tapes are a carefully edited version of a seminar given by Nolo Press founder Ralph Warner. They are designed to be used with *The Independent Paralegal's Handbook*.

$24.95 / GSIP

Marketing Without Advertising

MICHAEL PHILLIPS & SALLI RASBERRY
NATIONAL 1ST ED.

"There are good ideas on every page. You'll find here the nitty gritty steps you need to—and can—take to generate sales for your business, no matter what business it is."

—Milton Moskowitz, syndicated columnist and author of *The 100 Best Companies to Work For in America*

The best marketing plan encourages customer loyalty and personal recommendation. Phillips and Rasberry outline practical steps for building and expanding a small business without spending a lot of money on advertising.

$14.00 / MWA

The Partnership Book

ATTORNEYS CLIFFORD & WARNER
NATIONAL 3RD ED.

Lots of people dream of going into business with a friend. The best way to keep that dream from turning into a nightmare is to have a solid partnership agreement. This book shows you, step-by-step, how to write an agreement that meets your need. It covers initial contributions to the business, wages, profit-sharing, buy-outs, death or retirement of a partner, and disputes.

$18.95 / PART

How to Write a Business Plan

MIKE MCKEEVER
NATIONAL 3RD ED.

"...outlines the kinds of credit available... shows how to prepare cashflow forecasts, capital spending plans, and other vital ideas. An attractive guide for would-be entrepreneurs."

—ALA Booklist

If you're thinking of starting a business or raising money to expand an existing one, this book will show you how to write the business plan and loan package necessary to finance your business and make it work.

$17.95 / SBS

How to Form Your Own Corporation

ATTORNEY ANTHONY MANCUSO
CALIFORNIA 7TH ED.
TEXAS 4TH ED.
NEW YORK 2ND ED.
FLORIDA 2ND ED.

Incorporating your small business lets you take advantage of tax benefits, limited liability and benefits of employee status, and financial flexibility. These books contain the forms, instructions and tax information you need to incorporate a small business yourself and save hundreds of dollars in lawyers' fees. Each contains up-to-date corporate and tax information.

CALIFORNIA $29.95 / CCOR
TEXAS $24.95 / TCOR
NEW YORK $24.95 / NYCO
FLORIDA $24.95 / FLCO

The California Professional Corporation Handbook

ATTORNEY ANTHONY MANCUSO
CALIFORNIA 4TH ED.

Health care professionals, lawyers, accountants and members of certain other professions must fulfill special requirements when forming a corporation in California. Professional corporations offer liability protection, the financial benefits of a corporate retirement plan, and lower tax rates on the first $75,000 of taxable income. This edition contains up-to-date tax information plus all the forms and instructions necessary to form a California professional corporation. An appendix explains the special rules that apply to each profession.

$34.95 / PROF

The California Nonprofit Corporation Handbook

ATTORNEY ANTHONY MANCUSO
CALIFORNIA 5TH ED.

This book shows you step-by-step how to form and operate a nonprofit corporation in California. It includes the latest corporate and tax law changes, including expanded protection from personal liability for corporate directors. Includes forms for the Articles, Bylaws and Minutes you need. Contains complete instructions for obtaining federal 501(c)(3) tax exemptions and benefits, which may be used in any state.

$29.95 / NON

OLDER AMERICANS

Elder Care: Choosing and Financing Long-Term Care

JOSEPH L. MATTHEWS
NATIONAL 1ST ED.

Until recently, the only choice for the elderly in deteriorating health was to enter a nursing home. Now older people who need care and their families are faced with many more choices, ranging from care at home to residential facilities to complete care homes. This book will guide you in choosing and paying for long-term care, alerting you to practical concerns and explaining laws that may affect your decisions.

$16.95 / ELD

Social Security, Medicare & Pensions

ATTORNEY JOSEPH MATTHEWS & DOROTHY MATTHEWS BERMAN
NATIONAL 5TH ED.

When the Catastrophic Coverage Act was repealed recently, it drastically changed the kinds and amounts of government benefits for older Americans. While assistance with income and healthcare is still available, it requires more perseverance and understanding to get your due.

This new edition includes invaluable guidance through the current maze of rights and benefits for those 55 and over, including Medicare, Medicaid and Social Security retirement and disability benefits and age discrimination protections.

$15.95 / SOA

ESTATE PLANNING & PROBATE

Plan Your Estate

ATTORNEY DENIS CLIFFORD
NATIONAL 1ST ED.

"One of the best personal finance books of 1989." —Money Magazine

This book covers every significant aspect of estate planning, and gives detailed, specific instructions for preparing a living trust. *Plan Your Estate* shows how to prepare an estate plan without the expensive services of a lawyer and ncludes all the tear-out forms and step-by-step instructions to let people with estates under $600,000 do the job themselves.

$19.95 / NEST

Nolo's Simple Will Book

ATTORNEY DENIS CLIFFORD
NATIONAL 2ND ED.

It's easy to write a legally valid will using this book. The instructions and forms enable people to draft a will for all needs, including naming a personal guardian for minor children; leaving property to minor children or young adults; and updating a will when necessary. This edition also contains a discussion of estate planning basics with information on living trusts, death taxes, and durable powers of attorney. Good in all states except Louisiana.

$17.95 / SWIL

How To Probate an Estate

JULIA NISSLEY
CALIFORNIA 5TH ED.

If you find yourself responsible for winding up the legal and financial affairs of a deceased family member or friend, you can often save costly attorneys' fees by handling the probate process yourself. *How to Probate an Estate* shows you, step-by-step, how to actually settle an estate. It also covers the simple procedures you can use to transfer assets that don't require probate, including property held in joint tenancy or living trusts or as community property.

$24.95 / PAE

The Power of Attorney Book

ATTORNEY DENIS CLIFFORD
NATIONAL 3RD ED.

Who will take care of your affairs, and make your financial and medical decisions if you can't? With *The Power of Attorney Book* you can appoint someone you trust to carry out your wishes and stipulate exactly what kind of care you want or don't want. Includes Durable Power of Attorney and Living Will forms.

$19.95 / POA

GOING TO COURT

Everybody's Guide to Small Claims Court

ATTORNEY RALPH WARNER
NATIONAL 4TH ED.
CALIFORNIA 8TH ED.

So, the dry cleaner ruined your good flannel suit. Your roof leaks every time it rains, and the contractor who supposedly fixed it won't call you back. The landlord won't return your security deposit. This book will help you decide if you should sue in small claims court, show you how to file and serve papers, tell you what to bring to court, and how to collect a judgment.

NATIONAL $14.95 / NSCC
CALIFORNIA $14.95 / CSCC

Collect Your Court Judgment

GINI GRAHAM SCOTT, ATTORNEY STEPHEN ELIAS & LISA GOLDOFTAS
CALIFORNIA 1ST ED.

After you win a judgment in small claims, municipal or superior court, you still have to collect your money. If the debtor doesn't pay up voluntarily, you need to know how to collect your judgment from the debtor's bank accounts, wages, business receipts, real estate or other assets. This book contains step-by-step instructions and all the forms you need.

$24.95 / JUDG

Fight Your Ticket

ATTORNEY DAVID BROWN
CALIFORNIA 3RD ED.

Here's a book that shows you how to fight an unfair traffic ticket—when you're stopped, at arraignment, at trial and on appeal. No wonder a traffic court judge (who must remain nameless) told us that he keeps this book by his bench for easy reference!

$17.95 / FYT

The Criminal Records Book

ATTORNEY WARREN SIEGEL
CALIFORNIA 3RD ED.

We've all done something illegal. If you were one of those who got caught, your juvenile or criminal court record can complicate your life years later. The good news is that in many cases your record can either be completely expunged or lessened in severity. *The Criminal Records Book* shows you, step-by-step, how to seal criminal records, dismiss convictions, destroy marijuana records, and reduce felony convictions.

$19.95 / CRIM

Dog Law

ATTORNEY MARY RANDOLPH
NATIONAL 1ST ED.

Do you own a dog? Do you live down the street from one? If you do, you need *Dog Law*, a practical guide to the laws that affect dog owners and their neighbors. *Dog Law* answers common questions on such topics as biting, barking, veterinarians, leash laws, travel, landlords, wills, guide dogs, pit bulls, cruelty and much more.

$12.95 / DOG

How to Change Your Name

ATTORNEYS DAVID LOEB & DAVID BROWN
CALIFORNIA 4TH ED.

Wish you had gone back to your former name after the divorce? Tired of spelling V-e-n-k-a-t-a-r-a-m-a-n S-u-b-r-a-m-a-n-i-a-m over the phone? This book explains how to change your name legally and provides all the necessary court forms with detailed instructions on how to fill them out.

$19.95 / NAME

MONEY MATTERS

How to File For Bankruptcy

ATTORNEYS STEPHEN ELIAS, ALBIN RENAUER & ROBIN LEONARD
NATIONAL 1ST ED.

It's no fun having to think about declaring bankruptcy. But easy credit, high interest rates, unexpected illness, job lay-offs and inflation often conspire to leave people with a satchel full of debts. Here we show you how to decide whether or not filing for bankruptcy makes sense and if it does, we give you forms and step-by-step instructionson how to do it.

$24.95 / HFB

Simple Contracts for Personal Use

ATTORNEY STEPHEN ELIAS
NATIONAL 1ST ED.

If you've ever sold a car, lent money to a relative or friend, or put money down on a prospective purchase, you should have used a contract. Perhaps everything went without a hitch. If it didn't, you probably experienced a lot of grief and frustration.

Here are clearly written legal form contracts to: buy and sell property, borrow and lend money, store and lend personal property, make deposits on goods for later purchase, release others from personal liability, or pay a contractor to do home repairs.

$12.95 / CONT

Homestead Your House

ATTORNEYS RALPH WARNER, CHARLES SHERMAN & TONI IHARA
CALIFORNIA 7TH ED.

Under California homestead laws, up to $75,000 of the equity in your home may be safe from creditors. But to get the maximum legal protection, you should file a Declaration of Homestead before a creditor gets a court judgment against you and puts a lien (legal claim) on your house. This book shows you how and includes complete instructions and tear-out forms.

$9.95 / HOME

The Deeds Book

ATTORNEY MARY RANDOLPH
CALIFORNIA 1ST ED.

If you own real estate, you'll need to sign a new deed when you transfer the property or put it in trust as part of your estate planning. *The Deeds Book* shows you how to choose the right kind of deed, complete the tear-out forms, and record them in the county recorder's public records. It also alerts you to real property disclosure requirements and California community property rules, as well as tax and estate planning aspects of property transfers.

$15.95 / DEED

For Sale by Owner

GEORGE DEVINE
CALIFORNIA 1ST ED.

If you sell your house at California's median price—$200,000—the standard broker's commission (6%) amounts to $12,000. That's money you could save if you sold your own house. This book provides essential information about pricing your house, marketing it, writing a contract and going through escrow. With *For Sale by Owner*, you can do the job yourself and with confidence. Disclosure and contract forms are included.

$24.95 / FSBO

The Landlord's Law Book: Vol. 1, Rights & Responsibilities

ATTORNEYS DAVID BROWN & RALPH WARNER
CALIFORNIA 2ND ED.

The era when a landlord could substitute common sense for a detailed knowledge of the law is gone forever. Everything from the amount you can charge for a security deposit to terminating a tenancy, to your legal responsibility for the illegal acts of your manager is closely regulated by the law. This volume covers: deposits, leases and rental agreements, inspections (tenants' privacy rights), habitability (rent withholding), ending a tenancy, liability, and rent control.

$24.95 / LBRT

The Landlord's Law Book: Vol. 2, Evictions

ATTORNEY DAVID BROWN
CALIFORNIA 2ND ED.

What do you do if you've got a tenant who won't pay the rent—and won't leave? There's only one choice: go to court and get an eviction. This book takes you through the process step-by-step. It's even got a special section on local rent control laws. All the tear-out forms and instructions you need are included.

$24.95 / LBEV

Tenants' Rights

ATTORNEYS MYRON MOSKOVITZ & RALPH WARNER
CALIFORNIA 10TH ED.

Your "security building" doesn't have a working lock on the front door. Is your landlord liable? How can you get him to fix it? Under what circumstances can you withhold rent? When is an apartment not "habitable?" Moskovitz and Warner explain the best way to handle your relationship with your landlord and your legal rights when you find yourself in disagreement. A special section on rent control cities is included.

$15.95 / CTEN

Legal Research

ATTORNEY STEPHEN ELIAS
NATIONAL 2ND ED.

A valuable tool on its own, or as a companion to just about every other Nolo book. *Legal Research* gives easy-to-use, step-by-step instructions on how to find legal information. The legal self-helper can find and research a case, read statutes and administrative regulations, and make Freedom of Information Act requests. A great resource for paralegals, law students, legal secretaries and social workers.

$14.95 / LRES

Family Law Dictionary

ATTORNEYS ROBIN LEONARD & STEPHEN ELIAS
NATIONAL 1ST ED.

Finally, a legal dictionary that's written in plain English, not "legalese"! The *Family Law Dictionary* is designed to help the nonlawyer who has a question or problem involving family law—marriage, divorce, adoption, or living together. The book contains many examples as well as definitions, and extensive cross-references to help you find the information you need.

$13.95 / FLD

Patent, Copyright & Trademark: The Intellectual Property Law Dictionary

ATTORNEY STEPHEN ELIAS
NATIONAL 1ST ED.

...uses simple language free of legal jargon to define and explain the intricacies of items associated with trade secrets, copyrights, trademarks and unfair competition, patents and patent procedures, and contracts and warranties.

—IEEE Spectrum

If you're dealing with any multi-media product, a new business product or trade secret, you need this book.

$19.95 / IPLD

WillMaker

NOLO PRESS & LEGISOFT, INC.
NATIONAL 3RD ED.

"A well crafted document. That's even what my lawyer said ...noting that a few peculiar twists in my state's law were handled nicely by the computerized lawyer."

—Peter H. Lewis, The New York Times

"An excellent addition to anyone's home-productivity library."

—Home Office Computing

"A fertile hybrid that I expect to see more of: can-do software that lives inside a how-to-book. In this case, the book itself is one of the better ones on preparing your own will."

—Whole Earth Review

Recent statistics say chances are better than 2 to 1 that you haven't written a will, even though you know you should. *WillMaker* makes the job easy, leading you step-by-step in a question and answer format. Once you've gone through the program, you print out the will and sign it in front of witnesses. Because writing a will is only one step in the estate planning process, *WillMaker* comes with a 200-page manual providing an overview of probate avoidance and tax planning techniques. Good in all states except Louisiana.

APPLE II	$59.95	WA3
IBM PC 3 1/2	$59.95	W3I3
IBM PC 5 1/4	$59.95	WI3
MACINTOSH	$59.95	WM3
MACINTOSH 512K	$59.95	WM3K

For the Record

CAROL PLADSEN & ATTORNEY RALPH WARNER
NATIONAL 1ST ED.

This easy-to-use software program provides a single place to keep a complete inventory of all your important legal, financial, personal, and family records. Having accurate and complete records facilitates tax preparation and helps loved ones manage your affairs if you become incapacitated or die. The detailed manual offers an overview of how to reduce estate taxes and avoid probate, and tells you what records you need to keep.

MACINTOSH	$49.95	FRM
IBM PC 3 1/2	$49.95	FR3I
IBM PC 5 1/4	$49.95	FRI

California Incorporator

ATTORNEY ANTHONY MANCUSO & LEGISOFT, INC.
CALIFORNIA 1ST ED.

"...easy to use...the manual consists of far more than instructions for using the software...[it is] a primer that provides a great deal of background, including detailed explanations of the legal implications of each decision you make."

—Los Angeles Times

About half of the small California corporations formed today are done without the services of a lawyer. Now, this easy-to-use software program makes the job even easier.

Just answer the questions on the screen, and *California Incorporator* will print out the 35-40 pages of documents you need to make your California corporation legal.

Comes with a 200-page manual that explains the incorporation process.

IBM PC 3 1/2	$129.00	INCI
IBM PC 5 1/4	$129.00	INCI

The California Nonprofit Corporation Handbook: computer edition with disk

ATTORNEY ANTHONY MANCUSO
CALIFORNIA 1ST ED.

This is the standard work on how to form a nonprofit corporation in California. Included on the disk are the forms for the Articles, Bylaws and Minutes you will need, as well as regular and special director and member minute forms. Also included are several chapters with line-by-line instructions explaining how to apply for and obtain federal tax-exempt status. This is a critical step in the incorporation of any nonprofit organizaton and applies to incorporating in any state.

IBM PC 5 1/4	$69.95	NPI
IBM PC 3 1/2	$69.95	NP3I
MACINTOSH	$69.95	NPM

How to Form Your Own New York Corporation: computer edition with disk

How to Form Your Own Texas Corporation: computer edition with disk

ATTORNEY ANTHONY MANCUSO

More and more businesses are incorporating to qualify for tax benefits, limited liability status, the benefit of employee status and financial flexibility. This software package contains all the instructions, tax information and forms you need to incorporate a small business, including the Certificate of Incorporation, Bylaws, Minutes and Stock Certificates. The 250-page manual includes instructions on how to incorporate a new or existing business; tax and securities law information; information on S corporations; Federal Tax Reform Act rates and rules; and the latest procedures to protect your directors under state law. All organizational forms are on disk.

NEW YORK 1ST ED.

IBM PC 5 1/4	$69.95	NYCI
IBM PC 3 1/2	$69.95	NYC3I
MACINTOSH	$69.95	NYCM

TEXAS 1ST ED.

IBM PC 5 1/4	$69.95	TCI
IBM PC 3 1/2	$69.95	TC3I
MACINTOSH	$69.95	TCM